Investing in Your Life

Your Biggest Investment Opportunities
are Not Necessarily Financial

Ian Pollard

WILEY

First published 2009 by John Wiley & Sons Australia, Ltd
42 McDougall Street, Milton Qld 4064

Office also in Melbourne

Typeset in Berkeley LT 11/14pt

© Ian Pollard 2009

The moral rights of the author have been asserted

National Library of Australia Cataloguing-in-Publication entry:

Author:	Pollard, I. A. (Ian A.)
Title:	Investing in your life: your biggest investment opportunities are not necessarily financial / Ian Pollard.
ISBN:	9781742169316 (pbk.)
Subjects:	Self-realization.
	Self-acceptance.
	Happiness.
	Life skills.
	Interpersonal relations.
Dewey number:	158.1

Extracts on pp. 69 and 70 from *Newk* by John Newcombe and Larry Writer reprinted by permission of Pan Macmillan Australia Pty Ltd. Copyright © John Newcombe and Larry Writer 2002.

Printed in China by Printplus

10 9 8 7 6 5 4 3 2 1

Disclaimer
The material in this publication is of the nature of general comment only, and does not represent professional advice. It is not intended to provide specific guidance for particular circumstances and it should not be relied on as the basis for any decision to take action or not take action on any matter which it covers. Readers should obtain professional advice where appropriate, before making any such decision. To the maximum extent permitted by law, the author and publisher disclaim all responsibility and liability to any person, arising directly or indirectly from any person taking or not taking action based upon the information in this publication.

Contents

Part II: Empowering you to invest in your Life Capital

Part III: The application of your Life Capital to your career

Contents

To Tori,
For over 30 years of love, inspiration and challenge, patience
and support.

To Emma, Stuart and Jess,
For your futures and for the pleasure, satisfaction and pride
you have given your parents.

Acknowledgements

While *Investing in Your Life* is ultimately my work and my responsibility, I owe debts of gratitude to many people who have influenced the final text.

First chronologically are my late parents, Alf and Pearl, and my siblings John, Geoff, Graham, Christine and Anne, from all of whom I learned so much about opportunity, possibilities, relationships and learning.

My life and professional skills have been expanded materially, and continue to be expanded, by the support and constructive input of my personal friends and my professional colleagues in both business and coaching. Many of my clients have been willing to open up to me about their lives, aspirations and challenges, and have significantly enhanced my own life experiences and widened my circle of competence.

I owe particular thanks to those who have reviewed and commented on the manuscript, especially those who confronted the earliest and roughest drafts: Gillis Broinowski, Mark Burgman, Denise Fleming, David Gwynne, Peter and Sue Kaldor, Lukas Ruecker, Sandy Thomson and my brother Graham. Your encouragement and constructive input has been of great value.

Many people have been generous with their time, thoughts and frankness as I canvassed some of the concepts with them — Roland Burgman, Rebecca Dee-Bradbury, Peter Guy, Thos Hodgson, Narelle Kennedy, Rod Lester, Helen Lynch, Paul Murnane, Mike Perry, Rob Purves, Fiona Shand, Sandra Yates and my colleagues at Global Coaching Partnership.

I am particularly indebted to Bruce Hamilton who is the one person who has reviewed multiple drafts and provided me with constructive input and debate on the majority of the book. His input to my research efforts has also been very valuable, as has that of my daughter Emma and the librarians at JPMorgan Australia, Melissa Gavenlock, Jeanine Metcalf and Susan Shrubb. My PA Karen Miceli has also been of practical assistance in many ways.

Two of my relatives, Rowan Cook and Peter Kaldor, have been inspirational in their ideas and challenges and have introduced me to wider disciplines and supplementary frames of reference.

I would also like to recognise the professionalism of the John Wiley team on this project.

Writing a book can be a rather selfish pastime. I would like to recognise the patience and support of Tori, Emma, Stuart and Jessica for their endurance during my lengthy distraction by this project.

About the author

Over the past three decades Dr Ian Pollard has been chairman, director or CEO of more than 30 companies ranging from small to large and covering a diverse range of cultures, ownership structures and financial performance. In 1984 Ian founded DCA Group, which grew to become one of Australia's 100 largest companies.

Ian has also been extensively involved with youth development through the not-for-profit sector and, through Global Coaching Partnership, has coached around 30 CEOs and senior executives.

Since his youth, Ian has been interested in the development of people's capabilities and relationships, their identification of opportunities and the magnitude of what some people achieve and contribute in their lives. He especially admires those who have done this despite disadvantage and material adversity. Ian is particularly interested in the personal qualities and the events and processes which make these remarkable achievements possible. Ian has written a number of books on corporate finance.

Investing in Your Life is Ian's first book on the building of people's capabilities. Married with three adult children, Ian is an actuary and Rhodes Scholar and has represented Australia in tennis. He is currently Chairman of Corporate Express Australia and RGA Reinsurance Australia, and sits on the board of directors at Milton Corporation, the Purves Environmental Fund and the Wentworth Group of Concerned Scientists. Ian also serves on the advisory councils of both JP Morgan Australia and the Faculty of Business at the University of Technology, Sydney.

Preface

Identifying and investing in life's big opportunities

A senior partner in a major professional services firm, whom I was coaching, was successfully managing a significant team and major client assignments, but at substantial personal cost. All too often, Judy was working into the early hours of the morning, a commitment that wasn't shared equitably with those around her. Without reducing client service and practice growth, there had to be a better way.

Judy and I had discussed the importance of her 'negotiating' with her colleagues to find a more equitable way of sharing effort and expectations. However, she didn't seem to be taking up this combined challenge and opportunity with the passion that was required. She needed to overcome her own reserve, her anticipation of resistance and, most importantly, her view that it was often easier to do things herself. This approach may be easier in the short term, but is seldom the best course of action in the long term.

I happened to read a brief article in the financial press, and realised that its underlying principles, involving the accumulated impact of actions for the full term of a career, were fundamental to Judy's situation. I emailed her as follows:

> *Thought for the week—I saw a newspaper quoting a new book,* Women Don't Ask, *which estimated that women's coyness in negotiation costs the average US woman executive US$500k over a career. My extrapolation: if you assume that the same coyness in negotiation may be applicable to negotiations with clients re price and expectations, negotiations with colleagues (senior, junior and peer) re inputs/effort/allocation of responsibilities, negotiations with spouses and other family members (kids and siblings), then ... It emphasises the importance of someone in your situation (i.e. having vast demands on your time and energy) being clear on your own expectations from all of these relationships/stakeholders and having conscious decision-making processes/negotiations with your own objectives and priorities as a backdrop.*
>
> *It's worth thinking about the compounding effects of this and applying some devil's advocacy to some of the things you automatically take on just because you are a good, capable and productive person. Unfortunately, the well of energy can easily dry up.*

Women Don't Ask[1] made the potential financial prize of salary negotiation very clear. Its calculation drew on two core principles of wealth accumulation: the power of compound growth and the value of annuities.

My email to Judy challenged her to envisage her work–life balance, and to place some dimensions around her potential 'prizes' in terms of working fewer hours per working week and having reduced stress levels—and, as a consequence, increasing her effectiveness. This she did. Judy's conversations with me and with others then took on a different dimension and vigour.

My entire professional life has been associated with investing in and helping build businesses, and mentoring or coaching senior executives. Judy's story reveals how the richness of the link between my two principal professional interests suddenly became clearer to me. I realised something both simple and exciting: *people development is a process of investment, and a powerful analogy can be drawn between the highly measurable world of financial investment and the relatively unquantifiable world of people development.*

Investing in Your Life brings this analogy to the fore, inspiring you to view your own development through the prism of an investor. My aim in writing this book is to show you that the application of investment thinking to all aspects of your life will help you better identify the big opportunities for investment in what I call your Life Capital. By drawing on the lessons that the great investors apply in spotting financial investment opportunities, I hope to encourage and empower you to find greater opportunities in your own life, and to see how much bigger you can make them. As a result, you will invest more aggressively in the best opportunities, and make your life more meaningful, satisfying and rewarding.

For example, the thought of a $500 000 financial prize will no doubt get the juices going. But so too do Judy's five to 10 hours less work each week, along with less stress and her greater effectiveness. Your prizes will depend on your individual situation, and this book and the stories in it will provide you with the tools to identify the prizes that will suit you best. Seeing and sizing up the prize is important because it empowers you to feel good about the prospect. Once you deem the risks lower and the rewards higher, you are then more likely to act—to invest in your Life Capital.

Your Life Capital is made up of:
- → your human capital—who and what you are
- → your social capital—who and what you are surrounded by
- → your financial capital—what you own.

Collectively, they represent your capabilities and other aspects of your life that generate opportunity, income, contribution, companionship, satisfaction or pleasure for you.

Around the world, exceptional individuals have generated immense fortunes. Consciously or subconsciously, they have worked with the power of compound growth, the value of annuities and other core financial principles in order to succeed. Most of these principles are elegant in their simplicity—the ease with which they can be understood, the frequency with which they can be applied or observed, and their enhanced power when used in combination. I will demonstrate how these principles can be applied to the investments you make in your Life Capital and life's significant journeys.

I hope that *Investing in Your Life* will lead you to see conversations, relationships, opportunities, learning and decision-making through an additional lens—in an investment context. If you do so, you will re-evaluate the significance you place on many daily events, and probably change the way you invest your most limited resources, especially your time, energy and emotional capital. Initially, these will be conscious decisions, but they will later become more automatic. Assuming such behavioural change, there is significant potential for accelerating the growth of your Life Capital, and thereby generating additional and 'bigger' opportunities, income, contribution, satisfaction or pleasure.

In the course of this book, five key themes will emerge:

1 The potential returns from investment in your Life Capital are far bigger than you realise:

→ Most people overestimate their current capabilities, under-estimate their potential and hence underinvest in developing their capabilities. For example, on a scale of 1 to 10, table 0.1 compares estimated versus actual capabilities.

Table 0.1: estimated versus actual capabilities

	Current grade	Potential grade	Potential for improvement in grade
Your estimation of your capabilities	6	7	1
Actual capabilities	4	9	5

In this example, you have underestimated your potential return from investment in building your capabilities. Significantly, you estimate you have a potential for improvement of 1 grade, whereas your potential for improvement is actually 5 grades. You are therefore less likely to invest in this improvement, especially if it currently demands hard work for a result that will be achieved only in the long term.

→ Your consequent underinvestment in your human and social capital is further exacerbated in situations where it is competing with investment in your financial capital, because the latter is so highly measurable (for example, where you have a choice between a job that will pay more and one where you will learn more or meet more interesting people).

→ Even when someone invests energy and time in developing their capabilities, they tend to hope for quick, or at least consistent, growth. Instead, growth comes in fits and starts, and many people lose patience with the inconsistent returns on the investment and cease investing before the big returns are achieved. The time horizon for the achievement of your goals should therefore take this into consideration. The big returns over the medium and longer term are obtained by those who are patient, even though the short-term returns are inconsistent.

2 You can most effectively grow and develop your Life Capital if you strategically leverage off other people's Life Capital. The most effective way of doing this is through engaged conversation. I view what I call 'life-enriching conversations' as the fundamental catalyst for building Life Capital.

→ As John Donne said, 'No man is an island'. I am not, nor I suspect are you. The building of your Life Capital is accelerated by leveraging off others' Life Capital—their knowledge, their contacts, their ideas, their money … Your ability to do this is determined by your ability to engage effectively with other people—most commonly, but not exclusively, through conversation.

→ Effective engagement almost always simultaneously increases or reinforces your human and social capital. It may also lead to opportunities to increase your financial capital—either directly through an investment opportunity or indirectly through an income opportunity.

3 The potential to leverage off other people's Life Capital through conversation is widely and significantly underestimated and underutilised.

→ If you underestimate the potential from leveraging off others' Life Capital, you will suffer recurrent opportunity loss because of your failure to participate strategically in life-enriching conversations.

→ Some of your habits may minimise your ability to leverage off others' Life Capital; for example, such habits as always being in a rush, not listening or not having an open mind. Your ultimate loss of Life Capital from such habits can be vast if not detected or if no effort is made to change them.

4 Your life is your responsibility.

→ Responsibility for your career doesn't lie with your employer; responsibility for your retirement savings doesn't lie with your employer's pension fund; responsibility for your health and fitness doesn't lie with your doctor or your personal trainer. It's all in your court, as is the decision to grow and develop your Life Capital and to embark on any necessary behavioural changes.

5   In taking responsibility for your life, you can be empowered by:

→ *your individuality:* cherry-pick from this book whatever you find valuable and consistent with your preferences, dreams, goals, interests or profession.

→ *your interdependence with others and the power of reciprocity:* for simplicity, my focus is on *your* life opportunities and the building of *your* Life Capital. However, life and conversations are not one-way streets. Your life is enriched by the myriad people who contribute to it on a daily basis. You have many opportunities to talk with family, friends and colleagues about their interests, opportunities and challenges, and to introduce them to others. Anything you can do that may help them to enhance their lives may enhance your own. Firstly, if you help them, they are more likely to want to help you. Secondly, if you help them and their Life Capital grows, they will be better placed to help you. Finally, working through others' challenges can be valuable in anticipating or solving some of your own.

→ *your relief that Life Capital is not an exact science:* nor does it need to be. You won't need a calculator or complex formulae to spot the big opportunities.

So, dream big and think big ...

This book is ultimately about dreaming and thinking big. You have the right to do so and arguably also the obligation — we live in a world that needs us all to punch above our weight. I hope this book empowers you to do so.

... but base it around the long term

If you build your expectations of yourself too high in the short term, you're likely to place unreasonable pressure on yourself and to disappoint both yourself and those who share your expectations. As Australia's first female Governor-General Quentin Bryce often says to young women: 'You can have it all, but not all at the same time'.

Introduction

To most people, capital means a bank account, a hundred shares of IBM stock, assembly lines, or steel plants in the Chicago area. These are all forms of capital in the sense that they are assets that yield income and other useful outputs over long periods of time.

But these tangible forms of capital are not the only ones. Schooling, a computer training course, expenditures of medical care, and lectures on the virtues of punctuality and honesty also are capital. That is because they raise earnings, improve health, or add to a person's good habits over much of his lifetime.

—Gary Becker

Life Capital—the theory

Your personal capabilities and other aspects of your life that generate opportunity, contribution, income, companionship, satisfaction or pleasure collectively make up your 'Life Capital'.

Broadly, your Life Capital is a *function* of your human capital, your financial capital and your social capital. As table 0.2 sets out, these comprise the following:

Table 0.2: Life Capital

Human capital: Who and what you are (unique to you)	Cultural capital Emotional capital Intellectual capital Physical capital Sensory capital Spiritual capital Symbolic capital
Financial capital: What you own or control (arguably a commodity)	All your financial assets (such as shares, bonds, property and cash), less your borrowings (such as bank or credit card debt), plus the value of any businesses you own.
Social capital: Who and what you're surrounded by (partially unique to you and partially shared with those around you)	Your family Network capital (both personal and professional) Institutional and community capital (both bonding and bridging capital) Environmental capital

There is a vast amount of academic literature available on each of these three major categories of capital. Their precise definitions vary but what is important is their common theme — capital.

What interests me is your Life Capital, and the growth in income, opportunity, contribution, pleasure and satisfaction that it generates. I've tried to look at that growth mathematically but found no rigour whatsoever. Dealing with the three major categories of Life Capital is like dealing with dollars, apples and polar bears—and trying to add them together is a mathematical nonsense. Life Capital is further complicated by the many unquantifiable subsidiary categories of human and social capital.

Nevertheless, one aspect can be quantified—financial capital. Although in some circumstances financial capital can distort priorities or relationships, in this instance it is particularly valuable conceptually. It enables us to overcome the relatively poor measurability of both human and social capital, and the mathematical difficulties of adding things that have no common basis of measurement.

Financial capital offers three major opportunities for insight:

→ Its measurability enables you to see that capital can grow to be very substantial. You can, for example, marvel at Warren Buffett building each $1 invested in Berkshire Hathaway in 1965 to around $5000 (in market value) in 2009—evidence that, assuming strategically sound investment, the sky is the limit.

→ Its measurability also enables you to calculate rates of growth—in Berkshire Hathaway's case, compound 21 per cent per annum over 44 years.

→ Because of the amount of publicly available information and objective commentary surrounding financial capital, you can see roughly how Buffett and others achieve such financial growth.

The underlying objective of this book is to apply investment thinking to the building of both human and social capital, and therefore the building of Life Capital. For example, virtuous circles in building relationships are analogous to compound interest; recurring benefits from a skill or a change in behaviour can be viewed as annuities; opportunities are akin to financial options; and engaged conversations are opportunities to leverage off another person's Life Capital.

The core concept is that if you can identify opportunities to apply the same building principles, then surely the sky is the limit here too—even though human, social and Life Capital aren't so neatly measurable.

The capital of a business is made up of its assets (which generate income) less its liabilities (which reduce or absorb income). Your Life Capital is analogous: life assets are those things that generate opportunity, contribution, pleasure, satisfaction and income, while life liabilities do the opposite.

Some life assets are relevant to everyone, regardless of their work or career, and many are easily taken for granted until they deteriorate—such as your physical and mental health, your ability to get a good night's sleep, your memory and your five senses. There could be an almost mirror-image list of potential life liabilities.

Figures 0.3 and 0.4 (overleaf) show the processes by which an investor builds financial capital and the processes you use to build your Life Capital.

Figure 0.3: an investor building financial capital

Investor has:
1 financial capital
2 financial goals
3 time, energy and risk constraints
4 investment strategy to meet goals

Investor identifies/is introduced to investment or divestment opportunities

Financial capital generates income

Investor decides income allocation

Income reinvested

Income spent

Investment decisions

Opportunities taken up

Opportunities rejected

Good (bad) decisions lead to:
1 increased (reduced) financial capital
2 investor moving closer to (further from) achieving financial goals

Figure 0.4: building your Life Capital

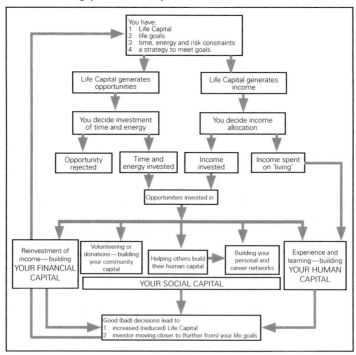

You have:
1 Life Capital
2 life goals
3 time, energy and risk constraints
4 a strategy to meet goals

Life Capital generates opportunities

Life Capital generates income

You decide investment of time and energy

You decide income allocation

Opportunity rejected

Time and energy invested

Income invested

Income spent on 'living'

Opportunities invested in

Reinvestment of income—building YOUR FINANCIAL CAPITAL

Volunteering or donations—building your community capital

Helping others build their human capital

Building your personal and career networks

Experience and learning—building YOUR HUMAN CAPITAL

YOUR SOCIAL CAPITAL

Good (bad) decisions lead to
1 increased (reduced) Life Capital
2 investor moving closer to (further from) your life goals

The detail of the two diagrams is less important than the analogy between the two, and the observation that the same key words appear in both diagrams: capital, goals, time, energy, opportunities, income, investment, decisions and building.

In applying this analogy, the lessons from the great investors become valuable tools to help you identify the magnitude of many life-enriching opportunities. You are then more likely to invest more of your limited resources—your time, money, energy, attention and risk—in capturing those opportunities. You'll also invest more strategically, recognising when the size and nature of the opportunity more than justifies the investment of those resources.

The analogy applies to any of life's significant journeys—career or business endeavours, travel, adventure, romance, hobbies, health and fitness. All of these important aspects of life involve the investment of your resources, and will therefore benefit from the analogy of building financial capital. By thinking in wealth-creation terms (like capital, assets and liabilities), you will increase:

- → your awareness of opportunities or options
- → your appreciation of their magnitude and therefore the consideration you give to the big opportunities
- → your confidence that you have the ability, the opportunity and the tools to reach, even exceed, your goals.

For example, you could focus on the parts of your Life Capital that are relevant to a particular journey, such as:

- → your 'career capital', those parts of your Life Capital that can be applied to your professional activities
- → your 'recreational capital', those parts that can be applied to your leisure activities
- → your 'family capital', those parts that can be applied to your family activities and relationships.

An important aspect of work–life balance is ensuring that you are not investing excessively in your Career Capital to the exclusion of your Recreational and Family Capital.

The 23 important Principles described in this book focus on the following aspects:

- → convincing you to invest in your Life Capital (Part I)
- → empowering you to invest in your Life Capital (Part II)

→ the application of your Life Capital to your career (Part III)
→ identifying and seizing opportunities (Part IV)
→ seeing how your Life Capital is influenced by building relationships (Part V)
→ the role of learning in growing Life Capital (Part VI)
→ making and implementing decisions (Part VII).

In each of these activities, the strategic use of conversations is a powerful catalyst in growing your Life Capital.

You will also come across a number of core principles of long-term financial investment that are also applicable to the building of human and social capital. Some of the principles are mathematical in nature (like the power of compound growth), while others are more like disciplines or learnings (such as accepting responsibility for your own investment strategy). Each principle's application to financial capital is explained in a box titled 'Wealth Insert'. You'll find a list of the Wealth Inserts at the end of this introduction, categorised according to the concepts they illuminate.

Because financial accumulation has been so widely researched and documented by others, financial capital is not the direct focus of this book. Accordingly, the Wealth Inserts in this book should not be applied unless they form part of a more comprehensive investment strategy aligned to your financial position, needs and goals. There are many excellent books on investment available that may help you develop a comprehensive investment strategy. This book does not purport to be one of them.

The Wealth Inserts could, however, be of value in causing you to reflect on your existing investment strategy. They might motivate you to develop a new strategy, or increase your interest in investment and long-term wealth creation.

Your financial capital is tightly linked to both your human capital and your social capital. For example:

→ your earnings from the application of your human capital, or more accurately the net savings from those earnings, are fundamental to building your financial capital, especially when you are young and your financial capital is growing from a small base
→ your experiences while you earn money also develop your human and social capital

→ if you overemphasise the earning of money, little of your time and energy will be left for developing your human and social capital

→ you can apply some of your financial capital to pay for tools or services to develop your human or social capital (for example, coaching), or to pay for services to free up your time so part of it may be committed to your human and social capital.

Life Capital—the practice

Ultimately, *Investing in Your Life* is about thinking bigger and empowering you to do so. Just as Warren Buffett has shown the potential for growth in financial capital, there is no limit to the potential growth of Life Capital. In fact, some people use it not only to change their circumstances, but to change the world.

Bono, the U2 rock star and campaigner for Third World equality, epitomises the building and application of Life Capital. Significantly, conversations have proved to be an important catalyst for him to do so.[1] Bono has always believed in instinct over intellect. What he does in practice, probably instinctively, I've sought to define as a process.

Interviews with Bono reveal the clarity of his vision—whether discussing music or third world development. From an early age, he was clear about who he was, what he stood for and where he was going. He had the courage to dream big, despite receiving little motivation from his home life or his schooling. His confidence in his ability to realise his dreams and his potential were instilled in him later on in life, by U2's manager Paul McGuinness. Subsequently, significantly influenced by Bob Geldof, he developed the confidence to be true to himself. He realised that he didn't have to live up to others' expectations, even today when treading the world's political and economic stages.

Bono and U2 also learned from McGuinness that, while they had to be focused on their art, they also had to be aware of the business issues. Thinking unusually long term for rock artists, the band took lower royalties from Island Records in the short term in order to retain ultimate ownership of their songs, copyright and master tapes.

While acknowledging McGuinness' great mentoring, Bono is proud that he and U2 have always been in charge of their own destinies. These days this also manifests itself in clear constraints when it comes to his own availability: 'I do all my business one day a week. And if I can't do it in one day, I don't want to do it'. Bono's political/economic and business work have given him an interesting balance, and returned music to a pleasant escape where he has the 'luxury to dream'.

Bono seems to have a natural talent for identifying the big points in life and playing them to their fullest. At the 1985 Live Aid concert, for example, he jumped off the very high stage and danced with a girl in the crowd, causing U2 to miss its next song but spontaneously creating a memorable image that became permanently associated with Live Aid. Bono's performance was more orchestrated and even more emotive in the lead-up to the July 2005 summit in Gleneagles, Scotland, where the G8 leaders agreed to cancel the debt of the 18 poorest African countries and to increase aid by US$50 billion by 2010. He appealed to the G8 civil service negotiators before the summit: 'Please go that bit further—in 20 years, this week is one of the things you'll be most proud of in your lives'. Just before the end of the summit, he appealed to George Bush: 'On so many issues it's difficult to know what God wants from us, but on this issue, helping the desperately poor, we know God will bless it'.[2]

Daring to be different and taking risks have been fundamental to U2 and Bono's success. Bono believes he has been 'open and vulnerable' in his music. While the band assumed that each of their new records risked 'commercial suicide', with each release they achieved more commercial success.

Bono has never feared failure, but he has sometimes failed to see obstacles and received a few 'black eyes'. He has been able to overcome these obstacles because he is objective about his own abilities and capacity, and surrounds himself with great people who fill the gaps. The band started when Bono (a self-described lousy guitar player and even lousier piano player) teamed up with lead guitarist the Edge (David Evans—'an extraordinarily gifted complex musician'), bass guitarist Adam Clayton and drummer Larry Mullen, without whom 'these melodies would not be grounded'. According to Bono, 'the blessing of your weakness is it forces you into friendships'. His approach of relying on others who are the best at their job remains key to his success today—whether they be musicians, business advisers or politicians.

In all that he has done, Bono has been a networker and connector extraordinaire, renowned for bringing diverse groups of interesting people together—whether for dinner, a meeting or a concert—and for finding the right entrees to decision-makers. In building relationships he recognises that you don't have to agree on everything—one single thing is enough. For example, a shared sense of humour has been one of the foundations of U2's success. Similarly, his belief that you only need to agree on the immediate cause has been fundamental to his effective collaboration with people from very divergent backgrounds and views—thus enabling his causes to benefit from a very wide congregation.

Bono's empathy is fundamental to reaching his audience. In his networking and relationship-building, his empathy gives him a better understanding of issues and challenges from others' points of view, and enables him to engage with people. Significant to this is his respect for 'people who stay true to their convictions, no matter how unpopular'. This makes it possible for those who might disagree with him in one context to be on his side next time—like former US Treasury Secretary Robert Rubin, who was philosophically against third world debt cancellation but later helped Bono get AIDS drugs to South Africans.[3]

Although gifted intellectually (and at chess), Bono lost interest at school and was not admitted to university because he failed Irish. He would have liked to study an arts degree in English and history, and was always interested in ideas. Years later, his work in development economics and the issues of the third world is a wonderful progression from the arousal of a genuine interest to passion, mastery and influence. Bono recognised that access to people in power would not be enough if he did not know the subject, and he stuck by his principles: Faith over fear. Know your subject. Know your opponent. Don't have an argument you can't win.

One of Bono's early 'connectors' to US political and financial circles was John F Kennedy's nephew Bobby Shriver, who introduced Bono to world-renowned development economist Professor Jeffery Sachs. Bono spent time with Sachs and with many other economists, mastering the issues. Fully versed, he then visited relevant people of power or influence. Bill Gates initially thought that meeting Bono would be a bit of a waste of time because the subject was so complicated. According to the *Time* magazine article naming Bono and Bill and Melinda Gates as *Time's* Persons of the Year for 2005: 'It took about three minutes with Bono for Gates to change his mind—Bono was hurling metrics across the table as fast as they could keep up'.[4]

Bono seems to have always shown the same curiosity and quest for learning and truth. As a teenager, he asked questions of record company executives about copyright, distribution, radio record selection and recording contracts.[5] Later, against the backdrop of violence in Northern Ireland, he studied Martin Luther King's philosophies of non-violence. Then, as a 25-year-old 'late developer trying to figure out a world view', he challenged his long-held belief in non-violence by studying the liberation theology of the Sandinista guerrillas in Nicaragua, which he visited so he could understand the situation first-hand.

Although Bono has described his intellect at this stage in his life as 'unschooled and haphazard', he always wanted to see things and find out things for himself. His intellectual curiosity inevitably led him 'to go round lifting stones until he found some really interesting creepy crawlies'. With an experimental nature and an open mind, Bono listens to and learns from sceptics and cynics. He likes being challenged: 'You're as good as the arguments you get—the friction of different points of view makes you better—The thing that'll make you less and less able to realise your potential is a room that's empty of argument'.

Following his mother's death when he was 14, Bono had to return to an empty home after school. Consequently, he likes being around people and fully engaging with them, tuning in to them. He appreciates great conversationalists, their hunger for ideas and their generation of ideas. The idea for Product RED (a marketing alliance between the Global Fund to Fight AIDS, Tuberculosis and Malaria, and a number of international companies) developed through conversations between Bono and Bobby Shriver—according to Shriver, 'over probably several glasses of wine, over one or two nights—and neither of us can remember who had this idea'. Shriver became CEO of RED, which on behalf of the Global Fund receives 40 per cent of the pre-tax profits from the companies' specially branded RED products.[6]

One of Bono's special personal relationships was with the late French painter Balthus—over 50 years his senior. Bono has always found older people more interesting, citing 'Frank Sinatra to Willie Nelson, to Johnny Cash to Balthus'. Balthus' painting was 'obsessed with the concept of youth—and innocence, and the moment of losing it'. The two men spent a lot of time together, just talking—ongoing discussions about 'God, death, sex, painting, music'. Interestingly, Bono reflected, Balthus 'didn't know our music. He knew my conversation. That's all that he knew—conversation to him was music. I don't think he had ever listened to a U2 song as well'. After Balthus' death in 2001, his Japanese widow Setsuko became a Catholic, with Bono as her godfather.

An Irish Catholic who values reflection, prayer and meditation, Bono believes that 'if you're gonna listen to yourself—and you discover stuff about yourself that you don't like—you have a duty to fix them'. According to Bono, 'the job of life is to turn your negatives into positives', and he admires the American ethos of redemption and reinvention.

Bono and U2 did not initially take charge of their own financial capital. In the late 1980s they received a substantial sum from the sale of their interest in Island Records. They invested it with people who they liked personally but 'weren't as expert as they thought in the areas they were investing in'. Much of the capital was lost. U2 learned a lot from this experience and they ceased their hands-off view of their financial capital.

Today Bono is an investor in a wide range of businesses, including as an active partner in a California-based private equity firm that invests in media and entertainment companies, especially those in a position to benefit as technological change disrupts the status quo. For Bono, apart from an investment opportunity, it is also a chance to keep at the forefront of his industry.[7]

Bono's story is one of long-term building of capital—his human capital by learning (both intellectually and emotionally), his financial capital by his income and the returns on his investments, and his social capital by his networking and relationship-building. Bono seems to build with a sense of urgency and a dislike for wasted opportunity, yet with an eye for the long term.

Central catalysts in Bono's story are his passion and his ability to engage with others—through his music and through his conversation in its many forms. Standing behind these remarkable capabilities are his strong family life (four children from his 30 years with his wife, Ali) and the stability of his U2 relationships. Bono's capacity to build and maintain relationships across so many fields suggests a richness of emotional capital, from a very obvious optimism to empathy and self-awareness. His understanding of his own strengths and weaknesses gives him sufficient self-belief to be able to understand and trust others, while his Irish Catholic spirituality features prominently in his reflections and his ever-evolving world-view.

When invested and applied wisely, all forms of capital grow rapidly. Bono invests and applies his Life Capital wisely—including his reputational capital from his celebrity, which he sees as a form of currency he can apply to raise the alarm on behalf of people who do not have a voice of their own. Ever optimistic, Bono prefers to describe Africa in terms of its myriad possibilities rather than its tragedies. He sees the world as being 'more malleable than you think. We can bend it into a better shape. Ask big questions, demand big answers'.

When Bono was around 25, U2's manager Paul McGuinness said to him: 'You have something very few artists have—You see the whole equation'. I'm convinced that Bono clearly sees the Life Capital–building equation and the catalytic role that life-enriching conversations play, both clearly and instinctively. Bono's rich life provides tangible evidence of the practical application of the principles espoused in this book—the results of making strategic investments in your Life Capital, especially with life-enriching conversations as a catalyst.

You might rightly say that you aren't Bono. You aren't, but the Life Capital approach can work for you just as it works for Bono, if not to the same extent. Knowing that I can't match Warren Buffett's investment performance doesn't discourage me from learning from him and applying his principles in my investments to the best of my ability.

Wealth Inserts

The Wealth Inserts provided in this book illuminate the following opportunities for building your Life Capital:

Frameworks for understanding your own situation

→ Accepting responsibility for your own investment strategy (Wealth Insert 5A)
→ 'I've got it, I've got it: what is it?'—categories of stocks (Wealth Insert 7)
→ S-curves and stall points (Wealth Insert 10B)

Your flow of opportunities

→ The power of leverage (Wealth Insert 12A)
→ A leveraged conversation with a broker (Wealth Insert 12B)
→ The value of options (Wealth Insert 13)
→ Qualified deal flow (Wealth Insert 19B)

Answering the question 'Is this a significant opportunity?'

→ The power of compound growth (Wealth Insert 3A)
→ The value of an annuity (Wealth Insert 3B)
→ Charlie Munger's 'latticework of mental models' (Wealth Insert 5B)
→ Opportunity loss (Wealth Insert 9)
→ Anything of the form A = B – C represents a special opportunity (Wealth Insert 10A)
→ Turning losers into winners (Wealth Insert 11)
→ Contested takeover bids bring bigger premiums (Wealth Insert 12C)

Maximising your probability of success

→ The circle of competence (Wealth Insert 5C)
→ Benjamin Graham's 'margin of safety' concept (Wealth Insert 19A)
→ Thorough analysis distinguishes investment from speculation (Wealth Insert 21A)
→ Diversification to spread risk (Wealth Insert 21B)
→ Put your eggs in one basket only if you control it (Wealth Insert 21C)
→ Expected value (Wealth Insert 22A)
→ Philip Fisher's scuttlebutt and the business grapevine (Wealth Insert 23A)

Maximising the size of success

→ Warren Buffett's 'If you were only allowed 20 investments in your lifetime' (Wealth Insert 20A)
→ Up the ante when the pricing or odds are favourable (Wealth Insert 20B)
→ Loss aversion: you can go broke taking profits (Wealth Insert 20C)
→ To achieve a high return, you need to take on some risk (Wealth Insert 22B)
→ Taleb's strategy for profiting from extreme events (Wealth Insert 22C)
→ Peter Lynch's two-minute monologue (Wealth Insert 23C)

Learnings/building confidence

→ Focus on the decision-making process, not the short-term outcome (Wealth Insert 5D)

→ Benchmarking (Wealth Insert 17A)

→ Performance attribution (Wealth Insert 17B)

→ Confirmation bias (Wealth Insert 19C)

→ Weight of money versus weight of competence and preparation (Wealth Insert 23B)

Part 1
Convincing you to invest in your Life Capital

The notion that our lives succeed or fail one conversation at a time is at once commonsensical and revolutionary. It is commonsensical because all of us have had conversations that, for better or worse, profoundly altered our professional or personal lives. It is revolutionary because a course on conversations won't be found in an MBA curriculum.

—Ken Blanchard[1]

In part I, I want to introduce two important points:
→ the life-enriching potential of conversations, through their role in building your Life Capital
→ the power of the analogy between the creation of financial wealth and the building of your Life Capital—in particular, as a guide to recognising the big opportunities in life.

I will achieve this by sharing a few stories and some logic based around three broad Principles:

→ *Principle 1:* Conversation has diverse rewards. The more you are engaged and the more strategically you view conversation, the greater the rewards.

→ *Principle 2:* You probably underinvest in strategic conversation because you don't see big enough rewards.

→ *Principle 3:* If you apply lessons from the great investors, you are more likely to see the size of rewards, target the biggest opportunities and invest more wisely.

Principle 1
Engaged strategic conversation

Conversation has diverse rewards. The more you are engaged and the more strategically you view conversation, the greater the rewards.

At our very first meeting, we talked with continually increasing intimacy. We seemed to sink through layer after layer of what was superficial, till both reached the central fire. It was an experience unlike any other that I have known.

—Bertrand Russell, describing meeting Joseph Conrad in 1913[1]

1.1　What is a conversation?

Many traditional writers on conversation argue that if it is a means towards an end, then it is not conversation. My definition contradicts that argument. In my view, conversations with anyone—family, close friends, fellow parents, club members, business colleagues or total strangers—are most engaging if they move naturally between the personal, the theoretical, philosophical or political and the individual's opportunities or problems of the day.

My definition, distinguished principally by the level of engagement rather than the content or motivation, is therefore: conversation is communication between people that offers opportunity for genuine engagement beyond any narrow functional purpose of the communication.

Face-to-face conversations in our personal and working lives take many forms and are held in many forums—from the dinner table, washing up and pillow-talk, to job interviews, performance appraisals and board meetings. There are also all those impromptu chats that take place in the bus, lift or airport lounge. However, a declining proportion of our communications are made face-to-face. Technology is taking over, offering so many alternatives through internet, video or telephone link-up.

So what constitutes a 'conversation' for our purposes? An endless list of situations qualifies, including almost any form of face-to-face discussion, regardless of location, and certainly including telephone and video hook-ups.

My definition excludes the majority of email communications and all texting. Email and texting often win when it comes to flexibility, efficiency and cost-saving, but their overuse results in the loss of real engagement, posing three major dangers:

→ loss of the opportunities that engaged conversation brings
→ absence of body language
→ the mistaken belief that you have understood complex situations when you have not.

Email plays a vital role in the globalised and networked business environment of the 21st century, especially for those working in multinational corporations or conducting global transactions across time zones. However, it disappoints (but does not astonish) me to hear about the young colleagues of friends who email each other from desks positioned just a few feet apart, or to learn about people being fired by email.

As those who value engagement know well, email, the internet and online social networking are valuable tools for keeping in touch, and planning and preparing for the real engagement. But as Bill Gates said in the early days of email (1994):

Email is not a substitute for direct interaction. Email helps out with other types of communication. It allows you to exchange a lot of information in advance of a meeting and make the meeting far more valuable.[2]

Many young people believe that a series of rapid-fire texts constitutes a conversation. They must be very adept at texting if they can conduct a well-engaged conversation by text! Such exchanges surely lack the breadth and depth of a great conversation, and the opportunities for spontaneity and instantaneous feedback offered by face-to-face or even telephone conversations.

While tone of voice may signal plenty in a telephone conversation, body language—the facial expressions, the confused look, the hand gestures, the stance, the group mood—communicates more than the spoken or written word. Efforts to resolve difficult business issues across time zones, cultures and perhaps languages are a particularly revealing case in point. The easiest things to communicate may be the facts, figures and logic but they alone will not achieve a resolution of issues, consensus or buy-in. The communication needs to be rich enough to achieve emotional engagement, and this is very difficult in the absence of the instantaneous feedback provided by body language.

From time to time world events significantly discourage long-distance travel—most notably in recent years following the terrorist attacks of 9/11 and the outbreak of Severe Acute Respiratory Syndrome (SARS) in 2003. At other times, pilot strikes have similarly restricted travel. During such periods, executives become more adept at using all sorts of tools for non-face-to-face communication. Yet after the impediment to travel is removed, most business people resume travelling as much as before, recognising that occasionally meeting face-to-face is essential.

1.2 Opportunity loss from efficient but narrow or disengaged communication

If you take pride in your efficiency, your communication habits may lead to substantial opportunity loss, as the following examples show.

Issuing an invitation

The simple invitation 'Would you like to come to the football on Saturday as my guest?' presumably merits a simple answer. It can be achieved in a few seconds or minutes through personal assistants or a brief email or text. Alternatively, through the positive engagement of a personal phone call, the conversation may be extended to include more wide-ranging subjects. Some of those subjects may be planned or anticipated by the caller; others may arise naturally in the ensuing conversation.

As a company director, I regularly receive invitations from accounting firms and investment banks. I value these business forums enormously, and appreciate the social invitations that include my wife, Tori. These firms' centralised marketing departments are so well organised that the invitations are generally sent out by PAs, email or post. I seldom receive a personal call to extend the invitation. Those firms are operating efficiently—minimising the risk of an embarrassing screw-up and not using their senior peoples' time. However, because of that efficiency, they miss opportunities by not having one of their senior people make personal calls for some of these invitations. Perhaps it's just too difficult, given the size of the firms and their functions.

As a sole operator, however, I don't have much choice. I always try to make the invitation personally by phone. If I already know the person well, this maximises the opportunity for some serendipitous outcome from the conversation. If I don't already know them well, it often helps in developing the relationship, increasing the chance that they will accept the invitation and increasing their awareness of me in the context of the upcoming function. Sometimes it helps to think like a sole operator or entrepreneur even if you work for a major corporation.

Reporting to the boss

One of the standard challenges/opportunities for executives is 'reporting up'—the effectiveness of the reporting relationship between an executive and their boss. A core part of such a relationship is the frankness of the feedback and encouragement provided by the boss, and the enthusiasm with which the executive responds. This is understandably challenging in some multinationals, separated by oceans and time zones—misunderstandings are easier to fix when you're only across the corridor!

One of my clients was not achieving genuine engagement with her boss. Although they worked in different buildings (one block apart), her standard mode of communicating with him was over the telephone. She saw it as being functional, efficient and respectful of her boss's time, but it was not effective in developing their relationship. After becoming aware of the issue, she made a point of arranging to meet more regularly in his office. She used that opportunity to explore more open-ended subjects than would be natural during their more functional telephone calls. Understandably, their engagement increased and the agenda widened. She soon better understood her boss's expectations, how she could help him and how she could capitalise on his broad experience. He had a better appreciation of how much she had to contribute, and also capitalised on it.

Thus, the greater the engagement, the wider the agenda and the greater the upside.

1.3 Good timing maximises engagement and opportunity

Whenever we delay important conversations, we delay achieving the direct benefits, any consequent relationship-building and any learning we might achieve. It also means there is more time spent worrying about the issue, resulting in big losses and opportunity costs all round.

Sometimes these losses can continue for years. My late aunt, Florence Kaldor, was the shared assistant for two mathematics professors of international eminence who never spoke to each other. These two Fellows of the Royal Society did not have the emotional intelligence to move on from a disagreement about their relative status. The result was years of emotional strain for everyone, and loss of collaboration.

On the other hand, sometimes a brief delay before talking about an issue can be a good thing. For example:

→ If your emotions would currently cloud an issue, do the verbal equivalent of drafting an angry letter and sleeping on it before sending it. If others' emotions could potentially cloud things, buy yourself some time and look for a good opportunity in the flow of events.

→ You can only engage effectively when the counterparty is ready to do so. Don't try engaging with someone in a rush. This was well demonstrated by a simulation of the Good Samaritan parable, conducted by two Princeton professors with a group of theology students. On their way to making their presentations, all the students were individually set up to pass a seemingly badly injured man. Of the students who had been told they were running late for their presentation, only 10 per cent stopped to help, compared with 63 per cent of those who were told they had a few minutes to spare. Ironically, those who were actually going to make a presentation about the Good Samaritan parable did not offer a greater level of assistance.[3]

→ You may also need to consult with third parties who have an interest in the matter—to get their input, engagement or support.

1.4   Conversation has many rewards

Bonjour. Je viens d'Australie. C'est Cowie, la petite vache de ma jeune fille Jessica, qui a neuf ans. Puis-je prendre une photo de vous avec Cowie pour Jessica?

Hello! I come from Australia. This is Cowie, my nine-year-old daughter Jessica's little cow. May I take a photo of you with Cowie for Jessica?

That's what you find yourself saying if you're on a Paris Metro platform and want to take a photo of your daughter's tiny bean-bag cow looking out of a Frenchman's shirt pocket. With a quizzical but positive response from the busking saxophonist, a great adventure is about to unfold. It turns out that Luis, actually from Argentina, speaks French.

You might well ask how a greying Australian businessman found himself in this situation. I was in Paris to visit the Organisation for Economic Cooperation and Development (OECD) for just one day—as the Chairman of an Australian think tank. I decided to extend my visit to four days to revive my French, a passion from my schooldays but untested in France for 25 years. On the day of my arrival, however, I had little luck speaking French with anyone.

My nine-year-old daughter Jess had asked me to take a photo of Cowie, her favourite fluffy toy, at the Eiffel Tower. Aiming, as always, to under-promise and over-deliver, I decided to get photos of Cowie at all the main Paris sights.

From the top of an open-air double-decker bus, I braved the embarrassed looks of other tourists as I held Cowie in my outstretched left arm and lined up the famous sights of Paris in the background—the Arc de Triomphe, Champs-Elysées, Notre Dame, Place de la Concorde, Musée du Louvre, Galeries Lafayette ... and, of course, La Tour Eiffel.

Unfortunately, that evening the one-hour Kodak man gave me a demoralising photography lesson—focal depth. In all the photos, the crystal-clear Paris scenes were partly covered by a blurred, over-exposed or shadowy Cowie. But the Kodak man's casual remark inspired me: 'You really need someone else to hold Cowie'.

Next morning, I left my hotel feeling optimistic but conscious that it was time to move beyond my comfort zone. I especially needed to forget all the stories I'd heard about the infamous unapproachability of Parisians.

When I saw Luis and his saxophone, I knew the worst possible outcome would be an expletive or a punch, so I summoned up the guts and asked him. My first experiment—and what a success it was! Not only did I get a great photo for Jess, Luis and I chatted in French for about 10 minutes. My photographic problems and linguistic barriers were suddenly lifted.

All that day I approached people around Paris using the same line—always with passion and commitment. Most were beautiful women I would normally not have had any chance of talking to (even in English) unless I was pushing a pram or walking a dog. In all cases, a Kodak moment and a chat in French ensued. They all seemed to appreciate, in whatever order, the enthusiasm of my approach, my child-based mission, my innocent little friend Cowie and my efforts to speak their language.

By evening, my spirits and confidence were so high that I walked uninvited into a small party at a fashion boutique called Michele C in Rue Lafayette, again seeking a photo and a chat. In no time I was drinking champagne with the other guests at Michele's birthday party. Several years later I returned unannounced to the boutique with my older daughter Emma and was warmly welcomed back. Michele recognised me immediately and proudly produced the photo I had sent her of Cowie's earlier visit.

My only knockback, late in the evening, was from two striking women who resembled the tennis-playing Williams sisters. I spotted them walking near the Gare du Nord, where the Eurostar train arrives from London. I walked about 100 metres with them, pleading for a photo for Jess. Serena wanted to; Venus didn't. Venus, who seemed to have had a bad day, won. Walking back, somewhat deflated, I realised that four enormous African men had been following us, and they approached me. Fortunately, their tone was inquisitive rather than confrontational. More French conversation ensued, along with photos of Cowie with the big men from Zaire.

Next morning, dressed in my business suit, I got out at La Muette Metro station, uncharacteristically early for the short walk to the OECD. With Cowie and my camera in hand, I was looking at things differently and noticing things I normally wouldn't. My unrushed mind was relaxed and ready to capitalise on serendipity.

The La Muette platform was adorned with giant advertisements. One, promoting an upcoming exhibition, attracted my attention. It showed a magnificent man of ancient Rome or Athens wearing nothing but a bunch of grapes and a shepherd's crook. Let's call him David. I invited one of the schoolkids on the platform to hold Cowie up to cover David's private parts, which he obligingly did.

A few minutes later I spotted a young woman carrying a pet in a cage—her black cat was off to the vet to have its teeth cleaned. Already late, the woman was waiting for a taxi in the peak-hour traffic, but despite her urgent mission, she could not resist the offer of a photo. We put Cowie in the cage with the cat—Cowie at the front behind the bars, and the ominous green eyes of the cat in the background. Then, after another pleasant conversation, I was off to the OECD.

When I arrived back in Sydney I was able to present Jess with an album full of photos of Cowie posing with the characters of Paris, complete with storyline and without any problems with focus. A special moment indeed!

The lessons I learned from my Parisian adventures with Cowie occupied my mind for some years. They significantly influenced my subsequent career interests and hobbies, and ultimately led me to write this book. Some of the lessons I learned reappear in this book in my telling of other people's stories—lessons about failure, experimentation, comfort zones, being brave, slowing down, finding serendipity, keeping an open mind, looking at things differently, speaking another person's language—and about the diverse rewards you can take from conversation.

Last, but not least, my visit to Paris with Cowie was a valuable lesson in self-awareness. It was a rude awakening to realise that it was a highlight of my life! Above all, it made me realise that I normally take myself too seriously. I could argue that this is justified because of the important responsibilities I take on as a parent and in my professional life, but that would be a cop-out.

The challenge and the opportunity is to take your responsibilities seriously while not taking yourself too seriously. You'll then have more laughs, and that's really valuable. According to neurologist Ross Mellick, there is substantial medical evidence that laughter is good for our physical and mental health:

> *Laughter stimulates the cardio-respiratory system: alleviates stress, sadness, anger and grief; enhances alertness, arousal, memory; increases the speed and accuracy of problem-solving and decision-making, stimulates the immune system, endorphin production and contributes to longevity.*[4]

1.5   Conversation is vital for you and those around you

My exploits with Cowie reminded me how much I enjoy chatting with people, listening to their stories and telling the odd tale myself. After the basic essentials of food and shelter, health and safety, there is nothing more important in life. This has been convincingly demonstrated in the work of those who study social capital, such as Professor Robert Putnam, author of *Bowling Alone*. Putnam defines social capital as 'connections among individuals—social networks and the norms of reciprocity and trustworthiness that arise from them'.[5]

Putnam has studied social capital in American communities over the past 100 years, and his studies show an almost continuous decline in most forms of social networks since 1965. More alarming than this decline are the consequences—for child welfare and educational outcomes, mental and physical health, life satisfaction, crime and tax evasion, economic performance and government effectiveness.[6]

Two of the many conclusions from his and related studies paint the following picture:

→ If you are socially connected you live longer. Social isolation is as big a factor in premature deaths as smoking.[7] In studies that were structured to remove the influence of isolation being caused by illness,[8] age-specific death rates for socially disconnected people were two to five times higher than for those of socially connected individuals.

→ If you are socially connected you are happier. Social capital is more important than financial capital in life satisfaction. In countries all around the world, those who are poor but well connected socially are more satisfied than those who are rich but socially disconnected.

Putnam's message is clear and disturbing in its magnitude, though you'll find it less surprising after you absorb the concepts and techniques discussed in this book. Indeed, the size of the opportunity loss for those who are socially disconnected or less connected will become very clear.

Conversation is one of the greatest and healthiest pleasures of life, lifting our spirits and strengthening our mind. We can easily take conversation for granted though, unlike those who have been denied this simple right by regimes such as Nazi Germany, Stalinist Russia, today's North Korea or the former East Germany with its secret police the Stasi, as portrayed in the 2007 Academy Award-winning film *The Lives of Others*.

Czech-born novelist Milan Kundera has commented:

> I learned the value of humour during the time of the Stalinist terror. I was 20 then. I could always recognise a person who was not a Stalinist, a person whom I needn't fear, by the way he smiled. A sense of humour was a trustworthy sign of recognition. Ever since, I have been terrified by a world that is losing its sense of humour.[9]

Principle 2
The impediments
and disincentives
to strategic conversation

You need to see big potential rewards in order to outweigh the impediments and disincentives to strategic conversation.

He who asks is a fool for five minutes, but he who does not ask remains a fool forever.

—Chinese proverb

Human behaviour, technology and the pace of 21st-century life conspire against fully engaged conversation. This is reinforced by the underdevelopment of your conversational skills, which are taken for granted by the education system and which you assume are better than they really are. Very often you do not see high enough rewards to overcome these impediments and disincentives, and so you are likely to systemically underinvest in strategic conversations.

2.1   Choosing not to talk

Some rare individuals have such clarity of vision that they can operate very successfully almost as an 'island'. My favourites are two shy and secretive geniuses, Pierre de Fermat and Andrew Wiles, linked by the 360-year history of mathematics' most famous riddle.

Fermat, a 17th-century French provincial civil servant and judge, avoided socialising in order to preserve his independence in court. In his hobby, mathematics, Fermat was also a recluse, 'sacrificing fame in order not to be distracted by petty questions from his critics'.[1]

In 1670 Fermat's son published a number of theorems he retrieved from his father's papers, including one remarkably simple proposition. It resembled Pythagoras's theorem and was expressed:

> The equation $a^n + b^n = c^n$ has no whole number solutions for n greater than 2. Thus, unlike in the examples of Pythagoras ($3^2 + 4^2 = 5^2$, $5^2 + 12^2 = 13^2$ or $20^2 + 21^2 = 29^2$), you can't find whole numbers a, b and c such that, for example, $a^3 + b^3 = c^3$ or $a^4 + b^4 = c^4$.

Thirty years earlier, Fermat had written in the margin of a book: 'I have a truly marvellous demonstration of this proposition which this margin is too narrow to contain'. He had not spoken about it to anyone, nor, therefore, told anyone his proof. It became known as Fermat's Last Theorem.

For the next three centuries, many of the world's greatest mathematicians tried in vain to prove the theorem, or find a counter-example. Their romantic and fateful stories are well told in Simon Singh's bestseller, *Fermat's Last Theorem*.

In 1908 awareness of the challenge escalated with the announcement of a reward of 100 000 German marks (equivalent today to several million US dollars) for the first to prove Fermat's Last Theorem. The reward was left in the will of German industrialist and amateur mathematician Paul Wolfskehl.

Obsessed by a beautiful woman but rejected by her, Wolfskehl planned to suicide at midnight. Having put his affairs and will in order, he was reading mathematical papers to pass the time, as you do. Reading someone's 'proof' of Fermat's Last Theorem, he identified a gap in it and then filled it. The theorem distracted Wolfskehl until after midnight had passed. He found in the theorem a renewed desire for life, and incorporated the reward in his will. Unfortunately, his reward became relatively worthless after the German hyperinflation of the 1920s. In the interim, however, it prompted vast interest and hundreds of 'proofs' were sent each year to the University of Göttingen, which administered the prize.

Three hundred years after the publication of Fermat's Last Theorem, man had landed on the moon but there was still no proof, nor any counter-example, despite mind-boggling levels of computer testing. Ten-year-old Andrew Wiles read about Fermat's theorem, and to solve it became his childhood dream. Virtually all his energies at school, Oxford and Cambridge, and then as a professor at Princeton, were focused on this goal. In the mid 1980s, Wiles moved into virtual professional isolation, discussing neither his ambitions nor his work with anyone. Seven years later, he emerged with a proof, tested it with one colleague and then presented it publicly.

Like all the other 'proofs' over the previous 320 years, it was found wanting. After another year, very much in the public eye, Wiles solved the gaps in his original proof and presented a valid proof, relying on branches of mathematics not thought of in Fermat's era.

As Simon Singh observed:

> His decision to work in absolute isolation was a high-risk strategy and one which was unheard of in the world of mathematics ... Without inventions to patent, the mathematics department of any university is the least secretive of all. The community prides itself in an open and free exchange of ideas and tea-time breaks have evolved into daily rituals during which concepts are shared and explored.[2]

Why you might choose not to talk

The factors that prompted Fermat and later Wiles to work so independently are clear in the above quotes from Simon Singh — shyness, avoiding distraction and achieving both focus and secrecy. There are endless reasons why you might choose not to talk to others before deciding or acting, including:

→ overconfidence in your own knowledge
→ at the other extreme, embarrassment that you don't know the jargon or the context well enough to engage

→ concern to protect the confidentiality or privacy of
others' information

→ knowing in your heart that your logic doesn't stack up and not
wanting to be confronted by some non-sequitur that someone
else will identify (as Nobel laureate Richard Feynman has said,
'The easiest person to fool is yourself')

→ a tendency to rush to put something into action

→ concern that you might not achieve what you tell someone about

→ thinking others won't be interested in your problem

→ not wanting to distract someone who has more important things
to worry about

→ thinking others may be distressed by your problem

→ not wanting to be perceived to be talking yourself up

→ a desire not to be seen to be 'talking shop'

→ in my case, just being male.

2.2 The underdeveloped and underutilised skill of conversation

In life, major assumptions are made about the development of your conversational skills — listening, talking, questioning, debating, persuading or joking. The education system assumes that you automatically develop these skills from experiences in the home, playground and classroom, in your social life and from the hard knocks of life. You might be 'getting by' but you're probably a long way from really capitalising on the gift of conversation until an event, most likely career-related, prompts you to hone your skills — perhaps it's a new job in sales, public speaking responsibilities, media training or promotion to management.

Writers have responded with dozens of effective 'how to' books on specific forms of conversation — negotiation, handling tough conversations, conflict resolution, networking, job seeking, selling, storytelling... nevertheless, most people, even those who spend a high percentage of their time sharing some form of verbal exchange, don't recognise the highly leveraged role of conversations. They remain unaware of opportunities they never saw coming, and continue that way until someone with a less impressive or less relevant CV gets a job or opportunity they were sure had their name on it.

2.3 You need a compelling 'Why?' to really capitalise on your conversational skills

Unfortunately, no book or course explains the collective life or career relevance of all these forms of conversation—the compelling question 'Why?'.

Why is it worth investing the commitment, effort and discipline necessary to converse effectively and strategically? After all, it has to be compelling enough to overcome the endless reasons you might choose not to talk (see 2.1), along with the major forces that pull you away from conversing effectively, including:

→ work preoccupation

→ the pace of modern life and your general over-commitment at home, at your children's schools, socially and at work

→ information overload and increasing specialisation, which challenge your perspective on issues, including the reason and need for conversation

→ back-to-back meetings, which leave no time for reflection

→ legacy or latent issues, unrelated to the matter at hand, which make you avoid conversations for fear that those particular issues will be raised.

Such forces prevail all too often and for too long…and then, when you've finally overcome them, the other party may not want to talk!

In addition to the long-standing distractions of radio and television, the modern world provides extra opportunities for you to avoid conversation. You can email, text or blog rather than talk, or you can focus your attention on your iPod, computer, BlackBerry or interactive games. In *The New Brain: How the Modern Age is Rewiring Your Mind* (2003), neurologist Richard Restak argues that the vast and competing stimuli forced on our brains by the modern world, including these conversation-avoidance devices, are actually causing our brains to change their organisation and function. In his view, this is challenging our ability to focus our attention, and attention deficit disorder is reaching epidemic proportions.

Interestingly, people tend to think they are better than they actually are at many activities, and so they underestimate how much more they could learn from others. For example, people think they are better than they actually are:

- as car drivers (80 per cent of Swedish drivers responding to a survey rated themselves in the top 30 per cent)
- in their ability to get on with others (less than 1 per cent of a US high school sample rated themselves as below average)
- at predicting the future
- as teachers
- as students
- as executives
- as lovers (I haven't found any survey results yet—but I can guess the answer!).

This tendency is sometimes known as the Lake Wobegon effect, after a fictional town in a US radio series where 'all the women are strong, all the men are good-looking and all the children are above average'. The same tendencies have also been well demonstrated in business situations, ranging from investment management to customer service, and presumably they also apply to conversational abilities.

According to Martin Seligman, the founder of positive psychology, people who are depressed are an exception to this trend. They are generally realistic about their skills, as they tend to be accurate about good and bad past events, whereas happy people remember and exaggerate the good events and forget more of the bad ones.[3]

Attend a well-presented specialist course in just about any subject and you will find it both a humbling and enlightening experience. At a recent conference, we were asked to form a semi-circle—those rating themselves one out of 10 in 'selling' were asked to stand at one end, and those rating themselves nine out of 10 at the other. Initially, I stood in the seven or eight section, but later realised that I had so much to learn that I was really a three or four. My potential may have been seven, eight or even nine, but I had never formally learned the key tricks of how to sell strategically. My experience at an excellent negotiation course 20 years ago was no different and I've since enjoyed 20 years of benefit from attending that course. The core messages from such experiences are very simple:

- this stuff (negotiation, selling or whatever) is really important—it can have a big impact, so treat it seriously!
- there are some fairly simple principles and techniques that can be acquired for minimal investment, which will enhance your skills and performance

→ your enhanced skills can be to your advantage for the rest of your life.

Making a minimal investment in having more engaged and more strategic conversations represents a great opportunity to achieve life-enhancing, ongoing returns. But how big are these opportunities? Their enormity is well evident in the examples relating to performance feedback that follow in Principle 3 and exemplify the compelling 'Why?'.

Principle 3
Seeing the size
of the rewards

By applying lessons from the great investors, you are more likely to see the size of rewards, target bigger opportunities and invest more wisely.

Sometimes big changes follow from small events ... sometimes these changes can happen very quickly.

—Malcolm Gladwell[1]

In my many years of coaching and mentoring senior executives, there has always been one principal determinant of the success of the assignment: the level of buy-in by the client to the process. My belief in this is so strong that I now have one overarching measure of the success of each coaching session—the extent to which it increased or decreased the buy-in of my client to their own personal development.

Three things are fundamental to such buy-in:

→ the client identifying an opportunity

→ the client working out how to capture that opportunity, and thereby believing they can achieve it

→ the client believing it's worth the trouble and consequently pursuing the opportunity.

Principle 3 focuses on convincing you that there are big opportunities to enrich your life that you can't afford to miss.

3.1 The compelling 'Why?', and lessons from the principles of wealth accumulation

In my preface, I referred to a newspaper article about the book *Women Don't Ask*, and the estimated US$500000 forgone by the average US woman executive as a result of her coyness in negotiation. When I later read the book, I realised the newspaper had represented as fact a theoretical calculation. It didn't matter. To me, it had provided a simple framework from which any person could get some measure of their potential prize.

The calculation drew on two core drivers of wealth accumulation: the power of compound growth, and the value of annuities. Both drivers are simple and powerful, but they are regularly underestimated. Their underestimation can lead to major opportunity loss—a vital theme of this book.

Wealth Insert 3A: the power of compound growth

'Compound growth' is exponential growth. One useful rule of thumb is that something growing at x per cent per annum compound will double in about 70/x years.[2] Hence, at 10 per cent per annum compound growth, something will double in around seven years, and quadruple in about 14 years. At 20 per cent per annum compound, values will grow much faster, as shown in figure 3.1.

Figure 3.1: value of $1000 initial investment

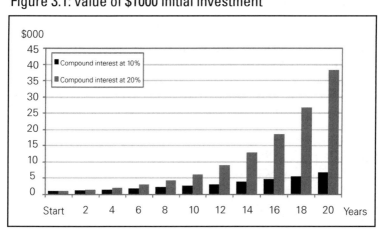

The longer the period, the more amazing the impact of compound growth. For example, over the 44 years since Warren Buffett gained control of Berkshire Hathaway, each share has increased in value around 5000-fold—a seemingly unbelievable increase—but the annual compound rate of growth over that period is 'only' 21 per cent per annum.

Over the whole of the 20th century, the Dow Jones Industrial Average Index increased from 66 to 11 497—seemingly enormous growth, but only 5.3 per cent compound![3]

Peter Minuit of the Dutch West Indies Company bought Manhattan Island from the native inhabitants in 1626 in return for goods worth 60 guilders (about US$24). What a steal! Or was it? Today, the total tax assessment value of Manhattan Island land is US$253 billion.[4] On this basis, Peter Minuit's 'steal' has achieved annual compound growth in capital value of only 6.2 per cent per annum.[5] Remarkable? Yes, the remarkable power of long-term compound growth.

Compound growth can be as severe on the downside as it is wonderful on the upside. Ask any borrower who is unable to pay off their debts. High and compounding interest charges over a significant period are ultimately crippling.

Wealth Insert 3B: the value of an annuity

An 'annuity' is a recurrent payment. For example, it could be monthly income received over a period of five years or a quarterly expense paid out for 10 years. The value of an annuity depends on the amount you will receive each year, how many years you will receive it and the rate of interest at which you value it. As shown in figure 3.2, the longer the term of an annuity, the greater its value.

Figure 3.2: present value of an annuity of $1000 pa valued at a discount rate of 8.0 per cent pa

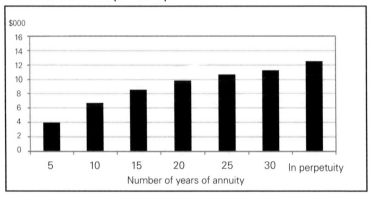

The value will obviously be greater if the annual payment increases with inflation or, as per the example in figure 3.3, increases at 3 per cent per annum.

Figure 3.3: present value of an annuity of $1000 pa valued at a discount rate of 8.0 per cent per cent pa.

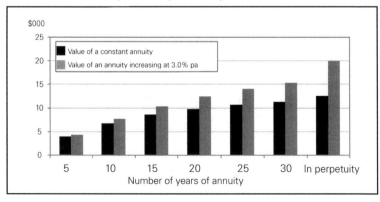

The key principle is that a long-term annuity may have a present value worth 10 or 20 times that of a one-off amount. This is why business leaders are forever looking for recurring and preferably increasing income streams or recurring cost savings for their businesses.

It also explains why major listed corporations tend to have stock market valuations at about 10 to 15 times their current-year maintainable earnings—or more if they have substantial profit growth prospects.

It also explains why companies in which my colleagues and I coach regularly use terms like 'seeking sustained behavioural changes, resulting in improved personal and business performance'.

An annuity's value is the financial equivalent of the old Chinese proverb: 'Give a man a fish and you feed him for a day; teach a man to fish and you feed him for a lifetime'.

Another annuity-based adage regularly comes into play in your working life: the name of the game is to stay in the game. If you lose your job because you take too big a gamble or focus too much on the short term, there may be no annuity for you. There is a delicate balance between the extent to which you should go out of your depth to learn and earn more in the short term without putting at risk your long-term income stream. The investment analogy of this was well demonstrated in the 2007–08 credit crisis by the number of good businesses that lost control of their futures because of excessive borrowings.

My objective in writing this book is not to achieve an accurate quantification of potential outcomes. Rather, my aim is to provide you with the tools for spotting substantial opportunities. Take the two extremely powerful tools in this section as examples: when you identify compounding opportunities for your life or your career, or you see an annuity of benefits, you should sense that the opportunity may be substantial and worth pursuing.

3.2 Receiving constructive performance feedback

People around us may tend to collude with our denial. Among the more difficult kinds of information to get in organisational life is honest, constructive feedback about how we are doing, especially about our lapses.

—Daniel Goleman[6]

One classic opportunity that everyone can take advantage of is performance feedback. How you handle this feedback can be a major determinant of your future performance and ultimate success. This applies whether you are the boss/teacher/coach/parent or employee/pupil/child. Even though performance assessments are becoming the norm in well-managed companies, their value is vastly underestimated.

A commonly held view is that performance reviews are solely a review of your current performance, and how that performance might be improved in the period ahead. Let's call those immediate period-ahead benefits Level 1. This one-dimensional view ignores the benefits that are potentially available to you at higher levels, assuming you take the constructive feedback positively and work to improve your performance.

Level 2 represents an *annuity* of direct benefits in your performance:

→ your improvement in performance may be permanent and thereby offer recurrent performance benefits (an annuity of higher contribution and higher reward)

→ your view of constructive performance feedback and therefore your reception of it will be positively reinforced.

If you focus principally on your own issues and decisions, it's easy to overlook or underestimate the impact that your constructive response will have on the person who gave you the feedback and your relationship with them—Level 3. For example:

→ by taking the feedback positively, you will distinguish yourself from others who react to critical feedback as though it is a personal attack

→ the person who offered you the feedback will watch to see if you put it into practice, will note your efforts and will probably offer more coaching until you master it

→ that person will probably offer you more (solicited or unsolicited) feedback in future in other contexts

→ over time, you will get better at 'managing up' (see 15.4), which in turn may give you a stronger base for managing your own team—better resources, clearer objectives, performance expectations and information; it also increases your circle of influence and hence your ability to impact the organisation positively

→ over time that person will become one of your 'champions' (see 15.5)—and you never know where that may lead.

These indirect, but nevertheless substantial, Level 3 benefits will *compound* with each other in a virtuous circle and compound with the *annuity* of direct benefits of improved performance (Level 2). Given this immense potential, the integrity of a company's performance review system is vital to ensure such discussions are undertaken in the right spirit.

The above analysis relates to just one performance review in a work context. The impact will be much greater still when the analysis is applied to the 'annuity' of regular performance reviews at work—formal or informal—as well as other constructive feedback at work or at home. This step involves a number of assumptions:

→ that you have regular performance reviews and receive other feedback, and that they are constructively presented (arguably both factors are outside your full control but within your influence)

→ that your response will be habitually positive if the feedback is constructive

→ that you will achieve the progress or changed behaviour that is suggested by the review.

If your response to performance feedback is typically positive, you have before you a lifetime of such valuable opportunities. If, however, you are habitually negative and defensive in such situations, you have a lifetime of opportunity loss. The potential magnitude of opportunity losses will be explored further in 9.1.

3.3   Virtuous and vicious circles

An alternative perspective on compounding positives in performance reviews is the concept of 'virtuous circles', as shown in figure 3.4.

Figure 3.4: a virtuous circle in performance feedback

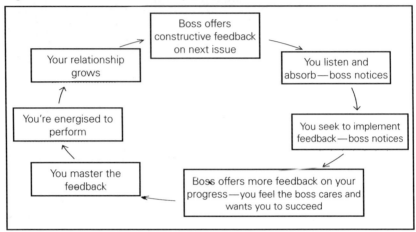

The reciprocity in performance feedback is fundamental. My positive analysis of valuable annuities and powerful compounding is based on key assumptions: firstly, about your positive response to the performance feedback; and secondly, about the positive ways your colleague/boss frames and communicates the feedback and, in turn, responds to your responses.

Figure 3.5: a vicious circle in performance feedback

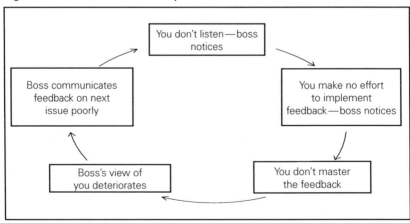

It's easy to envisage a 'performance feedback' scenario of compounding negatives if the person offering the feedback has preconceived views or is not objective, frames the feedback badly or communicates it destructively, resulting in a 'vicious circle', as shown in figure 3.5.

The almost inevitable outcomes are accelerating declines in both your performance and your relationship with your boss.

3.4 Giving feedback

Treat a man as he is and he will remain as he is. Treat a man as he can and should be and he will become as he can and should be.

—Goethe

In his 1969 paper 'Pygmalion in Management', J Sterling Livingston noted evidence from scientific research that a manager's perceptions, expectations and treatment of a subordinate largely determines the subordinate's performance and career progress.

These self-fulfilling prophecies are known as the Pygmalion effect, after the George Bernard Shaw play that became *My Fair Lady*. Pygmalion effects also occur in schools, with a teacher's perception of the ability of a student often influencing the efforts and performance of the student.

These are no small matters. Poor first impressions or a comment from someone in authority, such as 'You're no good at maths/selling/practical things', can start a vicious circle. On the other hand, being told by your coach/teacher/parent/boss how much they respect something you have done will probably leave you turbo-charged and may influence your self-esteem for years—as well as strengthen your relationship.

When you are the person presenting performance feedback, if you frame and communicate the feedback constructively, linking it to what's expected and the jobs and objectives at hand, and show that you care, you will increase the chances of the other person taking the feedback positively and acting upon it. If you subscribe to the 'always try to employ people smarter than yourself' approach, it is surely logical that you should do everything you can to build your people up. The investment of time, deliberation and emotional energy will generally be well rewarded in the growth of their human capital and the development of your relationship with them.

The importance of constructive feedback is seldom greater than for a person in their first job. Back in 1969, J Sterling Livingston observed:

> A young person's first manager is likely to be the most influential in that person's career. If managers are unable or unwilling to develop the skills young employees need to perform effectively, the latter will set lower personal standards than they are capable of achieving, their self-images will be impaired, and they will develop negative attitudes towards jobs, employers, and—in all probability—their own careers in business.[7]

This situation has changed little since 1969, except for the vastly reduced chance that today's Gen Y workers would choose to stay with such an employer.

3.5   Size matters

One of the unifying themes of this book is that the size of your return from an investment in your Life Capital matters. It matters in two respects. Firstly, your perception of the size of the return will be a major factor, both in your decision whether to make the investment and in your commitment to complete it. Secondly, maximising the actual return if you do complete the investment is obviously important.

The better your ability to objectively assess the size of your potential returns on an investment, the better your investment decisions will be; and when you choose to invest, the better your ability to assess whether you are achieving the returns you anticipated.

The ultimate objective is that your assessment of the size of the returns available from an opportunity becomes an automatic, almost subconscious discipline. It is not an exercise in mathematics or arithmetic; rather, it is an exercise in logic to identify the full dimensions of your potential return. You can reasonably achieve this by asking yourself a few basic questions:

→   If I make this investment, what are the direct benefits to me—in my performance, in the size of the success, the probability of success or in my increased human or social capital?

→   Are those benefits one-off or recurrent? If they are recurrent, for how long will they benefit me?

→ What are the indirect impacts on my human capital? On my confidence, my enjoyment or my capacity for risk-taking?

→ What are the indirect impacts on my social capital? On my relationships with others? Does it impact on one relationship or potentially on many?

→ What are the indirect impacts on the future opportunities that might be brought to me or which might be open to me?

The answers to these questions can then be matched to the relevant sizing concepts from the analogy of financial investment: principally, the power of compound growth, the value of an annuity, the value of options, the power of leverage and multiplicity—and, on the negative side, opportunity cost.

This approach was demonstrated in 3.2, in the example of receiving constructive feedback positively. A summary of the benefits gained from this investment is provided in appendix B.

My hope is that by the time you have finished reading this book, taking this approach to an opportunity to invest in your Life Capital will be somewhat automatic. To facilitate your development of this valuable discipline, I have included 'sizing exercises' relating to a number of the most common problems raised by my coaching clients—in other words, opportunities to invest in your Life Capital. Where appropriate, these exercises appear under the heading 'Action' at the conclusion of a Principle, asking you to analyse the potential benefits gained from an investment opportunity, and to think about their significance. Summarised sizings of these opportunities to invest in your Life Capital are provided in appendix B.

Part II
Empowering you to invest in your Life Capital

An important prerequisite for achieving some of the biggest opportunities in life is the ability to make behavioural changes. If you are not convinced that you can succeed in changing a behaviour, you are unlikely to try. And even if you try nevertheless, your lack of conviction will hold you back.

In part II, I want to empower you to take on the big opportunities in life with conviction, based on two principles:

→ *Principle 4:* Achieving the prize may depend on making behavioural changes. The odds of successfully changing your behaviour might seem low, but you can stack them in your favour.

→ *Principle 5:* If you recognise that your life is your responsibility, you are more likely to be successful on your own terms.

Principle 4
Stacking the odds of behavioural change

Achieving the prize may depend
on behavioural change. The odds
of successful behavioural change seem low,
but you can stack them in your favour.

*If I had not been in prison, I would not have been able to achieve the
most difficult task in life, and that is changing yourself.*

—Nelson Mandela[1]

If you analyse constructive performance feedback with a positive mindset
and take it on board, it's assumed that you will achieve the changed
behaviour suggested by the feedback. But how big is that challenge?

4.1 The odds seem stacked against behavioural change

You would think that a big prize (for example, an annuity of benefits)
would be a sufficient incentive to drive and sustain behavioural change.
Not necessarily so. Even your own life, the biggest prize you can possibly
envisage, is apparently not enough to overcome some behaviours.

In 2004 Dr Edward Miller, dean of John Hopkins University medical school, reported that 600 000 people had heart bypass surgery in the US each year, and of these, 90 per cent had not succeeded in changing their lifestyle two years later. What bigger incentive to change could there be? These alarming figures reflect the efforts of doctors to motivate patients with 'fear of death'. It works for a few weeks but then mortality becomes too frightening an idea, so their denial returns and they fall back into their old ways.[2]

Success rates with behavioural change are also inevitably low when people tackle the wrong problem; for example, tackling the symptom rather than the cause:

→ if you spend to counter depression, you are unlikely to curb your spending habits if you don't address the cause of your depression

→ if you drink to relieve stress, you are unlikely to change your drinking habits if you don't seriously focus on the problem causing you stress (for example, your excessive workload).

4.2   Restacking the odds in your favour

The odds of changing your behaviour seem to be stacked against you, but there is cause for optimism as there are many ways you can improve your chances.

Differentiate between adding or improving a behaviour and having to change a behaviour

In general, unlearning a heavily ingrained behaviour takes longer and is harder to achieve than adding a new behaviour. Those opportunities that do not require unlearning will be easier to achieve — metaphorically, they're 'the low-hanging fruit'.

The lowest hanging fruit will generally be those behavioural changes that depend on learning and embedding a limited number of new skills or disciplines. For example, time management is much easier to learn and master than energy management. In managing your use of time, you can rely on your watch to tell you how much of this scarce resource you have expended. In managing your energy, you have to depend on your self-awareness to account for your use of energy.

Stop to understand yourself and the best ways you learn

Your ability to target your low-hanging fruit will be greater the better you understand your own psyche and behaviour, and the ways in which you master change, gain satisfaction and learn.

Some people learn best by doing; others learn best by being taught. Some prefer discussion, others prefer the written word; some prefer books, others the internet. Finding the right environment, method or tools to suit you can double or treble your learning speed. This has two other important impacts:

→ you find the learning less draining, more satisfying and more likely to build your self-esteem
→ you have a much higher probability of persevering and taking something away from your learning.

The combined effect of these factors could be a five- or 10-fold increase in your learning for the effort required.

Identify objectively which of the low-hanging fruit are big and juicy, and prioritise them

There's nothing better for your self-confidence and performance than a few early and substantial wins.

Don't expect to capitalise on the opportunities overnight

Just as the greatest returns on an investment will be achieved over the long term, in talking lives or careers we're talking long-term investment — potentially over a lifetime.

My assignments with Global Coaching Partnership are set up as 12-month assignments, as in most cases such a time frame is necessary for the client to:

→ identify and buy-in to the opportunities
→ work on the opportunities for long enough so behavioural change takes place, is reinforced and ultimately becomes sustainable

→ identify new skills and learn and apply them for a long enough period of time, so they become part of a permanent, almost subconscious 'toolkit'.

You don't have to do all this on your own

Others can really help you achieve your goals—your boss, a team member, a colleague, a friend, a coach, a mentor, a personal trainer, your partner … The importance of having people help you is highlighted in Alan Deutschman's *Change or Die: The Three Keys to Change at Work and in Life* (2007). In his book, Deutschman rejects the traditional trust in facts, fear and force ('the three Fs') as drivers of change, and replaces them with his 'three keys of change—the three Rs':

→ relate—you form a new emotional relationship with a person or community that inspires and sustains hope

→ repeat—the new relationship helps you learn, practise and master the new habits and skills you've learned

→ reframe—the new relationship helps you learn new ways of thinking about your situation and your life.

Deutschman uses a range of examples to demonstrate the three Rs, from heart bypass patients to released prisoners and factory workers. In the context of bypass patients, he notes the mid-1990s experience of a couple of hundred patients with severely clogged arteries who could have had bypasses or angioplasty covered by their insurance plans. Instead, they signed up for a trial funded by their insurance company, Mutual of Omaha—a one-year program arranged by Dr Dean Ornish, a professor of medicine at the University of California, San Francisco.

Staffers helped the patients quit smoking, change to an extreme vegetarian diet, get together for group conversations twice a week, and take classes in meditation, relaxation, yoga and aerobic exercise. These steps became part of their daily routine. After a year, they were on their own. After a further two years, 77 per cent had stayed with their lifestyle changes. While this sample had been self-selected, the improvement from only 10 per cent of the patients achieving a change in lifestyle in the experience of Dr Miller (see 4.1) to 77 per cent is a significant reflection of the value of the alternative approach.

There are many variations on such support structures, some based on mutuality, such as Alcoholics Anonymous and Gamblers Anonymous. Both examples are fellowships of people who share their experience, strength and hope, aiming to solve common problems and to help each other recover from their addictions.

Victory in achieving behavioural change is more likely if it's a clear 'no'

Taking another concept from Alcoholics Anonymous, it's probably easier to achieve a goal of 'no smokes' rather than 'no more than five per day', or 'no alcohol' rather than 'no more than two drinks per day'. The more clearly the line is drawn, the less the continual indecision, temptation or discomfort—even when it is not a matter of addiction.

Make a public commitment while accepting inner responsibility

The effectiveness of such mutual support organisations often capitalises on public commitments made by individuals not to drink or not to gamble. Such public commitments can be significant in steeling the individual's resolve. For example, President General de Gaulle announced to the French people that he had given up smoking so that 'there could be no turning back'. However, the success of the public commitment really depends on the individual accepting inner responsibility for the necessary change.

Make binding decisions in advance

Many decisions in life weigh up investment (short-term pain for long-term gain) versus consumption (short-term pleasure).

The investment decision will be guided by the cognitive system of the brain, whereas the consumption decision will be guided by the brain's impatient dopamine system, which operates faster. Nobel Laureate game-theorist Thomas Schelling characterised his personal battle with cigarette addiction, which he ultimately won, as follows:

> People behave sometimes as if they had two selves, one who wants clean lungs and long life and another who adores tobacco ... The two

are in continual contest for control ... How should we conceptualize this rational consumer whom all of us know and who some of us are, who in self-disgust grinds his cigarettes down the disposal swearing that this time he means never again to risk orphaning his children with lung cancer and is on the street three hours later looking for a store that's still open to buy cigarettes ... [3]

Schelling noted that economics texts see the consumer as a single person, when perhaps the ordinary person isn't a single-minded individual at all—rather, they are a person with two cerebral hemispheres that have come from different evolutionary paths, 'giving us two ways of perceiving our little universes'.

According to Tim Harford in his book *The Logic of Life*, Schelling's 'view of addiction as a kind of mental civil war'[4] is gaining support from brain research. He says that we combine information from both the cognitive and dopamine systems in a compromise that has evolved from natural selection.

Harford then describes experiments where the type of food a person chooses to eat, the movie they choose to see or the level of savings they choose to commit to vary widely, depending on how long they have before the moment of consumption or investment to make the decision. He notes that where a binding decision is made in advance, 'the forward-thinking person outwits the impatient or weakly-willed person who inhabits the same body'[5]; this is less likely when the decision is made on the spur of the moment. When offered a snack to enjoy right now, seven out of 10 people chose chocolate instead of fruit. When offered a snack for next week, three quarters chose fruit instead of chocolate.

It would seem, therefore, that if you are trying to beat an addiction, improve your savings, eat healthier food, get more exercise or change bad habits, the more you can lock yourself into commitments well in advance of the moment of truth, the more likely you are to win your 'mental civil war'.

Public commitment and changing leadership style

In 1997 around 100 Lion Nathan leaders, including CEO Gordon Cairns, attended change and development workshops with the human development company Human Synergistics. The workshops included feedback (called an LSI—Life Styles Inventory), giving the managers insights into their self-reported thinking styles and their behaviours as perceived by others. The Lion Nathan leaders' styles were primarily described as aggressive-defensive and were low in constructive behaviours. In the main, these managers had been promoted on the basis of their financial and operational performance, regardless of how this had been achieved, and they tended to hire people who shared their style.

Cairns' style was reported as aggressive, oppositional, demanding and insensitive—consistent with most of the leadership feedback he'd received over the past 20 years. Previously, he'd largely ignored such feedback because he'd continued to be promoted regardless, because of his results. When his wife asked him what he'd learned at the conference, and he told her about the feedback, she told him it came as no surprise to her. Her next question was how much the company had paid to discover this remarkable information, and she wondered why they hadn't just asked her!

Cairns realised he had to change or he would be 'a failure at home and a failure at work'. One key to his and the company's ultimately successful transformation was his public commitment to change. He published his LSI feedback and asked people in the company to help him change. This made his commitment to change public, and encouraged others in Lion Nathan to do the same. Ten years later, *Fortune* magazine named Lion Nathan as one of the top 10 Asia-Pacific companies for leadership.

Having a wonderful role model

Understanding your weaknesses and being aware of the potential areas for improvement is one thing. Doing the hard yards and taking the risks involved in making the necessary changes is another league of commitment. I have heard of a number of international sportsmen and sportswomen who realised that in order to make it to the very top they would have to make major changes to their game—physical, mental or both. Perhaps the biggest challenge they had to overcome was to recognise that their performance was probably going to worsen before it would improve.

Major change is never easy, and it must be hardest to contemplate for those already at the top. They must question the hard work, the uncertainty of the outcome, the likely deterioration of their performance in the short term, and the potential of very public embarrassment, disappointment or failure.

At age 21, after winning the Masters by a record 12 strokes, Tiger Woods studied a video of his performance and concluded that his swing 'sucked', and that his great performance had been due to his good timing—something he could not always rely on. Tiger told his coach Butch Harmon that he wanted to rebuild his swing. Harmon was confident Tiger could do it but cautioned him about the length of time it would take, along with the likely drop in results and consequent negative press coverage he would receive. Tiger and his coach made the journey together. He changed his grip and improved his strength, with the objective of maintaining power while gaining more control. It took 18 months of poorer results.

During that time, however, Tiger insisted he was a better golfer than before, commenting: 'Winning is not always the barometer of getting better'. After that 18 months, he won 10 of the next 14 events he played and went on to become the youngest ever winner of golf's Grand Slam. He was ranked world number one in seven of the following nine years.[6]

Tiger believed he could improve his performance, and knew that he might be forever frustrated if he didn't give it his best shot. Perhaps he also anticipated that the competition would get better, and that he wouldn't stay ahead of the game in the longer term without making that change.

Such a leap of faith, that by making a major change you will ultimately perform significantly better, takes real courage and maturity. If you take it on lightly, you're more likely to be consumed by the short-term deterioration of your performance and end up in 'no-man's land'. If you give it your full commitment, you have a big chance of taking your performance to a new, higher level on a sustainable basis.

Most importantly, it's all under your control. Your challenge is to put in place the framework, models and processes that suit you, your make-up, your commitments and opportunities, your time horizons and your ability to tap into support from others.

4.3 Stopping to ask 'What of it?'

I benefitted enormously from reading the 400 pages of Mortimer J Adler's 1940 classic *How to Read a Book*—especially thanks to one three-word question: what of it? This question has transformed my reading habits. The action of stopping to ponder the significance of what I've finished reading inevitably leads to other questions that beg answers—which I can then search for in wider reading, targeted conversation or on the internet. I apply the same question to things I hear on the radio or television, or things I observe. In all these contexts, this simple and logical discipline—arguably instinctive but too easily cast aside by a frenetic approach to life—has great rewards. And if you find it doesn't, it's time to question what you're reading or your preferred media!

A significant aim of my book is to encourage you to recognise that conversations are fundamental catalysts in growing your Life Capital. They fulfil that role most effectively if you take a few minutes after having an important conversation to review (and, where appropriate, note down) its strategic significance, instead of just rushing off to your next commitment.

For me, developing the habit of stopping to ask 'What of it?' has been a classic case of low-hanging juicy fruit. To do so, I have not had to unlearn any habits, so the behavioural change has not been difficult. In addition, its impact for me has been material and become permanent. My reading is now more valuable. It is also more efficient, as I have developed a better view of which writers or reporters will best challenge my views or broaden my knowledge.

You may have been brought up never to write in the margins of a book. Adler takes the totally contrary view that marking a book expresses your differences or your agreements with the content, and so is the highest respect you can pay the author. In my view, the more a book influences or challenges your thinking or learning, the more you should underline or write in it. It makes rereading, cross-referencing or comparative reading more efficient. I have always written in books, except, ironically, the *Encyclopaedia Britannica*, of which Adler was chief editor.

Investing in Your Life is ultimately about you, so your 'What of it?' questions will be personal and individual. Each Principle hereafter concludes with a section titled 'Over to you...', to help you ask 'What of it?' and to consider some actions I propose as a consequence.

Some of the suggested actions may be quite time consuming, especially if you feel motivated to do some comparative reading of other books, including some of the titles from which I quote. You'll obviously judge what is of value to you and come up with your own version of the 80/20 rule (see 10.3), whereby you probably get 80 per cent of value from undertaking 20 per cent of the actions that are most relevant to you.

Over to you...

Reflection

- Think of a behavioural change you've made and successfully sustained. What were the key factors that enabled success? What was the nature of the investment you had to make? What ongoing investment are you still having to make? What is the nature and size of the rewards from your success (sustainable/annuity or virtuous circle/compounding)?
- Think of a behavioural change you achieved but didn't sustain. Why didn't you sustain it? What might have helped you succeed? What have been the costs or opportunity costs of not succeeding?
- When you read a book or a newspaper or watch a documentary, do you ask yourself 'What of it?' If you've spent four hours reading a book or an hour watching a documentary, how much more time do you need to invest to form a 'What of it?' view, and then determine whether some action or comparative reading, watching or conversation is justified?

Action

- Buy a new exercise book or open a new Microsoft Word document or any equivalent. If it will help your focus on and passion for personal growth, put a picture of Tiger Woods swinging a golf club on the cover, or an equivalent image that inspires you. As you read and work through *Investing in Your Life*, record any important personal reflections and any suggested actions you consider important enough for you to undertake.

- Identify a situation in which your current solutions are addressing symptoms rather than fundamental causes. Decide what you think are the fundamental causes and plan what you are going to do about them, including any strategies or external inputs to enhance your chances of success. When your personal commitment to the plan is strong enough, implement it.

- Identify some habits you would like to change on a sustainable basis. For each habit, think through what is needed to achieve this change. Rank the habits according to how easy they are to change (for example, whether they involve unlearning) and how significant they are (for example, whether they are things you can both reinforce and benefit from on a daily basis). Appendix B3 may prompt further thoughts. Choose an easy but significant change (a juicy piece of low-hanging fruit). Plan how you will achieve the change, including anticipating any limiting factors and any external input that would be helpful. Implement the plan, perhaps followed by other significant habit-changing opportunities.

Principle 5
Your life is your responsibility

If you recognise that your life is your responsibility, you are more likely to be successful on your own terms.

We are all individuals!

—Monty Python, *Life of Brian*

When our children were growing up, Tori and I treated them as individuals capable of making their own decisions from an early age. They chose which high school they went to, what they studied and what sports, arts or hobbies they pursued. This, we felt, empowered them to design their own school careers, increasing their buy-in to schooling and the enthusiasm with which they got out of bed each day. Now adults, our children have remained individuals, with distinctly different personalities, and they are keenly pursuing totally different careers.

From this, you would think we intervened little in their education. On the contrary, we intervened quite a lot. Firstly, we tried to ensure that they were exposed to any alternatives and received objective information about them. Secondly, while we did not generally exercise the parental right to veto their decisions, we regularly questioned whether they were 'setting themselves up for failure' in some context, or whether their school was doing so. If we thought so, and the matter was important enough, we would intervene—either with our child or with their school.

This chapter expands your perspective on life-enriching conversations by focusing on these same three concepts:

→ recognising your individuality
→ consequently, recognising your responsibility for your life
→ empowering you to set yourself up for success on your terms.

5.1 It's all about you and your preferences so it's your responsibility

Wealth Insert 5A: accepting responsibility for your own investment strategy

For decades, Charles Ellis was a global leader in strategy consulting to professional financial service firms. In the 1970s, Ellis noted the increasing domination of institutional investors and the vast talent coming into investment management. He concluded that in order to outperform others, managers would have to be skilful enough to regularly catch others making errors and quick enough to exploit those errors faster than anyone else. He thought the high quality of many professional investment managers made it nearly impossible for any one person to outperform the market they together dominated.[1]

The next step in Ellis's logic is a key one for our purposes: 'The exciting truth is that while most investors are doomed to lose if they play the loser's game of trying to beat the market, every investor can be a winner. All we need to do to be long-term winners is to reorient ourselves and concentrate on realistic long-term goal setting, sound policies to achieve our goals, and the requisite self-discipline, patience, and fortitude required for persistent implementation'. The rest of his book tells how.

But who is responsible in this scenario? Ellis' view is that it's unrealistic to assume that a portfolio manager can construct portfolios matched to the goals and objectives of each client. He argues that you know the most about your overall investment and life situation, so you should know what you want and should take responsibility for making it happen.

Ellis's principles for winning as an investor translate naturally as principles for making your life a success in the context of your preferences: making realistic long-term goals, incorporating sound policies to achieve them, and the disciplined, patient implementation of those policies—with you taking charge.

So how do you take charge of your life? Because you are responsible! You can't delegate this task.

5.2 Your personal mission, your rules, your values

I must create a system or be enslaved by another man's.

—William Blake

For 25 years, my cousin Peter Kaldor has worked with National Church Life Survey Research. Peter and his colleagues have researched patterns of church life and spirituality in Australia, surveying church communities in over 20 denominations. Their research also included a survey of the wider community, the *2002 Security and Wellbeing Survey,* carried out jointly with Edith Cowan University. Not surprisingly, the survey revealed that if you have a spiritual dimension to your life, you are likely to have increased self-esteem, sense of control, prioritisation of your personal growth and sense of purpose in your life.

Significantly, their research also indicated that *how* you develop your spirituality is also important. Those who arrived at conventional religious beliefs in an uncritical, unquestioning or dogmatic way tended to have significantly lower levels of wellbeing, self-esteem and sense of control in their lives than those who arrived at potentially similar orthodox religious positions in a more *reflective* way. The former were also less likely to trust others and contribute to wider society or help others in crisis.

Mahatma Ghandi's life was one of reflective spirituality. In his autobiographical work *The Story of My Experiments with Truth,* published in 1925, Ghandi wrote that his experiments in spirituality were the source of his power for working in the political field. The more he experimented and reflected, the more vividly he felt his limitations, yet this strengthened him as he worked towards his very long-held goal of self-realisation and salvation. 'I live and move and have my being in pursuit of this goal', he wrote. 'All that I do by way of speaking and writing, and all my ventures in the political field, are directed to this same end.'

'Absolute truth' was Ghandi's sovereign principle, fundamental to his qualities of leadership, which ultimately brought India to independence in 1947. Not surprisingly, the principle was also a core foundation of his professional life as a lawyer:

> During my professional work it was also my habit never to conceal my ignorance from my clients or my colleagues. Wherever I felt myself at sea, I would advise my client to consult some other counsel, or if he preferred to stick to me, I would ask him to let me seek the assistance of senior counsel. This frankness earned me the unbounded affection and trust of my clients. They were always willing to pay the fee whenever consultation with senior counsel was necessary. This affection and trust served me in good stead in my public work.

Ghandi set rules consistent with his principles; his clients respected him for it and worked with those rules. So, in your life or your career, *you* can set the rules, especially your goals — your definition of success.

Investment in spiritual capital

The term 'spiritual capital' has emerged only in recent years but already it has multiple definitions. I like the simple concept that your spiritual capital is whatever ultimately makes your life meaningful for you at the deepest level. It's what you ultimately draw on when the going gets tough and you face hard decisions. It underlies your sense of purpose and values, and therefore how you use the other components of your human capital, and how you decide what is important or what is good. Your spiritual capital may be based on or linked to a religious tradition but it need not be.

Some years ago, Peter Kaldor attended a leadership development program that included many presenters who had been selected because they exercised significant leadership, in many cases at great cost or well against the odds. Those presenting regularly talked about the challenges of leadership, the importance of commitment, the costly nature of working for change, and the importance of clarity of purpose. Kaldor observed that while many of those presenting did work from a spiritual base (whether religious, quasi-religious or from a strong connection with the land or the environment), not once was this deeper aspect of their leadership discussed—either by the presenters or the attendees. This is not particularly surprising in Australia, however, where spiritual capital is seldom discussed other than between those who have similar sources of spirituality, those who disagree vehemently or those whose lives have been affected by spiritual charlatans or unhelpful religious upbringings.

Kaldor argues that it is essential to regularly take some time to reflectively explore and grow your own spiritual capital. It provides a compass for your life and decision-making, a framework for understanding your limitations and difficulties, and is a source of resilience. Whether that reflection is in prayer, in conversation, sitting on a rock looking at the sea, mountains or wilderness, or lying on a beach looking at the stars, it is time well spent—even if some of it is spent wrestling with ultimately unknowable questions.

The importance of finding a meaning in life

The most basic measures used by Western governments to calculate our standard of living are GDP per capita and life expectation. Despite these two aspects improving consistently for decades, and people also having more leisure time, happiness has not improved and mental health problems have escalated.

Richard Eckersley, a leading Australian researcher and commentator on happiness and wellbeing, attributes much of this unhappiness to people's struggle or failure to find meaning in life in modern society:

> Meaning in life is a crucial aspect of human well-being. For most of our existence as a species, meaning was pretty much a social given ... Much of life was predictable and what wasn't was explained in terms of the supernatural ... Today things are different ... The speed, scope and scale of economic, social and cultural change have made the past seemingly irrelevant, the future uncertain. Family and community ties have been loosened. We know much more of the rest of the world and how differently others live and think ... Meaning in life is no longer a social given, but a matter of personal choice; it has to be constructed, or chosen, from a proliferation of options ... the openness and complexity of life today can make finding meaning and the qualities that contribute to it—purpose, direction, balance, identity and belonging—extremely hard, especially for young people, for whom these are the destinations of the developmental journeys they are undertaking.[2]

Eckersley notes that wellbeing doesn't come from positive emotions alone. It also depends on your satisfaction with life, the fulfilment of your potential, your relationships and interests, and the feeling that your life is worthwhile and has meaning.[3]

Undertaking a conscious quest for life's meaning is ultimately an important investment in life itself—even though your hectic family life and your personal and professional ambitions may, in the short term, leave little time for such a quest, and may make you feel you have already found it.

Pursuing a quest for meaning may be one of the hardest investments for you to consider. We live in a society that promotes materialism and individualism, even though these qualities are quite contrary to many people's professed values. According to Eckersley:[4]

→ materialism is bad for wellbeing, because it breeds dissatisfaction, depression, anxiety, anger, isolation and alienation

→ individualism encourages some qualities that are good for wellbeing (personal control, self-esteem and optimism), while discouraging others (intimacy, belonging, self-restraint and meaning in life).

This contradiction is what ultimately makes the search for meaning a challenging but important investment. It seeks to answer a key question: what ultimately matters to me?

5.3   Your framework of mental models for building your Life Capital

A key to building your Life Capital is to have a number of core principles or models that work for you and with which you are comfortable.

While there may be many such principles that work for you, the 80/20 rule (see 10.3) will probably apply, and a few key principles will dominate. The important principles are those that work strongly for you in the situation at hand. Regardless of how many core principles you have, it's obviously even better if they work well in combination (compounding) and on a recurring basis (annuities).

The great long-term wealth builders didn't need to combine all the great financial principles and strategies, just the ones with which they were comfortable. Take a leaf out of the book of Charlie Munger, vice-chairman of Berkshire Hathaway, and Warren Buffett's long-term investment partner. Buffett sometimes calls Munger his 'junior partner in good years and senior partner in bad years'. One of Munger's many gifts to investment thinking is his concept of a 'latticework of mental models' (see Wealth Insert 5B).

Wealth Insert 5B: Charlie Munger's 'latticework of mental models'

In 1994 Charlie Munger presented a lecture to business students titled 'A lesson on elementary, worldly wisdom as it relates to investment management and business'. His key theme was the power of an investor drawing from a range of disciplines a number of models to describe how the world works, and how the people in it behave. From these models Munger developed his 'latticework of mental models' to which his accumulated experiences were added.

Munger's purpose in this approach was to look for investments where he could identify a number of his models operating in the same direction—their effects combining to produce a major upside.

Munger emphasised: 'You don't have to be an expert in any of those fields. All you've got to do is to take the really big ideas and learn them early and well...so they become part of your ever-used repertoire'.[5]

Three of his key observations on this approach were:

- You need multiple models. If you have only one or two, 'you'll torture reality so it fits your models or at least you'll think it does...like the old saying "To the man with only a hammer, every problem looks like a nail."'
- 'The models have to come from multiple disciplines because all the wisdom of the world is not found in one little academic department...80 or 90 important models will carry about 90 per cent of the freight in making you a worldly wise person...only a mere handful really carry very heavy freight.'
- 'It is important to understand the relative reliability and limitations of the models and the assumptions on which they are based.'

Wealth Insert 5C: the circle of competence

Munger continued:

> There's a model that I call 'surfing'—when a surfer gets up and catches the wave and just stays there, he can go a long, long time. But if he gets off the wave, he becomes mired in shallows...people get long runs when they're right on the edge of the wave—whether it's Microsoft or Intel...

> However, Berkshire Hathaway, by and large, does not invest in these people that are 'surfing' on complicated technology...We tend to avoid that stuff, based on our personal inadequacies...Again, that is a very, very powerful idea. Every person is going to have a circle of competence. So you have to figure out what your own aptitudes are. If you play games where other people have the aptitudes and you don't, you're going to lose.[6]

For you to be truly comfortable with a model or principle, it needs to be within or closely adjacent to your circle of competence. If you are passionate about matters outside your 'circle of competence', or your personal mission takes you outside it, maybe it's time to focus on expanding your circle of competence. I am enjoying doing that very thing as I research and write this book—reading, thinking about and experimenting with many disciplines that are somewhat new to me.

The models I'm presenting to you have been influenced by my passions, my growing circle of competence, my successes and failures, and an ongoing study of the people I admire. While I find my set of models extremely powerful in combination, you will be able to build something more powerful for your own purposes. Use this book as a starting point—a solid framework that you can significantly enhance by focusing on your own interests, experience and competence in other disciplines and other models, and your observations of the people you admire.

Some of your models will be timeless and certain—like the power of compound interest and the value of annuities—while others will be simplifications or uncertain, built on assumptions that need to be regularly retested in a changing world. Even the timeless models need to be tested for their application to the context at hand. While it can be very powerful to apply a model almost subconsciously, it can be dangerous if you do so without having an open mind, without recognising the underlying assumptions or with little reference to reality.

The good news ...

The *good news* is that you can derive your own approach, suited to your career, personal interests, circle of competence and, most importantly, your personal qualities and areas of comfort. The concepts of building Life Capital and life-enriching conversations can be adapted to fit *your* ambitions, priorities, risk-tolerance, energy levels and time commitments. You can also adapt them to the different dimensions of your life. For example, you can apply them to your aspirations to be a world-class golfer or research scientist, while also applying them to your love of occasionally playing guitar at local gigs, searching for a great wave for surfing or your journeys as a keen traveller.

The *even better news* is that you can expect higher returns, however you choose to define and target them, for your chosen amount of effort and risk taking.

Better still, those higher expected returns will then encourage you to make greater effort and take more risk or show more courage. If you are willing to invest significant time and energy, and take managed risk, the upside is potentially exponential — in fact, it's almost unlimited!

... and the bad news

The *bad news* is that nothing here proclaims that you can succeed without hard work — only that you can achieve greater success (however *you* choose to define it) for a given amount of application and initial Life Capital. As Benjamin Franklin said, 'Diligence is the mother of good luck', which has been restated by a number of famous golfers as 'The harder I practise, the luckier I get'.

Belief in yourself and your framework is essential to motivate you to invest the time, effort and courage necessary to achieve *your* goals. The rewards will occasionally come in the short term, but most certainly and most significantly in the longer term if you are patient and persist.

Wealth Insert 5D: focus on the decision-making process, not the short-term outcome

Market values are generally continuously available, but many great investors don't monitor such values regularly. Their rigorous investment processes and their comfort with a number of key principles underlying those processes give them confidence in the long-term results. Regular, exact valuations serve little purpose for such investors. It's an example of how focusing on short-term outcomes rather than the process can be misleading.

Michael J Mauboussin, author of *More Than You Know*, emphasises the importance of process in investment management:

> *Investment philosophy is important because it dictates how you should make decisions...But even a good investment philosophy will not help you unless you combine it with discipline and patience. A quality investment philosophy is like a good diet: it only works if it is sensible over the long haul and you stick with it...*
>
> *Quality investment philosophies tend to have a number of common themes. First, in any probabilistic field—investing, handicapping, or gambling—you're better off focusing on the decision-making process than on the short-term outcome. This emphasis is much easier announced than achieved because outcomes are objective while processes are more subjective. But a quality process, which often includes a large dose of theory, is the surest path to long-term success.*
>
> *That leads to the second theme, the importance of taking a long-term perspective. You simply can't judge results in a probabilistic system over the short term because there is way too much randomness.[7]*

5.4   Your process

In many of the things we undertake, our philosophies and processes are key determinants of our ultimate success. This is certainly so in managing an investment portfolio.

Lives and careers, like stock markets, are probabilistic systems. Just like investment management, life-enrichment is not about regularly quantifying outcomes and performance. Nor can it generally be about some highly quantifiable or clearly defined endgame. It is about committing to a framework and approaches with which you are comfortable, and then proceeding with confidence that the long-term results will be rewarding—rather like the changes Tiger Woods made to his swing.

Whether or not you're aspiring for elite performance like Woods, your approach to many of your challenges and opportunities in life may benefit from the efforts of people who have devoted most of their careers to the study of top performers. From my exposure to such people, I've taken away three core messages about process:

→ right up front, be clear on the steps in the process, all the way through to the finish line
→ visualise or mentally rehearse the process, so when it comes to the real thing you are comfortable and familiar with it
→ when the performance time arrives, focus on your process—not the ultimate goal. Just concentrate on what you have to do in the present, and do it with passion and to the best of your ability.

If you have focused on process, you are also better placed after the event to deconstruct your successes and failures, thereby learning and building more effectively.

5.5   Your stories

Many writers expand their knowledge through research, and they clarify their thinking as they write. Even after they've published their book, they might not yet consider themselves to be experts because there's always so much more to learn. I am one of those people.

This book reflects my thinking about life-enrichment and career development, and the important role of conversations. It reflects my own life and career, my experiences and the stories I've seen or heard. Initially, I felt self-conscious about including some stories from my own life, even the story of Cowie, which motivated it all. However, I realised that including autobiographical vignettes is integral to my argument. They provide a context to the conclusions I've reached as a result of those experiences and stories—but it's my framework, not anyone else's. I'm unable to avoid the fact that this book is actually about *me*—but my aim in publishing it is about *you*, encouraging and empowering you to develop your own framework and tools for expanding your own horizons.

What's ultimately important is that you construct your own framework, and that you're comfortable with it. My stories are included to prompt you to reflect. Your reflections, your stories and those of the people you admire will be the building blocks of your own framework of Life Capital and life-enriching conversations. They may bear little resemblance to mine, and you certainly don't have to spend years and hundreds of pages documenting them. However, the stakes are big, and they justify some deep reflection.

5.6   Your labels and your language

As an actuary, I am trained to think and talk in terms of annuities and compounding. I view many situations in this way, and in my mind (and, selectively, in conversation) I label them using actuarial or financial terms. There are plenty of alternative labels I could choose for both concepts:

→   for 'annuity', I could use repeating, recurrent, frequent, regular or multiple

→   for 'compounding', I could use combining, synchronising, reinforcing or virtuous circles.

Alternatively, I could borrow powerful terms from others; for example, I could use Charlie Munger's term 'lollapalooza' to describe the compounding positive impact of a number of his mental models coming into play together (see 9.3).

'Annuities' and 'compounding' work as labels in my case, and that's what matters for me. You're different. Label them in your own way to better reflect your ownership, perception or use of these concepts—perhaps in ways that will motivate you or will be more likely to prompt you to act.

5.7 Your commitment and persistence

Occasionally in sport the oldies rule, and this can be truly inspiring to witness. In 1983, 61-year-old farmer Cliff Young won the inaugural Westfield Sydney to Melbourne Ultra-marathon run. He won the 875-kilometre event by a big margin from his younger rivals, finishing in a remarkable five days and 15 hours. He just shuffled along and didn't sleep.

In 1994, by knocking out his 26-year-old opponent, 45-year-old George Foreman regained the world heavyweight boxing championship title he had lost 20 years earlier, also by knockout, to Muhammad Ali in the historic 'Rumble in the Jungle' bout in Zaire.

What qualities enabled athletes like Cliff Young and George Foreman to overcome the effects of both ageing and boredom? Presumably, if you continue the same physical routines day after day, year after year, it should be possible to retain most of your physical youth. But that would surely drive you insane! Cliff Young managed to keep up his regime by always rounding up his sheep without a horse, bike or four-wheel drive. But in order for most of us to persist, we probably need to find something deeper in the daily grind itself, something to invigorate us, as exemplified in the following stories of survivors Andre Agassi (tennis), James Tompkins (rowing) and Garry Kasparov (chess).

With a real commitment to process, Andre Agassi made a step-by-step recovery from a career-low world tennis ranking of 141 in November 1997 to be number one in 1999. In that year he won the French Open to become only the fifth man to have won all four Grand Slam events in his career, he made the final at Wimbledon (losing to Pete Sampras) and won the US Open. 'My so-called comeback was a difficult journey for me', Agassi commented. 'But one I never lost focus on. It was important for me on a daily level, regardless of the ultimate accomplishment...I was proud of myself along the way. Results come as a by-product.'[8]

James Tomkins rowed in six Olympic Games, winning three gold medals. He also talks process rather than outcome, but with a twist. 'The Olympic Games is the end point, but it's the enjoyment and preparation leading up to it that I love. When I was younger, I did the hard yards because I had to in order to get there. Now I actually like the hard yards.'[9] The key to this enjoyment, Tomkins finds, is a cross-training regime that engages his mind as well as his body.

Garry Kasparov, another survivor — the world's highest rated chess player for the 20 years 1985 to 2005 — showed the same love of the process. 'I learned to enjoy the study and the analysis process itself and not just to see it as a necessary evil or means to an end.'[10]

Taking inspiration from Agassi, Tompkins and Kasparov, you may be better able to commit to and persist with your process of building Life Capital if you have had a major hand in designing it, have consequently bought into it, and enjoy studying it and refining it.

5.8 Your learning strategy

Your future stands on a tripod of human, financial and social capital. The stronger each leg, the easier it is to build that tripod. Some people say 'it's not what you know, it's who you know' — that your social capital is more important than your human capital. Others might say that 'it's not what you know, it's what you own' — that your financial capital is more important than your human capital.

On balance, I believe your most powerful weapon in building your Life Capital, apart from luck, is your human capital. It is your human capital that determines how much you earn and how wisely you invest your financial capital; it is your human capital that determines how effectively you build your social capital. Therefore, the building of your Life Capital is fundamentally dependent on your ability to build your human capital — which, almost by definition, is your ability to learn. Thus, your strategy for building Life Capital must include learning as a fundamental plank.

The *good news* is that after years of experiments, successes and failures, you know more than anyone else how you best learn and what you want to learn. So who better to be responsible for your learning strategy?

There's *even better news*, according to anthropologist Edward Hall: 'Humans are the learning organism par excellence. The drive to learn is as strong as the sexual drive — it begins earlier and lasts longer'.[11]

The *bad news* is that at primary school and high school, students are principally spoonfed. They are taught much too little about learning processes, and not given enough encouragement to explore their own learning. Soon thereafter the spoonfeeding stops, and life becomes more and more about self-teaching and self-starting — but most young people don't have the tools to understand the strengths and weaknesses of their own learning.

I have never studied a formal course on learning but I have been interested in the subject since I was quite young. I used to think I was an excellent learner, and I did have a very good capacity for self-teaching, which I overdeveloped and overused. One of the unfortunate results of this was a feeling that I didn't need to discuss the things I was learning with others. Given that the subjects were mainly mathematical, statistical or actuarial, that may come as no surprise, and you might think that my friends were well spared that opportunity. Who, after all, discusses such subjects at the pub or at a party!

On reflection, I now realise that intellectual development was a rather solitary pursuit for me at that time. The result was that, as a student, I developed little awareness of the benefit of discussing my ideas with others. What a great opportunity loss for me! For a long time I lived in a far narrower world of ideas than I might otherwise have enjoyed.

So I entered the workplace with my own learning strategies. These strategies were very effective for the self-teaching of my range of academic subjects but less well suited to studies of the liberal arts or wider learning about life and business. However, I did have a genuine interest in learning processes on my side, and, as a result of my self-teaching, a tendency to be a self-starter and an independent thinker. As a consequence, I've reasonably fulfilled Garry Kasparov's expectations:

> There are guidelines for what works, but each person has to discover what works for him. This doesn't happen by itself. Through practice and observation, you must take an active role in your own education.[12]

I will return to the subject of learning methods in Principle 16, which I trust will encourage your interest in developing further your own learning strategies. As Warren Bennis and Robert Thomas explain in their book *Geeks and Geezers*, your learning strategies need to evolve:

> All our geeks and geezers devised their own learning strategies, applying their creativity to devise new ones at each stage of their lives... For lifetime leaders, learning is as natural as breathing. They squeeze all they can out of every new acquaintance and encounter. They regard life's sterner less pleasant side as a particularly instructive classroom.[13]

5.9 'Life-enriching conversations' as your catalyst

Every good process needs a catalyst—something that either initiates events or accelerates them. Conversations about the negotiation of work–life balance and the communication of performance feedback are major catalysts in building Life Capital, as are many of the other conversations described or envisaged in this book.

However, they are not always easy. They can require self-confidence and courage—but, most importantly, they have the potential to transform lives. Accordingly, I call them 'life-enriching conversations'. I recommend that you view life-enriching conversations (or whatever you choose to label them) as the fundamental catalyst in your framework for building Life Capital.

Over to you …

Reflection

- Do you take full responsibility for your life? Are you in charge? If not, in what ways are you not in charge?
- What ultimately matters to you?
- Is your passion outside your present core competencies? Do you need to expand your circle of competence?
- Do learning and training invigorate you like they did Agassi, Tompkins and Kasparov? If not, why not? Is it because you don't have a learning strategy?
- When have you experienced significant returns from an investment in your personal development? Did those significant returns spur you on to invest more?
- When has taking a short-term perspective diminished your opportunities in life? What can you learn from that experience?

Action

- Recognise your responsibility for your own life.
- Write down your plans, including the processes needed to fulfil them.

- Identify any new core competencies you think are important to your plans. Analyse how these new core competencies would benefit you and how significant those benefits are (appendix B6 may prompt further thoughts).
- Talk to people about your plans—both to reinforce your commitment to your plans and to leave yourself open to benefit from their wisdom.
- Start a list or analysis of how you best learn.
- Start a list of your mental models of how you built, or intend to build, your Life Capital. As you do so, consider how powerful each of those models is for you, why it's powerful and what assumptions that power is built on.

Part III
The application
of your Life Capital
to your career

In Principle 3, I discussed the power of compounding and the value of annuities—two wonderful concepts when it comes to wealth accumulation. I also demonstrated the size of the potential prize arising from strategic conversation, using the example of the multiple levels of benefits achieved by taking constructive feedback positively.

In part III, I want to probe a little deeper into the wealth-accumulation lessons from the great investors by applying the Life Capital concept to one of life's significant journeys. I could have chosen travel, hobbies, health and fitness or even romantic endeavours. However, I have instead chosen to focus on careers in order to demonstrate the application of Life Capital. The field of careers is rich with public precedents and lends itself more naturally to the quantitative analogy with financial capital.

Part III presents the following three principles:
→ *Principle 6:* Understanding your life assets and liabilities enhances your performance.

➜ *Principle 7:* It is possible to achieve and sustain very high annual growth rates of both human and social capital. Life is more satisfying if financial capital is not the only measure.

➜ *Principle 8:* Life assets and liabilities regularly morph. Your greatest strength in one area may be your greatest weakness in another.

Before discussing these principles, it is vital to distinguish between a career and a job. Decades ago, the two concepts were somewhat confused. A career banker, for example, would probably have had a long-term career at a single bank, but that would be a rarity today. Our Gen Y need to anticipate not only having multiple jobs in their lifetime, but also multiple careers.

At another level, there is an important distinction between a career and a calling. A calling is something you are passionately committed to because of some greater good, where the work itself is your focus rather than your own financial rewards or status.

I will be focusing on careers, rather than callings or jobs, because the measurability of career capital through its surrogate (annual income) is vital to my demonstration in Principle 7 that it is possible to achieve and sustain very high annual rates of growth in both human and social capital—just as Buffet and others show it is possible in respect of financial capital.

Principle 6
Understanding life
assets and liabilities

**Understanding your life assets
and liabilities enhances
your performance.**

*Being wrong about your own competencies can be just as destructive
as being wrong about what game you are playing... This regularly
happens to companies that have had a degree of success but
misunderstand the reason why.*

—Sydney Finkelstein[1]

Like the capital of a business, your Life Capital is made up of your
assets, less your liabilities. The part of your Life Capital that can be
applied to your professional activities is your 'career capital'. Hence
your career assets are those things that generate for you opportunity
in your career, contribution, pleasure, satisfaction and income; career
liabilities do the opposite.

6.1   Opportunities for and from self-discovery

Writing this book has led to a deeper understanding of my own life. Given the overarching subject matter—lives—that's perhaps understandable, as I've made new discoveries and crossed new disciplinary boundaries. In particular, major limitations in my own thinking and self-expression—and therefore great opportunities for personal growth—have been revealed to me.

In an early draft, I put together a general list of career assets and then broke the list down into the categories of intellectual assets, emotional assets and so on. To my amazement, not one item came under the heading of spiritual assets. Perhaps this reflected the lack of depth of my own spiritual capital, or my lack of understanding of it.

When I mentioned this gap to my cousin Peter Kaldor, he immediately bombarded me with questions as diverse as 'How do you feel when you are in a wilderness area?', 'Have any paintings really moved you?', 'What would you really celebrate?', 'Why are we here?' and 'What would you be prepared to die for?'.

His questions made me better appreciate what was meant by spiritual capital, and that my own, while far from being the wasteland I first feared, merited significant further reflection. That I was so vague on the meaning of spirituality is not unusual in Australia, where the subject is little discussed. Around 20 per cent of Australians rank themselves as not spiritual at all, and more than half rank their spirituality at less than five out of 10.[2]

My poor understanding of spirituality revealed opportunities for exploration, growth in my Life Capital, and gaining more pleasure and satisfaction from life.

This fairly recent experience reminded me of a similar situation that had occurred years earlier. My wife Tori had asked me how I felt about something important to us both, and at the time I could not adequately define or describe my emotions. I realised that I just did not have the vocabulary, and this started a challenging, interesting and personally vital journey. Relevant in both contexts was my inability to define or express clearly my thoughts or feelings at that stage in my life—a major step to overcome in any learning journey (see 16.1).

6.2 Understanding career assets and liabilities enhances performance

Your challenge, like mine in 6.1, is to become conscious of the assets that are most significant in your career progress, and the liabilities that will most impede your career. Just like your spiritual capital or your personal mission, this requires ongoing soul-searching.

Here's an example. In his tennis career, John Newcombe won 21 grand slam singles and doubles titles, including nine at Wimbledon. He is regarded as one of the most mentally astute and tough tennis players of the last 40 years, and exemplifies the power of understanding your own assets and liabilities. He has used those qualities to become an outstanding commentator and coach, as well as an astute businessman. Millions of dollars of his endorsements were said to be contingent on him not shaving off his trademark moustache.

When Newk was a 16-year-old protégé in 1961, a pioneer in sports psychology phoned him. He told Newk that he'd watched him play, and felt that some mind-training exercises could help his game. It says something special about the young Newk that he gave it a go:

> He was right—some of the things we tried together did improve the way I played tennis, and they made me want to know more about how my mind worked and the role it could play in my physical performance... My mental strength was one reason for my success. Knowing that I knew my game (and myself) very well indeed gave me the confidence to compete at any level. I could tough out the gruelling matches, cope with the crowds that heckled me, and face down tennis's worst sledgers, bullies and mind-game operators. If things were going wrong for me, I had the ability to go into another mind zone, clearly consider the problems I was facing, then reprocess my body and mind to overcome the adversity.[3]

The most memorable tennis point I have ever seen was halfway through the fourth set of Newk's 1971 Wimbledon final against American Stan Smith. Down two sets to one, Newk fell heavily trying to reach a short ball. He lay there. Smith came over, looking confident. As Newk describes it:

With a pained grimace I gingerly got to my feet holding my arm at a crazy angle as if I'd broken it ... I groaned to Stan: 'Ohh, you've got me ... I'll have to default.' Then I straightened my arm and burst out laughing and 15 000 fans roared with mirth at my antic. Stan was less amused. The object of my little game was to let him know that his air of supremacy was misplaced, that I wasn't sweating it and had no fear. He stopped swaggering and I saw a flicker of doubt cross his face.[4]

Newk went on to win.

Understanding your strengths and weaknesses can be a major contributor to your performance on the day, and can also help you identify areas for improvement in the long term.

Career assets and liabilities can be surprising

The strengths that determine career progress are often more obvious than the weaknesses that impede it. For example, success in international swimming would appear to be most influenced by physical attributes, commitment to their development through training, and injury-free good health. Yet the swimming careers of a number of the world's greatest swimmers have been cut short by interesting non-physical limitations.

Dawn Fraser was for eight years the fastest woman freestyle swimmer in the world, but she left competitive swimming after a disagreement with officialdom over Olympic flags in Tokyo.

Ian Thorpe, winner of five Olympic gold medals and breaker of 13 world records, retired just as he was developing a 'lethal new stroke'.[5] He said he retired because his head and heart were telling him that swimming wasn't what he wanted to keep on doing, and that he was happily developing his professional life beyond swimming. Thorpe believes that traditional swimming training is too Spartan, and does not allow swimmers to develop any 'real life', preventing them from balancing other pursuits outside the pool. It's interesting to contrast Thorpe's view of Spartan training with the invigoration Agassi, Tomkins and Kasparov were able to take from theirs (see 5.7).

For me, the most intriguing retirement of a swimming legend was that of Shane Gould. At the 1972 Munich Olympics, Gould won five individual medals, including three gold, and was named best sportswoman in the world at the age of 15. At the one time she held the world records in all the freestyle events, from 100 metres to 1500 metres, plus the individual medley. On her 17th birthday, Gould shocked her fans, including me, by announcing her retirement from competitive swimming, even though she still loved it.

More than 30 years later, and some years after Gould's return to public life, I finally heard a key reason for her decision:

> If you're in a situation where you're not feeling confident, standing up in front of a group of people and talking is the most scary thing... For me, being in the pool, talking to cameras about swimming, that was no sweat, but when I was asked to be a 15-year-old talking to people at a bowling club, I wasn't trained for it. It was scary... I felt dorky and stupid.[6]

This seemingly minor factor had apparently become a major career liability for Gould—possibly undetected or misunderstood, but certainly underestimated by those close to her.

6.3   A major life or career asset is the ability to make good decisions

Most people found it hard to understand Shane Gould's decision to quit when she had so many opportunities in front of her. They probably thought her decision was irrational, but perhaps it was more a reflection of her physical and mental exhaustion, somewhat similar to the decisions made regularly by:

→ burnt-out executives who feel less motivated by their job, less satisfied by their rate of career progress and increasingly intimidated by monthly performance expectations and their responsibilities for others' careers

→ pressured professional advisers such as accountants and lawyers who become worn down by the demands of recording timesheets in six- or 10-minute intervals

→ fatigued people in social-support and personnel-support roles who ultimately are wearied by imbalanced or unreciprocated communications and probably work in under-resourced organisations—seemingly always being the listeners, the empathisers, the investors of energy in a world of complex personal problems

→ executives in multinational companies challenged by the long hours of executive life, compounded by jet lag and international link-ups at antisocial hours and the resultant challenges to work–life–family balance.

Career burnout breeds poor decisions and can make major change seem essential. If your working life is hectic and over-committed, the challenge is to see burnout coming—to find the time, awareness and thought needed to spot and understand the emerging symptoms that spell physical or psychological fatigue, and to make changes early on so they don't need to be too dramatic. The solution may then lie in making modifications and ensuring your resilience, rather than changing your job or career. In such a situation, it is always valuable to talk to others before making any dramatic decisions—preferably including someone who has walked the same path.

The ability to make good decisions is an essential life asset. Neurologist Antonio Damasio was taught early in life 'that sound decisions come from a cool head, that emotions and reason did not mix any more than oil and water'.[7] Damasio's work with patients debunked this theory, and led to his revolutionary 1994 book *Descartes' Error: Emotion, Reason and the Human Brain*. He argued that emotions and feelings play an essential role in rational thinking: 'At their best, feelings point us in the proper direction, take us to the appropriate place in a decision-making space, where we may put the instruments of logic to good use'. Reciprocally, impaired feelings take us to the wrong place, and we fail to concentrate on the things that really matter.

In *Blink: The Power of Thinking Without Thinking*, Malcolm Gladwell focuses on a different dimension of decision-making, challenging the traditional view that 'the quality of a decision is directly related to the time and effort that went into making it'. He presents a wide array of snap judgements, made by people's 'adaptive unconscious', which proved to be more effective than those made on the back of research, logic, soul-searching or lengthy exposure. Speed-dating is one popular example. As Gladwell notes, those who are speed-dating don't need a whole evening, just a few minutes to answer the key question: whether they want to see the other person again.[8]

Gladwell examines when we should trust our instincts and when we should be wary of them. Instinctive judgements, such as recognising a face or playing a shot in sport, can be blurred by going over them in too much detail or trying to explain them to someone else. The opposite applies to logic problems—although here you can still become swamped with too much information and ultimately have to reduce the problem to its simplest elements. Finally, Gladwell discusses how we can control those first impressions by controlling the environment in which rapid cognition takes place—by acknowledging 'the subtle influences that can alter or undermine or bias the products of our unconscious'.

This he demonstrates through stories of the selection of horn players for orchestras—a traditional male domain. The innate prejudice against female horn players, especially diminutive females, was only overcome when auditions were conducted anonymously behind a screen. Some real surprises emerged.

Few life assets are more important than the ability to make good decisions. Decision-making is revisited in Principles 19 to 23.

6.4 The diminishing lives and real values of knowledge assets

When contemplating making any investment, it is fundamental to understand the expected useful life of the asset in which you are investing. An asset with a useful life of two years has to be viewed differently from one with 20 years of useful life. Also important is how well the asset retains its real value in an inflationary environment, and how much reinvestment it requires if it is to maintain its output.

The real values of our human capital and social capital are not generally diminished by inflation. However, the values of many career assets may diminish over time from lack of use or the pace of change. Many career assets have shorter useful lives than in previous decades, requiring you to capitalise on them more quickly and more effectively. Paradoxically, the most rapidly wasting asset in the modern knowledge economy seems to be knowledge itself.

Knowledge as a rapidly wasting asset

The rate at which the knowledge you built up at university becomes obsolete will vary from discipline to discipline. Nevertheless, you can be confident that its obsolescence is accelerating. The same short life cycle applies to:

→ your knowledge of your specific employer, due to more frequent job and career changes

→ your industry knowledge, due to the impact of changes in industry structure through mergers, technology or fashion.

Many employers shorten these life cycles even further by restructuring and retrenching, often resulting in the loss of corporate memory.

Behavioural scientist Professor Peter Kelly has commented that:

> *A big issue for young people is increased credentialism, which is the idea that you need higher and higher qualifications for entry level jobs... For young people who are not in education and training, youth unemployment runs at between 30 per cent and 40 per cent on average in OECD countries.*[9]

What a paradoxical 'arms race' in qualifications! A knowledge economy, with accelerating obsolescence of that knowledge, and yet higher and higher qualifications being demanded for first jobs—and also for top jobs. But is this increased credentialism fully justified? Is there a counter-argument that, in the knowledge economy, what matters is not specifically what you know, it's how you use your knowledge to engage effectively with others and their knowledge?

French sociologist Pierre Bourdieu suggested that those who rely mainly on their educational qualifications and less on their social capital will be most at risk in a period of 'credential deflation', partly because they lack connections and also because they will be less aware of changes in the market for those credentials. It's also important to note that, because of the ready availability of facts and figures on the internet, detailed, fact-based knowledge is less valuable than the principles, models and processes you learn and evolve through experience.

Keeping your knowledge up to date

If you work in an area where detailed knowledge is important, keeping up with the latest research is vital. Nowhere is this more important than in the practice of medicine.

Whenever I think about professionalism or vocational excellence, I immediately think of Dr Raff, a surgeon at Sigmaringen in south-west Germany who saved my mother's life after a near-fatal car accident in 1972. Among other things, Dr Raff sewed Mum's severed hand back on using micro-surgery techniques that were in their infancy back then, and which he had only read about in a journal. Not only had Dr Raff kept up to date with the latest techniques, he also had the courage to attempt the procedure—in a small regional hospital and without the optimum equipment usually required. Three years later I visited Dr Raff with Mum, and he immediately quoted the date of the operation. It had obviously been an important moment for him professionally.

Long inspired by Dr Raff, I was amazed to read that in 2000 the lag between the discovery of a more effective treatment and its widespread adoption in US patient care was typically 15 to 20 years. As Ian Ayres in *Super Crunchers* observed, 'If doctors didn't learn about something in medical school or in their residency, there was a good chance they never would'.

Before reading this, I had assumed that the internet made it easier for the next generation of medical professionals to keep in touch with developments. I now realise that this is not necessarily the case. The medical literature available on the internet is vast, scattered and of varying quality. Consequently, the challenge of accessing that information effectively can be quite overwhelming, but it can also be very rewarding.

Ayres has reviewed the progress made since 2000 in the practice of evidence-based medicine—decision-making based not on intuition or personal experience, but on systematic statistical studies. He has noted that information-retrieval technologies on the internet have enabled doctors while treating patients to 'cruise through dozens of internet search results and distinguish anecdotes from robust multi-study outcomes', enhanced by a 15-category scale of the quality of evidence.

The bottom line is that the internet is making it easier and more efficient than ever before for professionals in all fields to keep up with the latest developments. As a result, the gap will now widen more rapidly between those who do their research and those who are not so committed.

6.5 Life assets need to be refreshed, updated and nourished

If you adopt a pattern of life that focuses on golden eggs and neglects the goose, you will soon be without the asset that produces the golden eggs.[10]

—Stephen Covey

'Sharpen the saw', the seventh of Stephen Covey's seven habits of highly effective people, is critical. Your life assets will deteriorate rapidly if they are not refreshed or nourished. Covey emphasises the balanced renewal of body, mind, heart and spirit, and notes that renewal in one of these dimensions will have a positive impact in others—a strong foundation for a virtuous circle.

The most fundamental contributor to the refreshment and nourishment of our assets is our use of them. For example, our intellectual and physical assets are likely to deteriorate more rapidly the less we use them. It is thought that if you keep your brain active with varied, interesting and reasonably complex activities, you will build reserves of healthy brain cells and connections between them. You are fortunate indeed if you achieve the necessary rejuvenation of mind, body and spirit in the ordinary course of your preferred daily life and work, without having to undertake conscious investment to do so.

Some assets can easily become 'liabilities' if they are seldom part of your typical day and significant extra effort is required to maintain them. My visit to Paris with Cowie (see 1.4) rejuvenated my interest in languages. Luckily for me, my hobby and labour of love is an investment for my occasional travel. However, living in Australia, opportunities to speak foreign languages in business or in the streets are rare. Hence, for most Australians, foreign languages are a significant negative sum proposition. A vast amount of time is required to maintain your progress to date, and if you don't practise, your grammar, vocabulary and fluency rapidly deteriorate—and, importantly, so does your confidence. This vicious circle of deteriorating competence and confidence can also apply in many other situations if you don't make the ongoing investment.

Over to you ...

Reflections

How well do you understand your principal life assets and life liabilities?

Do you commit much time to refreshing your principal assets? How are you doing that? How can you do it more effectively?

Are you caught in a vicious circle of deteriorating competence and confidence in some context? If that context is important to you, what can you do to reverse the decline?

Actions

- Analyse how you benefit from understanding your assets and liabilities, and how significant these benefits are (appendix B7 may prompt further thoughts).
- List your principal life assets and life liabilities, then look at appendix A as a further thought-prompter.
- With an open mind, examine your assets and liabilities, and evaluate them for relevance, significance and currency for implementing your plans.
- Make a diary note for 12 months hence to do another evaluation.

Principle 7
A more satisfying life

It is possible to achieve and sustain very high annual rates of growth of both human and social capital. Life is more satisfying if financial capital is not the only measure.

I never could be content with a fixed salary, for mine is a purely speculative disposition, while others are just the reverse; and therefore all should be careful to select those occupations that suit them best.

—PT Barnum[1]

One major constraint on your career choice is the need to generate income from your labour to feed yourself and your family. However, this constraint may be reduced or removed if you have significant financial capital, freeing you to pursue your preferred career and commit more of your energy to it. Financial capital may also make wider career opportunities available; for example, through the capacity to buy a business.

Life Capital and career capital are much deeper and richer concepts than financial capital. Apart from capital tied up in a family business, financial capital is arguably a commodity, whereas Life Capital and career capital are unique to the individual. However, for my immediate purposes, financial capital has three major strengths:

→ it is a highly measurable and familiar commodity
→ its accumulation is well understood and demonstrates the power of a long-term building process
→ a strong analogy can be drawn between the building of financial capital and the building of career or Life Capital.

This chapter fleshes out that analogy, specifically in a career context.

7.1 Buying a share in someone's career income

Various writers on share investments have drawn theoretical analogies between making an investment in someone's career earnings and buying a share in a company.

In his 1958 investment classic *Common Stocks and Uncommon Profits,* Philip Fisher used the prospective careers of classmates to demonstrate the importance of holding on to your winners (a subject you'll come to in Principle 10). He asks you to envisage your graduation day. It's a day on which all of your classmates have an urgent need for immediate cash and they all offer you the same deal: 'If you would give them a sum of money equivalent to 10 times whatever they might earn during the first 12 months after they had gone to work, that classmate would for the balance of his life turn over to you one-quarter of each year's earnings'.

With only enough money to make three such deals, you would analyse your classmates solely on the likelihood of how much money they might make, not on your liking for them or their talents outside earning money. Ten years later, one of the three classmates in whom you have invested has done sensationally, winning promotion after promotion in a major corporation. To demonstrate his point of 'hold on to your winners', Fisher then asks whether you would consider selling out of that classmate if someone offered you a 600 per cent return on your original investment. In Fisher's graduation-day scenario, the individual's earning capacity is the only relevant measure.

Legendary Fidelity investor Peter Lynch used a similar analogy to develop his readers' thinking about companies and their earnings and assets: 'If you were a stock, your earnings and assets would determine how much an investor would be willing to pay for a percentage of your action'.[2]

Lynch also noted that:

→ Your assets would include your real estate, cars, jewellery, golf clubs etc, and you would subtract your mortgages, loans, unpaid bills, IOUs and poker debts etc. The result would be your positive net worth as a tangible asset.

→ You also have the capacity to earn income, depending on the basis of your wage and how hard you work—with potentially huge differences in the cumulative results over a career.

A version of Fisher's and Lynch's theoretical concepts became a reality in 1997 with rocker David Bowie's US$55 million personal bond issue. The buyer of the Bowie Bonds (Prudential Insurance Company) was entitled to a portion of Bowie's future income stream, made up of royalties on previously recorded material and receipts from future live concerts. Bond issues by other recording artists followed.

Caroline Ilana, a young London actress, funded her tuition fees by offering shares in her future income. The subscribers included composer Andrew Lloyd Webber and actors Bob Hoskins and Emma Thompson. In their book *Blur: The Speed of Change in the Connected Economy*, Stan Davis and Christopher Meyer raised some of the less palatable issues regarding such a deal:

→ Could Caroline's shares fall into the hands of strangers who, disappointed with her results, might pressure her to pursue unpalatable career options? This would be especially relevant if she sold more than 50 per cent of her shares.

→ If Caroline is successful in her career, it will cost her more to buy back her shares.

7.2   If your career were a stock, what kind of a stock would it be?

When Peter Lynch posed this question to his readers, he suggested it would be a 'halfway decent party game' to put yourself in one of his six categories of stocks, described in Wealth Insert 7.

Wealth Insert 7: 'I've got it, I've got it: what is it?' — categories of stocks[3]

When Peter Lynch gets a lead on a stock (such as the time, decades ago, when he was impressed with a Taco Bell burrito on a trip to California or when his wife came home to him raving about L'eggs stockings), he sees what he's got as 'simply a lead on a story that has to be developed'.

Lynch's first step in 'developing the story' is to put the stock into one of six categories he has identified to cover the useful distinctions that any investor has to make: slow growers, stalwarts, fast growers, cyclicals, turnarounds and asset plays. He then fills in the details that will help him guess how the story will develop.

In the context of his party game, Lynch draws the following analogies, shown in table 7.1.

Table 7.1: categories of companies and analogous careers

Category of company and description	Financially analogous career
Slow growers: large and ageing; started out as a fast grower and eventually pooped out because they had gone as far as they could, or else got too tired to make the most of their circumstances; example, electrical utilities.	Librarians School-teachers Policemen
Stalwarts: multibillion-dollar hulks that are not exactly agile climbers but they're faster than slow growers; examples, Coca-Cola or Procter and Gamble.	Middle managers in corporations
Fast growers: small, aggressive new enterprises that grow at 20 to 25 per cent per annum, not necessarily in a fast-growing industry; in a slow-growing industry, all it needs is the room to grow; examples (in the 1980s), Taco Bell, Anheuser Busch, Marriott, Gap.	Actors Musicians Small business-people Inventors Property developers

Category of company and description	Financially analogous career
Cyclicals: companies whose sales and profits rise and fall regularly and somewhat predictably; examples, auto, airline, steel and chemical companies.	Farmers Resort emp-loyees Jai alai players
Turnarounds: companies that have been battered or depressed and are potential fatalities; example, Chrysler in the 1980s.	Bankrupts Down-and-outers Unemployed
Asset plays: a company sitting on something valuable that you know about but the stock market has overlooked.	Those living off family fortunes and contributing nothing from their own labour

Lynch's categorisations from 1989 omit one significant category of stocks—the purely speculative plays in areas such as resources exploration or technological research. Such stocks can have little value for years, then suddenly increase tenfold in a matter of weeks on the back of a discovery, and then perhaps return to being worthless. The risks and rewards of such speculative stocks are more analogous to careers in the performing arts and sport, or as an inventor.

Graphical representations of the growth of these categories of companies, and implicitly the income-generating capacity of the analogous careers, are shown in figure 7.1 (overleaf)

When presented with such choices, what model of career are you interested in? How does that fit with the career you're actually pursuing? Are you being true to yourself?

Figure 7.1: graphical representations of company growth

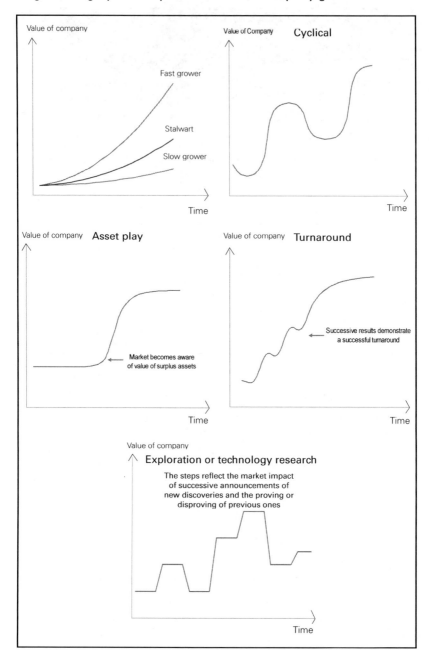

7.3 A world where annual income is the only measure

Imagine a neatly measurable world in which everyone is in a race to maximise their income. Presumably, this is an unbalanced and therefore unpleasant world full of investment bankers, property developers, plastic surgeons, personal injury and class action lawyers, pop stars and professional athletes.

Also imagine that it's a world where your career assets and career liabilities are measurable in dollar terms and can be added together (career assets) and subtracted (career liabilities). As I explained in the introduction to this book, such a concept is a mathematical heresy—you can't find mathematical meaning by adding oranges and lemons and then subtracting tomatoes and carrots! Nevertheless, for the purposes of this example, I'd like you to think this way. The number you would come up with is a 'quantification' of your career capital—your career assets less your career liabilities.

You are now in a world where income maximisation is everyone's sole objective. Everything is measured in dollars and cents. Person A with $1 million of career capital can earn $100000 per annum. They are perfectly happy until they realise they are only half as successful as person B with $2 million of career capital earning $200000 per annum. Unfortunately for person B, their neighbour person C has $4 million of career capital and earns $400000 per annum...and so it goes on. In such a world, are there any winners?

You'd never get caught up in a world like that, would you? Not only do comparisons with your neighbour make you feel unhappy, the more you earn, the more you think you need as you start to grow tired of your house, your boat and your car, which are all too small compared with those of your peers.

7.4 Climbing the ranks in a world of inequality of income

In today's world, inequality of income is increasing:

→ In 2006, three hedge fund managers each earned more than US$1 billion—more than the GDP of Burundi (population

8.1 million), Eritrea (population 4.8 million) or Mongolia (population 2.6 million).

→ Goldman Sachs's 2006 bonus pool of US$16.5 billion averaged US$623 000 per employee, prompting the *New York Daily News* to comment: 'In this city, 1.5 million people live below the poverty line of US$16 000 a year for a single parent with two kids. Goldman's bonus pool could raise each of their incomes by more than US$10 000. Something is wrong when one firm's bonus pool is enough to end poverty in America's largest city'.

→ In 2001 Charles Handy noted that statistically America was the most unequal society in the world after Nigeria. He commented: 'America seems to be proof of the theory that the faster an economy grows, the greater is the gap between rich and poor, because the poor get left behind in a race where knowledge and skills count so much more than mere muscle'.[4]

Will Smith's 2006 movie *The Pursuit of Happyness* was inspired by a true story, which somewhat mirrored the above Goldman Sachs–New York single parent contrast. Chris Gardner (played by Will Smith) sank all his family's savings into expensive scanning devices, which he sold very irregularly to doctors. In 1981, he saw a man getting out of a red Ferrari convertible and stopped him:

'I've got two questions. What do you do and how do you do it?'

'I'm a stockbroker.'

'Man! Stockbroker! Do you have to go to college?'

'No. You don't have to. You have to be good with numbers and good with people.'

Gardner applied for an internship at stockbrokers Dean Witter but his wife put him down: 'Stockbroker. Why not astronaut?' When his scanning device business failed, she moved to New York, leaving Gardner and their son (played in the movie by Will Smith's son Jaden) in San Francisco, broke. As she left, she remarked: 'Salesman to intern is backwards!'

In contrast, Gardner said to his son:

'Don't ever let anyone tell you, you can't do something. Not even me ... You got a dream, you gotta protect it. People can't do something themselves, they wanna tell you that you can't do it. You want something? Go get it. Period.'

In the movie, the internship offered no salary and no promise of a job. After six months, only one of the 20 interns would get a job—mainly based on an exam and their on-the-job performance selling stockbroking services via cold calls from sheets of contact details. Gardner was at a major competitive disadvantage in this hyper-competitive environment: committed to pick up his son, he could spend only six hours per day making calls, compared with the other interns' nine hours. After the six-month internship, Gardner was selected for the permanent job, and several years later he founded his own successful investment firm, Gardner Rich.

I was delighted to see how many of the principles of *Investing in Your Life* were fundamental to Gardner's story. Some, like time management, were taken to extremes—Gardner made his selling time more effective by not hanging up the phone between calls, which he figured saved eight minutes per day, and not drinking water, which saved wasting time in the bathroom. After-hours Gardner studied wherever he could—whether in trains or cafés or at the refuge where he and his son had to live when he ran out of money. The film also highlighted the way Gardner engineered and handled conversations—persistent, strategic, resourceful and fully engaged, whether kerbside, in interviews, networking at ball games or cold-calling on the phone.

The Pursuit of Happyness vividly demonstrates the power of life-enriching conversations and their compounding impact on your career capital. It's an approach that has significant potential value whether you are Gen Y, Gen X or a baby-boomer. The Gen Y person has plenty of years over which to capitalise on those compounding benefits, so the impact for them is potentially immense. If career capital were a measurable concept, a 20 per cent per annum compounding in career capital would equate to a sixfold increase over 10 years (a realistic career horizon for a baby boomer), 38-fold over 20 years (realistic for a Gen X) or 237-fold over 30 years (realistic for a Gen Y)![5]

A test of realism—CEO remuneration

At first glance, these figures seem completely unrealistic—especially a 237-fold increase in career capital over 30 years. How might we test this?

If career capital is measurable, it is only roughly so and only indirectly. If you are happy to measure your life by money (and therefore live in the world of 7.3), one reasonable surrogate measure of career capital would be annual remuneration. This measure obviously has to be treated with some care, as when it comes to remuneration potential, not all professions are created equal. For example, it would be wholly illogical to use annual remuneration as a surrogate measure across professions and compare the career capital of an investment banker or commercial lawyer with a nurse or teacher by comparing their salaries. However, it may be reasonable to apply annual remuneration as a rough relative measure within an industry.

Is it realistic for an ambitious youngster in an industry to aspire to a 237-fold increase in their career capital or its surrogate (annual remuneration) over a 30-year career? Let's test this.

Since the days of ancient Greece, leaders in many fields have remarked on the relationship between highest wages and average or minimum wages. In 400 BC, Plato argued that no-one should earn more than five times the wage of the ordinary worker. In 1903, JP Morgan reportedly said that he would never invest in any company where the highest paid employee earned more than 10 times the wage of the lowest paid employee. In 1984 management consultant Peter Drucker recommended that boards limit CEO compensation to no more than 20 times the pay of their average worker. These early signs of growth in acceptable CEO remuneration relative to an average worker's pay gave no hint of what was to come.

In recent years, the average CEO of a Fortune 500 company, including top and poor performers, has earned around 300 to 400 times what the average US worker earns. Presumably, some of those 50-year-old CEOs started their careers at age 20, earning the wage of an average worker, and achieved a 300- or 400-fold increase in real (that is, inflation-adjusted) remuneration over that period. Therefore, maybe a 237-fold increase in career capital over 30 years doesn't seem so far-fetched after all! It is possible, even though:

→ it's somewhat illogical, given such a large proportion of company performance is determined by external factors

→ it's obscene, says Warren Buffett, reflecting 'a tendency to put cocker spaniels on compensation committees, not Doberman pinschers'.

A person's career capital is principally dependent on their human and social capital, not their financial capital. Hence, the fact that US CEOs have achieved such high rates of growth in career capital gives me further confidence that very high rates of growth in human and social capital are achievable and sustainable, and are fundamental to the contribution of people like Bono.

7.5   A far more satisfying world — where you choose your unit of measure and you're building those units

Only two things are needed to make your world far more satisfying than a world where annual income is the only measure.

First, you need to choose your own way to measure the output you want from your Life Capital. It may be based solely on your annual dollar income, or on the reduction in infant mortality from your work in Somalia, the growth of your business, the survival rate of your cancer patients, the size of the congregation in the church where you preach, the number of hours each week you have free to pursue your special hobby or golf handicap, the number of times you (or your partner or your children) smile each day — or a combination of the above. Given that we're all different, the field of economic analysis has come up with a concept called 'utils', which measure our satisfaction with alternative outcomes or alternative goods.

Second, the more rapidly you're growing your utils, the happier you'll be. You'd be very happy if you were doubling them every five years (the equivalent of a 15 per cent per annum compound increase). In order to double your utils every five years, however, you have to double the underlying driver — your Life Capital.

Selecting your own unit of measure also changes the dynamics of your relationship with your neighbours. If you're all focused on the same measure, the inevitable emotion is to hope that you do better than them — otherwise you will feel like an underperformer. If you each have your own individual measures, which are not directly comparable, it becomes more rational to hope they do really well so you might be able to leverage off their Life Capital some time in the future. The more successful your neighbours, and the closer your relationship with them, the greater your opportunities in the future.

Over to you ...

Reflections

- Imagine your career as a share in a company: which of Lynch's categories would you place it in? What implications does that have for how you need to approach your career?
- For how many more years do you anticipate pursuing that career? What implications does that have for your investment in it?

Actions

- Write down the goals that you rank more highly than financial success.
- Write down how you would measure the life assets you need to fulfil those goals, and the investment you make into those life assets.

Principle 8
Morphing assets
and liabilities

**Life assets and liabilities
regularly morph. Your greatest
strength in one context may be your
greatest weakness in another.**

*Dualism underlies the nature and condition of man... For every
grain of wit there is a grain of folly. For everything you have missed,
you have gained something else; and for everything you gain, you
lose something... As no man had ever a point of pride that was
not injurious to him, so no man had ever a defect that was not
somewhere made useful to him... Our strength grows out of our
weakness... Whilst he sits on the cushion of advantages, he goes to
sleep. When he is pushed, tormented, defeated, he has a chance to
learn something.*

—Ralph Waldo Emerson[1]

Your greatest strength in one context may be your greatest weakness
in another. Your strength, if overused, may become a weakness. It can
require a special maturity and self-awareness to recognise this yourself,

and significant courage to do something about it. This dichotomy is challenging and multi-dimensional.

8.1   Asset or liability?

The questions that follow all relate to perceived assets that have the potential to be liabilities. My aim is to whet your appetite for this fascinating subject and to encourage you to contemplate your own situation. There are no definitive answers.

Is it an asset or a liability to:

→ *Have ability in a number of fields?* Having ability in a number of fields may lead to so many options that you find it hard to focus on just one. You are then more likely to become a happy 'jack of all trades', rather than a master of something.

→ *Have an alternative career or Plan B to fall back on?* The existence of a Plan B may influence your commitment to Plan A—your real passion. Are young people well advised to get a (safe) commerce or accounting degree so they will have something to fall back on if their real (but higher risk) ambitions in the arts, music or sport are not fulfilled? In his book *The Origin of Wealth: Evolution, Complexity and the Radical Remaking of Economics*, Eric Beinhocker suggests that strategies become more effective when we deliberately cut off our options. By way of example, he notes the commitment of the Spanish conquistador Cortes in ordering his men to burn their ships after landing in Mexico, thus forcing them to march inland.

→ *Be a specialist in one narrow field?* Being a specialist may increase your likely contribution in your field. It may also reduce the range of your opportunities unless you intentionally seek alliances with others who bring wider experiences.

→ *Have a quick wit?* Humour can be a major asset in building relationships or diffusing difficult situations. However, when accompanied by poor emotional intelligence or just plain arrogance, a quick wit can lead to terrible interpersonal relations. The Duke of Edinburgh is so renowned for his inappropriate comments that reporters Phil Dampier and Ashley

Walton compiled his gaffs, slurs and politically incorrect remarks into a book, *Duke of Hazard: The Wit and Wisdom of Prince Philip*.

→ *Trust others?* This can be a valuable asset, but taken to an absolute level it can be a fatal flaw; for example, King Lear's trust in his daughters.

→ *Have your parents involved in your career?* We regularly read in magazines and tabloids about international celebrities whose parents have been one of their greatest assets in the formative years of their careers, but who ultimately become major liabilities. Moving on from those relationships or changing them so they become a form of asset once again takes special courage. However, making no changes at all can be a very rocky road (generally downhill).

→ *Have great quantitative or theoretical skills?* Excessive focus on the numerical, theoretical or philosophical aspects of a situation or discussion may cause you to become blind to the emotional, practical or political issues.

→ *Grow up in a well-off family?* If you are not wanting for anything in your childhood, will you have the same hunger to succeed or win as those from disadvantaged backgrounds? Abject poverty in childhood and youth brings out some people's determination and ingenuity in earning, saving and learning—often leading to business and wealth creation.

→ *Be respectful?* It may make you good at institutional politics but may be less valuable if you are to play devil's advocate.

→ *Answer clearly the question you're asked?* You may be excellent in exams but you might not perform so well in answering questions from the press, where the challenge is to get your key messages across, regardless of the question.

The morphing of assets into liabilities and the converse comes as no surprise when viewed from the Chinese yin and yang perspective—the two opposite and correlated states, which in combination create a unit. Any opposites we experience, such as poverty and wealth, are explained by reference to the temporary dominance of one principle over the other. All phenomena have within them the seeds of the opposite: for example, poverty contains the seeds of wealth; missing something often leads to gaining something; and strength brings out weakness.

From confidence to overconfidence

According to Norman Vincent Peale in *The Power of Positive Thinking*, 'self-confidence leads to self-realisation and successful achievement'. However, it is very easy for the wonderful asset of self-confidence to morph into a dangerous liability—overconfidence. Your ultimate protection from this potential risk lies in objectivity, 'keeping your feet on the ground'. There are many tools to assist in this, including having objective benchmarks of your performance and surrounding yourself with a few people on whom you can rely for objective comment.

As Nelson Mandela has said:

> To achieve those goals to which one is committed and chooses to dedicate one's life, belief in yourself is essential. That self-belief becomes vain and egotistical, and ultimately self-defeating, if it does not derive from a dedication to and a faith in a common goal. The necessary self-belief of the true leader or champion is tempered by respect for broader concerns.[2]

Leadership qualities may become liabilities

Leadership qualities that are great assets at one time can become liabilities as circumstances change. For example, cost-cutting or culture-change experts may achieve major turnarounds in businesses but they are often not the best people to lead a company through the next stage of growth. It takes a perceptive board to realise that it may be time for a change of CEO just when the company has been turned around and the results look good.

The contrast can be even more glaring in politics, especially as a country moves from war to peace. A change of leader is to be expected where the war has been lost, as was the case for Napoleon Bonaparte. However, despite the Allies' victory in World War II, and the massive contribution of Churchill's leadership to it, his government was rejected at the 1945 election, due in part to a perception that post-war reform required a new leader.

What career assets should we aspire to?

Sydney Finkelstein, Professor of Management at Dartmouth's Tuck School of Business, studied 51 major corporate collapses for his book

Why Smart Executives Fail. He notes: 'For managers, many of the qualities we aspire to emulate, or feel guilty for not having, turn out to be the ones we're better off without. For investors, many of the signposts of success that we strive to identify turn out to be markers for failure'.[3]

Where is the line between the asset of 'a bias for action' (which my generation of management learned from Tom Peters and Robert Waterman's 1982 bestseller *In Search of Excellence*) and the liability of 'not stopping to think'? Or the line between the asset of 'strong charismatic leadership' and the liability of 'excessive power'? Finkelstein has identified both as being significant in Samsung's history.

The company was founded in 1938 with capital of 30 000 won (equivalent to US$30). Lee Kun-hee, the son of the founder, succeeded his father as chairman in 1987 and by 1999 had grown Samsung to be the second largest corporation in Korea. As the company's chairman and major shareholder, Lee then took Samsung into auto manufacturing, with disastrous results. Despite all the board members being against the move, none went against Lee's will at official meetings. As Finkelstein states:

> Though few deny that his strong charismatic leadership contributed greatly to Samsung's previous successes, it is clear that this strength became a liability. Lee wielded extreme power that enabled him to quickly dismiss organisational resistance and bypass conventional procedures in decision making.[4]

Lee ultimately resigned in 2008, after being indicted on tax-evasion charges.

It seems it can be dangerous to focus too much on the development of certain strengths—there's a risk you might take them to excess unless you develop other strengths that keep them in check. This is one dimension of the question of whether it is more valuable to focus on building your assets/strengths or on overcoming your liabilities/weaknesses (see Principle 11).

8.2 Your greatest weakness may be the foundation of your career

Many leading international sports stars took up their sport as a form of therapy to overcome a major injury, physical problem or illness. For example, dual Olympic 1500-metre swimming champion Kieren Perkins, who won gold in Barcelona (1992) and Atlanta (1996), followed by silver in Sydney (2000), came to swimming for rehabilitation following the major leg injuries he received when he fell through a glass door at the age of nine.

There are also many examples of people who make major discoveries while trying to understand and overcome their own problems. In the late 19th century, Frederick Alexander found that his promising acting career was in jeopardy because he regularly lost his voice during performances. His voice was absolutely fine during his everyday encounters, and doctors could find nothing wrong with him. Determined to understand the cause, he arranged a system of three-way mirrors to study what he did while he was reciting. Through extensive observation and experimentation, he developed principles of body use, body re-education and coordination, which he applied to solve his voice problems. These principles also improved his general health, and he taught them for decades internationally to actors, musicians and other performers. His principles became known as the Alexander Technique, and today they are widely applied to activities in everyday life.

Albert Einstein's life is a classic story of his liabilities becoming great assets. Because his verbal skills were slow to develop, he learned to think in pictures and noticed things that everyone else took for granted. This capacity later became a major asset in his scientific endeavours. His contempt for authority, which led to missed opportunities in his youth and early working life, later differentiated him from others in a positive way. It gave him the capacity to move beyond Newton's laws and discover the General Theory of Relativity.

The slow development of skills as a child, such as Einstein's verbal skills, is one thing. Complete loss of one or more senses is in another league altogether. The absence or weakness of one sense, especially from birth, can strengthen other senses and be the foundation of a career. This is exemplified by many wonderful blind blues and jazz musicians, including Stevie Wonder, Ray Charles and Art Tatum. British-born jazz pianist George Shearing gained a better education than his parents could afford for his eight older siblings because he was able to attend a school for the blind. In his autobiography, he remarked:

> Maybe we miss a lot, but for the most part that's more than made up for by what we have to replace sight—the ability to

conceptualize the world through sound, or our other senses, and the close connection with all those other people who help us to get our bearings in unfamiliar surroundings, whatever they may be.[5]

8.3 Your employer—career asset or liability?

Your employer can in some contexts be one of your major assets, in others, they can be a major liability.

Charles Handy, the renowned British management philosopher and author of *The Elephant and the Flea*, spent 30 years or so working for organisations with then unquestioned job security. In 1981, at the age of 49, Handy ceased working as an employee and began a portfolio of interests. He predicted significant declines in the proportion of the population holding conventional full-time and relatively permanent jobs. His predictions, then widely scoffed at, were soon vindicated. In most Western countries today, few can realistically assume the job security implicit in Handy's 30-year career as an employee. Even substantial corporations, whether Shell, Microsoft or BHP Billiton, no longer offer job security; nor these days do most academic posts.

Many big organisations offer the trappings of office. At the extreme, they can include corporate jets and fawning subordinates; more commonly, such trappings include cars, expense allowances, titles, offices and the corporate brand. The trappings come with the office, regardless of who holds it, and with two dangerous features.

The first is that you may find yourself having to make a significant investment in order to maintain these trappings:

→ long hours, which potentially distract you from important non-work interests

→ conformity—institutional or peer group pressure to place a very high value on certain aspects of your make-up, or to change others. This may put at risk some of your independence of character, thought or behaviour, and inhibit experimentation, risk-taking and, consequently, innovation.

The second feature is that those trappings are ephemeral. When you leave that particular job, you lose them. You may not find them in your next job, leaving you without any long-term return on your significant investment.

Identity through your job — asset or liability?

Your work is likely to be an important component of your personal mission, but it is possible to confuse what you *do* with who you *are*, so much so that your identity is inextricably linked to your job. The warning signs are evident in the so-called 'Sunday neurosis', defined by psychiatrist Viktor Frankl as 'that kind of depression which afflicts people who become aware of the lack of content in their lives when the rush of the busy week is over and the void within themselves becomes manifest'.[6] That job-based identity is lost when you retire, leaving a big gap — a gap that arose from the long-term subordination of your other interests to your work.

Today, this gap is so common among sports men and women that it has been given a name — Sports Retirement Stress. It's a phenomenon that has probably always been common but is perhaps even more prevalent today, due to the professional domination of modern sport. The elite athlete's identity, sense of purpose and daily routine are totally tied up in their sport, and they are often in the public eye. On retirement, most of that changes, leaving a worrying void for such highly achievement-oriented people. Some elite athletes miss out on the exploratory behaviour of a typical misspent youth because of their early and strong commitment to their sport. As a result, they may lack career maturity and confidence outside being an athlete, and so are not well prepared for this transition. Today's sports psychologists use conceptual models of retirement from sport, which take into account the entire career transition process, including the reasons for retirement, development during the transition and coping resources post-retirement.[7]

As an employee, the most important thing to recognise is that it is you, not your employer, who is responsible for your personal development. Your employer doesn't own you — and good employers wouldn't want to own their people. The good employers are those who want you to have a fertile life outside work so you are invigorated and balanced when you walk into the office — and so your contribution is enhanced by your outside interests. Good employers don't want you to be the same and think the same as your colleagues. They want you to be yourself and to be different. If this doesn't sound like your employer, then it's time to ask yourself a question — is your employer an asset or a liability?

In *Blur: The Speed of Change in the Connected Economy*, Stan Davis and Christopher Meyer encourage you to think of yourself as a free self-employed agent. Even if you are on a company payroll, think of yourself not as a wage slave but as being currently under contract to one team, which you may stay with forever or for just one season. This mind-set change, they say, brings you new freedom but also makes *you*, not your boss, responsible for your future. The point, they say, is not how often you might change jobs, but what's going on inside your head.

Whether you are an employee, a 'portfolio' person like Charles Handy, self-employed, an athlete or an artist, the key is the balance you maintain between job-related obligations and your other interests—the interests that remain with you as you move from job to job. I sum up this 'work–life balance' issue in one expression: 'Don't give up your night job!' Don't overcommit to work to the exclusion of the things outside it that give you friendships, self-esteem, resilience and a wider perspective. These other dimensions of your identity are wonderful assets at all times, and are particularly valuable when your work environment disappoints you significantly, as it no doubt will from time to time.

Being comfortable in your job—asset or liability?

Comfort in your job is likely to be an asset if you use it as a base from which to challenge yourself—to give you the confidence to work with others from different disciplines or to work in settings less familiar to you, and thereby enjoy powerful growth opportunities. On the other hand, comfort in your job can be a liability if you choose to restrict yourself to existing comfort zones.

Reciprocally, discomfort is a liability if you do not respond to it, but it can be a major asset if it spurs you into action.

8.4   Born into a successful family business—asset or liability?

Successful family businesses and family trades have been the backbone of world economic development for thousands of years. You might think it must be an asset to be born into a successful business, offering plenty of opportunities and providing useful capital or income. However, this simple question has many dimensions.

Over 35 years ago, Jason Kimberley's father Craig, his uncle Roger and their wives Connie and Chrissie founded Just Jeans. The company has since grown into Australia's and New Zealand's largest speciality fashion retailer, the Just Group—a wonderful business. (Having until recently been the chairman, I'm biased!) The Kimberley family sold its controlling interest in 2001, and Jason left the Just Group to focus on his passions of photography, writing and adventure. In the book he wrote on his cross-country adventures in Antarctica with two mates, Jason pondered why children work in their parents' businesses:

> *Is it just a remarkable coincidence? Do we love the same industry with the same passion as our fathers? Are we unwittingly pushed there? Does it just happen that way? Is there a certain feeling of obligation? The prospect of following in my father's footsteps always seemed unsatisfactory to me. Furthermore, as the son of the boss, you feel obliged to set a perfect example, work long hours .... in short, conform, which I am not very good at ... When the family decided to sell the business, I was at first a little disappointed that it was all over, but then the exhilarating feeling of total freedom washed over me. I thought about how this opportunity could be embraced in a way that would set me free to follow my own path.*[8]

With the vast choices available to children in modern Western society, it's a positive coincidence if, of all the available alternatives, a child chooses the same career or profession as the parent—had it not been for the existence of the family business.

Is the development of the child enhanced by working in the family business? Or is the parent so dominant that the child's independence will be crushed? The story of Henry Ford's son Edsel is salutary. Henry forbad Edsel from enlisting in World War I, discouraged him from going to college (Henry himself had not gone to college and he believed work experience was more important for Edsel), reacted strongly against Edsel's plans for the business and regularly put him down, both publicly and privately. Edsel's career was crushed. In *Family Wars*, the authors Grant Gordon and Nigel Nicholson proffered the advice: 'For sons of towering figures the best advice is, get out from under the shadow ... take an independent path and find your own way to make a mark'.[9]

Similar issues plagued the relationship between IBM CEO Tom Watson Sr and his son Tom, who later succeeded him. One core difference between the Watsons and the Fords was that Tom joined the US Army

Air Corps during World War II and received the confidence-building outside experience and mentorship that Edsel Ford never had.[10]

Some parents discourage their children from becoming involved full time in the family business, as they aspire for greater things for their children. Other parents almost demand their involvement in order to secure succession. In some cases generational involvement occurs from a sense of obligation to the business, as in the Guinness brewing business. The Guinness family felt that as the company had brought them fortune, they had a responsibility to continue as stewards. This led to Rupert Guinness, whose son died in World War II, staying on as chairman until the age of 88, to ensure he was directly succeeded by his 25-year-old grandson.[11]

Some children are so turned off by their early exposure to the family business that they can see nothing worse as a career. Others compete with each other to succeed their parents; for example, on farms that are not large enough to be subdivided on a commercially viable basis.

Reciprocally, is it good for the future of the business? While there are some businesses that have operated successfully under family management for many generations, there are many more examples of the 'rags to riches to rags' scenario in three generations—or less!

8.5 The people you surround yourself with— assets or liabilities?

One of the most important determinants of your career luck, opportunity and satisfaction, and also of your self-awareness, is the people you choose to surround yourself with and the way you engage with them. They provide you with a different and potentially more objective mirror than self-analysis, thereby increasing the chances that you will become aware if you are overplaying your assets, or if those assets are deteriorating and becoming more like liabilities.

In work relationships

In work relationships, do you tend to choose to be surrounded by people who are different from you? If so, you defy social psychology research, which shows that we prefer people who are similar to us as they reaffirm the validity of our own persona. We also prefer to work with people with whom we are familiar, and who, we think, like us.[12]

Do you tend to choose to be surrounded by people who are smarter than you? Who bring different skills? Who are likely to disagree with you but with whom you can constructively engage? Or do you tend to choose to be surrounded by 'yes men' or by people who are likely to think the same as you?

Although you are (or feel) less empowered to choose your boss, their leadership qualities and emotional intelligence are fundamental to your personal growth. Your boss's moods, attitudes, competence and leadership have a major impact on you directly and, through their impact on your peers, also indirectly. The contagious effect of your boss's behaviour has a compounding impact on team dynamics and performance. If your boss is an emotionally intelligent leader with a clear commitment to developing the team, you are on a winner. If not, your challenge is to determine how you can change your game—whether by influencing your boss to change or modify their behaviour, by seeking a transfer or by looking elsewhere.

In personal relationships

In personal relationships, are you surrounded by people:
- → who build your emotional strength and awareness, or are forever tapping into it and sapping it
- → who believe in you and encourage you to set ambitious goals, work hard and take risks, or discourage you so you won't be disappointed or so they won't be left behind?
- → who are as passionate about things as you are, or would like to be?

In your advisory relationships

How often do you re-evaluate whether your doctor, accountant, solicitor, tax adviser, investment adviser or fund manager is the right person for you? Probably not very often—at least, not unless they get something terribly wrong! If you do not regularly re-evaluate their performance, you run the risk of getting an *annuity* of average advice or average service. If you do ask yourself that question, then:
- → what are the things you should be reasonably expecting from such a relationship?

→ how do you benchmark it?

→ do you have the conviction necessary to make the change?

You have zero control over the two big 'lucky dips' in your life—your genetic make-up (your starting human capital) and the family/ community/society/country into which you are born (your starting social capital). As an adult, you have considerable control over who you choose to live with, socialise with, work with and take advice from—and, more than ever before, where in the world you choose to live and bring up your children. We return to social capital in greater depth in Principles 14 and 15.

8.6   Your generosity with your time, energy and attention—asset or liability?

To give your money to a charity that you know will use it well is generosity; to give it to a charity that will not respect the value of your donation is arguably foolhardy. Similarly, to give your time, energy and attention regularly to those who show no appreciation of their value is ill-advised.

If you value your time, energy and attention appropriately, you will generally have more of these resources available for the most significant people or situations in your life. To be known as a person who appreciates the value of your own (and others') time, energy and attention, but who nevertheless is generous with them, can be a valuable asset. It sends a positive signal, implying 'feel free to approach me about something of importance to you and we can certainly commit the time to discuss it'. Principle 15 further explores the importance of valuing another person's time and energy if you are to build a deep relationship.

A level of generosity with your time will often be well rewarded through the reciprocal efforts of others, or through the serendipitous outcomes of your engagements, a topic which is visited in some depth in Principle 13. However, if you are indiscriminately generous in being available to others, the risk that your generosity will be regularly abused is high. Your generosity may soon become a significant liability.

After learning he was terminally ill with an inoperable brain tumour, KPMG USA CEO Gene O'Kelly drew up a series of concentric circles, listing the people with whom he wished to achieve some closure. His wife and children were in the innermost circle, followed by his immediate family, lifetime friends, close business associates and friends who, because of shared experiences and shared passion, enhanced his life and vice versa. His consequent reflections in his book *Chasing Daylight* are revealing:

> *I might have unconsciously been too consumed by the outermost circle ... Had I somehow been inspired to draw my map of concentric circles earlier in my life ... perhaps it would have guided me in how to allocate my time (or my energy) ... I realised that being able to count a thousand people in that fifth circle was not something to be proud of.*[13]

Over to you ...

Reflections

- Which of your life assets could potentially turn into liabilities, and which life liabilities might you be able to turn into assets?
- Which of the people you surround yourself with (at work, personally or as advisers) are liabilities, or perhaps not as big assets as they might be? Reciprocally, for whom can you be a bigger asset? How can you change the dynamics of these relationships?
- Do you share your time or energy indiscriminately? Is it valued by those with whom you share it?

Actions

- Take your list of life assets and liabilities and see how they fit with the plan you prepared from Principle 4. With an open mind, seek feedback on your list, especially the potential to turn liabilities into assets or vice versa.
- Draw your equivalent of Gene O'Kelly's concentric circles of relationships. Review the composition of each circle, and the relative time, energy and attention you invest in each.

Part IV
Opportunities

The opportunities you capitalise on are fundamental drivers in the growth of your Life Capital. There are four key steps:

→ finding the opportunity, whether intentionally or serendipitously
→ realising it's an opportunity worth considering
→ deciding to pursue it seriously
→ managing to capture it and maximise it.

The first three Principles in part IV focus on what you can learn about the size of opportunities by applying the principles of financial wealth creation:

→ *Principle 9:* Your opportunity losses may often be much greater than your actual losses. Your blind spots are recurrent sources of major opportunity loss.
→ *Principle 10*: If you apply some elementary mathematical thinking, the big opportunities may become more obvious.

→ *Principle 11:* Your Life Capital will grow faster if you take opportunities both to grow your assets and overcome your liabilities.

The final two principles demonstrate the role of engaged conversations in helping you to identify or capture opportunities:

→ *Principle 12:* Any engaged conversation offers you multiple potential benefits, most fundamentally the opportunity to leverage others' Life Capital.

→ *Principle 13:* Engaged conversations lead to many opportunities. These free options cost you nothing other than your time and energy but they may be very valuable.

Principle 9
Opportunity losses and blind spots

Your opportunity losses may often be much greater than your actual losses. Your blind spots are recurrent sources of major opportunity loss.

In the long run, people of every age and in every walk of life seem to regret not having done things more than regret things they did.

—Daniel Gilbert[1]

9.1 Opportunity loss is often much greater than actual loss

Regret for not having done things, for an opportunity lost, is common across business, family, educational or social issues. This is not surprising because, as shown by my investment experience described in Wealth Insert 9 (overleaf), opportunity losses are often much greater than actual losses. They can also be the most insidious of losses, in that you often don't realise that you are missing out on these opportunities.

Wealth Insert 9: opportunity loss

Investors in shares face two types of loss. The one that stands out is a capital loss — the sale of a share well below its cost. A capital loss can have only three potentially redeeming features: first, it may offer some tax benefit; second, the worst you can lose is the money you invested (unless you've sold short or geared your investment in some way); third, you might learn something from it. As Fred Schwed Jr wrote in his 1940 investment classic *Where are the Customers' Yachts?*, 'like all of life's rich emotional experiences, the full flavour of losing important money cannot be conveyed by literature'.[2]

The other form of loss is opportunity loss. It may not be a rich emotional experience, as you may not even be aware of it happening, but it can be much more significant than a capital loss.

Two contemporaneous poor investment decisions of mine make the contrast between real loss and opportunity loss very clear. I invested in a high dividend-paying company, but only a few months later my shares were worthless when the company lost the confidence of its bankers. It hurt! At virtually the same time, a friend showed me a list of companies with high returns on capital over the previous five years, trading at prices well below their historical highs. Near the top of the list was a company I knew well from my work, which had fallen from grace as a result of poor governance. Despite my understanding of the company's competitive advantages, I failed to look into it because I was busy on other things and so did not purchase any of its shares. They later traded at up to 20 times that price. The opportunity cost of not buying those shares far exceeded the capital loss on the other shares I did buy. It hurt big time!

On a grander scale, Warren Buffett included a 'confession time' in his 2007 Annual Letter to Shareholders, and described the three worst mistakes of his career. His first mistake was a potential opportunity loss when he was adamant about not going above US$25 million in purchasing See's Candy in 1972.

Fortunately, the vendor gave in, so Berkshire Hathaway was able to buy See's for US$25 million. See's has since generated US$1.35 billion in profits.

> His second mistake was an actual opportunity loss. Buffett was offered NBC's Dallas-Fort Worth media station for US$35 million in the 1970s and declined. It has since earned at least US$1 billion in pre-tax earnings.

The outstanding success of JK Rowling's book *Harry Potter and the Philosopher's Stone* would have really hurt the many publishers who rejected the original manuscript. The ultimate opportunity cost of their decision must vastly exceed the downside from all the other bad decisions they've ever made, and their regrets must have compounded with each sequel.

In 1793, Lord George Macartney was sent to Peking by King George III to open up trade relations with China. Macartney was unlikely to have been aware that China had invented most things well before the West.[3] The Chinese emperor Qianlong, perhaps blinded by China's proud record, said to Macartney 'We possess all things... I have no use for your country's manufactures'. What an opportunity loss! China remained economically isolated for almost another 200 years, and its GDP per person dropped materially whereas Britain's rose fivefold. It's probably a little unfair to attribute almost 200 years of poor economic performance to Qianlong alone. There must have been many subsequent opportunities to reverse China's stance, all of which were lost until the leadership and vision of Deng Xiaoping!

9.2 Comfort zones and some bad habits cause recurring opportunity loss

One of the greatest sources of opportunity loss is the comfort zone. It may be:

→ the job you have done successfully, or at least adequately, for many years
→ the company of those who think like you and who share your values
→ books you can read easily or those in your area of expertise
→ the sport you have played for years, against people of your own standard

→ functions and occasions where you socialise with those you already know well.

In some respects it is the quest for a comfort zone or an opportunity to relax that drives you on. But if you always stay well within your comfort zone, you will have little exposure to negative feelings like fear, pain, frustration or boredom, which can spark action. As a result, you are likely to suffer opportunity loss on a recurring basis.

Recurring opportunity losses (or 'annuities of opportunity loss') may also be caused by such habits as:

→ not listening to others
→ not having an open mind
→ not giving others the opportunity to talk about their experiences
→ retreating into your shell when you strike a problem, thereby not allowing yourself to benefit from others' input
→ not taking note of ideas as they occur to you
→ restricting most conversations to their original purpose because of time pressures.

Reversing any one of these habits is reasonably achievable and may be of real value, hence falling into the category of 'low-hanging juicy fruit'. Further, you have daily, even hourly, opportunities to practise the right behaviours and to capitalise on them.

9.3   Blind spots

The early-20th-century American slang word 'lollapalooza' means 'something outstanding of its kind'. The word was revitalised in 1991 with the launching of the Lollapalooza music festival, featuring mainly alternative rock, hip-hop and punk rock bands. In 1996, Charlie Munger said that he looks for 'lollapalooza investments', where he can identify a combination of factors operating in the same direction—their effects combining and reinforcing to produce major upsides.[4]

Lollapalooza ...

In 3.2 you saw the compounding benefits and the annuity of benefits that result if you take constructive feedback positively and work to improve your performance. These very powerful concepts apply each time you are offered the opportunity of constructive feedback. Whether over a lifetime or just over a few years, they offer a lollapalooza of benefits. Imagine that every December you have a performance review at work or with your life partner. As table 9.1 shows, each year you take away one item of behavioural change that becomes your New Year's resolution, and you work hard over the following year to achieve that behavioural change and make it sustainable.

Table 9.1: key items of behavioural change from annual performance reviews

Year	Sustainable behavioural change
1	Listening with a more open mind—ensuring you first understand the other person
2	Setting aside time to check your activities are aligned with your mission
3	Improving your preparation for meetings
4	Communicating more clearly your enthusiasm—enhancing your influence
5	Managing your time and energy better—valuing others' time and energy highly
6	Learned optimism
7	Confronting and dealing with the difficult issues—building your resilience
8	Greater preparedness to experiment and take reasonably managed risks
9	Searching for why things can be done rather than why they can't
10	Developing a greater comfort at working across disciplines

How big is the upside? If sustained, each of these 10 changes in behaviour will benefit you for the rest of your life. Each therefore has a life annuity of value for you. If you stick by your 10 New Year's resolutions, you have created 10 life annuities of value—definitely a lollapalooza!

...or Lollapaloser

Then imagine the vast dimensions of the opportunity loss over a lifetime or career if you are a person who:

→ is unable to take constructive feedback positively
→ avoids feedback for fear it may not be positive or
→ works in an environment where feedback is seldom offered and you do not seek it.

If this is the case, you will not buy into the above opportunities for behavioural change and you won't make the New Year's resolutions. Consequently, over the next 10 years you will miss out on 10 life annuities of value, adding up to the ultimate lollapalooza opportunity loss.

In 5.6 I referred to the merits of using your own language or jargon — whether for motivation, for inspiration or for clarity of thought. I've modified Charlie Munger's concept and come up with the term 'lollapaloser' to refer to something that is an annuity of major opportunity loss, when one of our habits causes us to repeatedly miss out on big opportunities. If you're a listener with an open mind, you're likely to enjoy lollapaloozas; if you're not a listener, you're likely to suffer lollapalosers.

Lollapalosers are often caused by negative habits resulting from underlying personality traits. Often these are blind spots, serious weaknesses of which we are unaware.

Lack of self-awareness

Self-awareness is a major factor separating the unsuccessful from the successful. Research shows that those who rate themselves more highly than they are rated by others tend to be underachievers. They are also:

→ more likely than others to fail
→ more likely than others to fail or underperform after enjoying success for a period
→ less likely to learn from management development programs
→ less likely to bounce back from career derailment.[5]

Blindness to your own performance or behaviours is obviously a major contributor to such ratings. Organisations have all sorts of feedback mechanisms to help you in that regard, including 360-degree feedback, peer reviews and performance reviews. The best approaches include an opportunity for self-assessment before you receive feedback or are influenced by feedback from colleagues. Your family won't have formal 360-degree assessments in place, but they'll be happening there informally and regularly.

Blind spots, where your assessment of yourself is well above that of your raters (at work or at home), may offer big opportunities, so they're worth taking really seriously. While they can have many sources, I'd like to focus on one source — the overuse of a strength. This is probably the most common source of a blind spot, as it is often easy to slip into and almost as easy to get out of, provided you become aware of when and how you're guilty and how serious the implications are. It also offers significant potential for conversion from a blind spot back to the wholesome asset it should be. All in all, it's a wonderful example of the principle of turning your liabilities into assets (see 11.3).

Almost every strength you can think of can become a blind spot if taken to an extreme or relied on too much. For example, if your mathematical talent enables you to mentally assess the accuracy of numbers mentioned by others in a conversation, you can easily annoy people and disadvantage yourself by focusing on whether the calculation was correct. You will miss the real point being made in the conversation, as well as the next couple of sentences, then interject to correct the maths, which was probably irrelevant and had already been forgotten by everyone else. Similarly, if your quick mind enables you to always see a few steps ahead, you might regularly annoy others by interjecting to finish their sentences for them or, if you have the floor, losing them by not taking them methodically through all the steps in your logic.

The list of overused strengths that may become blind spots is endless — from humility, listening or asking for feedback, to courage, questioning, entertaining or having a quick mind.

9.4   Minimising opportunity loss

Luck is when preparation meets opportunity.

—Seneca the Younger

While we will all suffer regular instances of major opportunity loss, often without being aware of it, a number of steps can be helpful in minimising opportunity loss.

Preparation

→ Having a picture of what you are looking for or aspiring to.

→ Being on the lookout for opportunities that are reasonably matched with your aspirations.

Engagement with others

→ Having an open mind.

Stopping to take stock of an opportunity

→ Looking at all of its dimensions—particularly the upside if you're a pessimist or comfortable with the status quo, and the downside if you're an optimist.

→ Getting others' perceptions on the situation and the opportunity.

Having the confidence to act

→ Ultimately, not missing out on an opportunity depends on your confidence to act, in the knowledge that you have the necessary capacity and competence to achieve your goal. While this confidence will have been enhanced by your strategic preparation, it is influenced by your self-regard. Positive self-regard will increase your awareness of positive feedback and opportunities, while poor self-regard increases your awareness of negative or embarrassing factors and challenging situations.

Finally, when it comes to minimising opportunity loss, don't forget the other guy. As swimming legend Ian Thorpe has said: 'Sometimes we question things that we have done in our lives, but how many times do we question what we haven't done in someone else's?'

Over to you …

Reflection

• Have there been any major opportunity losses in your life? If you had your time over again, what would you have done differently, given what you know now? What does that tell you about how to identify a major opportunity or looming opportunity loss in your life?

- Have you missed opportunities because you wanted to stay in your comfort zone? Have others taken up those opportunities? What can you learn from what they have done with them? Were they big opportunities?
- When are you a good listener and when are you not? When do you have an open mind and when do you not?
- Are any of your habits regularly causing someone else opportunity loss?

Action

- Find a partner you know well, with whom you can mutually explore your own and each other's blind spots, the size of any potential opportunity loss and the potential to change those blind spots into assets. This is not for the faint-hearted!
- Identify one (or more) of your own habits or a comfort zone that regularly causes you opportunity loss. Put dimensions around that opportunity loss. Decide what you will do about it.

Principle 10
Elementary maths
but big opportunities

If you apply some elementary mathematical thinking, the big opportunities may become more obvious.

The essence of mathematics is not to make simple things complicated, but to make complicated things simple.

—Stan Gudder

In Principle 3 we looked at two simple mathematical concepts that are fundamental in building both financial capital and Life Capital:

→ the power of compound growth
→ the value of annuities (or the importance of repeat events).

The impact of these concepts was demonstrated through examples related to constructive feedback. There are a number of other elementary mathematical concepts, which may help you to identify significant opportunities.

10.1 Use of your time

Each week of your life gives you 168 hours to spend. These hours belong to you, and ideally you should control how you use them. In this context, the concept of 'A = B – C' is very powerful and has numerous potential applications that influence your Life Capital.

Wealth Insert 10A: anything of the form A = B – C represents a special opportunity

Many aspects of business and wealth accumulation are determined by the small difference between two numbers. For example, your savings = your income – your expenditure. If you earn $200 000 per annum after tax and spend $190 000 per annum, you have net savings of $10 000.

The business equivalent of this calculation is profit = revenue – expenses. Accordingly, $200 million of revenue less $190 million of expenses leaves $10 million of profit.

In these two simple examples, a 5 per cent increase in B (income or revenue) combined with a 5 per cent reduction in C (expenditure) would lead to an approximate trebling of A (savings or profit). Improvements of 10 per cent in each of B and C would increase the savings or profits fivefold, as shown in figure 10.1.

Figure 10.1: savings = income less expenses

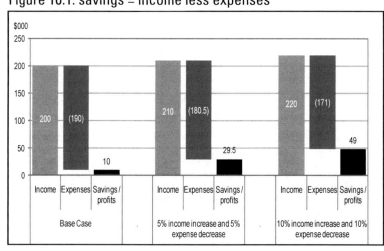

The A = B − C has two versions offering highly leveraged opportunity. The first is similar to those in Wealth Insert 10A, where it is possible to engineer a small percentage change in each of B (income) and C (expenses) to produce a much higher percentage change in A (savings). The second is where B or C is fixed, such as where B is your 168 hours in the week, but, because C is of a similar size to B, A is small. Consider the following example:

Picture yourself as being young, single and harbouring ambitions as a musician. Unfortunately, you are working 40 hours per week in a supermarket in order to afford the coaching and travel that your musical development demands. You wisely assess how you are spending your allocated 168 hours:

➡ 56 hours for sleep, 15 hours for meals and personal hygiene, 15 hours for socialising and exercise, 10 hours for TV and seven hours for household chores, including shopping

➡ 40 hours at work and 10 hours getting ready and travelling to and from work

➡ 15 hours on your musical ambitions, of which three are spent catching up with where you last left off—warming-up, focusing or getting into a rhythm.

Your net effective allocation to your real passion is therefore around 12 hours. Will you make real progress on that basis? Are you setting yourself up for failure or disappointment? How much more progress would you make if you could change the 12 hours to 24? Is that feasible?

As that 12 hours is the small difference between large numbers—168 minus 103 (the necessities) minus 50 (work etc) minus three (warm-up etc)—there is enormous potential to increase it by carrying out any of the following:

➡ Plan A: by working four days instead of five, you could reduce your work hours from 40 to 32 and your travel time from 10 hours to eight—giving you an extra 10 hours per week to spend on your music.

➡ Plan B: if your budget doesn't allow Plan A, you could look at working a higher proportion of overtime hours at a higher rate, or finding a different, better paid job.

➡ Plan C: you could take a good look at those other 103 hours. A 10 per cent cut in each category (sleep, meals, TV and so on)

would almost double the time you could commit to your real passion and accelerate your progress towards your special goal.

→ Plan D: you could decide which of those activities are really necessities. If you're really serious about your passion, perhaps those 10 hours of watching TV are not as essential as you originally thought.

A great first step would be to have some financial capital so you don't need to work in the supermarket at all! This would free up the majority of your time to pursue your musical ambitions, so all you would need is passion, commitment, focus, ability and lots of luck!

Spending quality time with your family

'The difference between two numbers' also applies to the amount of quality time a busy executive has left to spend with their family. By overcoming feelings of guilt at leaving the office before the boss or the team, and exercising sufficient discipline, the well-organised executive may be able to double the amount of quality time they can spend with their family during the five days of the working week. They then also set a great example for their colleagues, who in due course may follow suit or at least start to arrange meetings at more sensible hours.

This is one dimension of the work–life balance issues faced by those working in senior positions in large organisations—and especially those with families—already exemplified in the preface by my client Judy.

Time spent in meetings

The same leverage applies to the allocation of time at meetings—a major consumer of the working week. For example, there is much debate these days about the balance between board meeting time spent on conformance (for example, checking that the company is meeting its legal, statutory and financial reporting obligations) and time spent on performance (building the business, growing profitability and strategic development). If the board of a company meets for four hours every month there will be a vast difference in performance between a company that needs to spend three of those hours on conformance and governance issues, and a company that only needs to spend one hour on them. The latter can devote three times as much attention to performance, or leave early to pursue other opportunities. Inevitably, the spirit and invigoration of people dedicating at least three-quarters of their meeting time to business building and performance are much more positive than those of people managing to dedicate only one-quarter of their time.

Time spent meeting today's needs versus time investing in your capabilities and building for the future

How you manage your time is fundamental to how well you can build your capabilities. The key question is whether the time you have for growing your capabilities is determined by the amount of time you have left after you have opened the mail, read the newspaper, done your emails and so on. If this approach is followed, the result is an $A = B - C$ situation, and your aim is to maximise B and minimise C.

Alternatively, you can take control of the situation and recognise that if you're going to make serious progress, you must spend 20 hours per week on growing your capabilities. Then, every working day, those all-important four hours need to come before the mail, newspaper etc. You then overcome the natural human tendency to defer the important but non-urgent matters so much that you never get around to doing them!

A variation on this theme is faced every day by most people building businesses or careers. In a professional services firm, it is the balance between the time spent by the firm's leaders on daily client matters (chargeable hours) and administration, and the time they spend on planning and marketing, developing new products and ideas or looking for new team members.

All hours are not equal

The above analysis assumes that all hours are equal. For me they are not. Most days, I find that I'm least effective between 2 pm and 3 pm. Circumstances permitting, the optimum use of my time during that period would be power-napping rather than making important decisions or trying to be innovative. It's important to recognise when you are least effective and, if circumstances allow, match your most effective hours with your most demanding challenges, and your least effective hours with your routine work.

Similarly, for meetings, the first half-hour is likely to be more productive than the second, the second more productive than the third and so on—so it's important to prioritise your agenda accordingly.

10.2　Managing your energy and your attention to the moment

I wish there were more than 24 hours in a day.

—Everybody

The bad news is that there aren't. The good news is that you can make those 24 hours more meaningful and more valuable by managing your energy levels.

As Tony Schwartz points out:[1]

→ You have four main sources of energy: your body (physical energy), your emotions (which determine the quality of your energy), your mind (which focuses your energy) and your spirit (which taps into your sense of meaning and purpose).

→ Each source of energy can be expanded and renewed by the right habits—of eating, drinking, sleeping, taking breaks, regular exercise, deep relaxed breathing, seeing events in your life through alternative lenses, tackling the most important things first, keeping focus on one thing at a time, understanding what matters to you most, and making technology like mobile phones and email work for you rather than the opposite.

→ To recharge yourself, you need to recognise the costs of energy-depleting behaviours and then take responsibility for changing them.

Schwartz also notes that companies focus on developing employees' skills, knowledge and competence but few help build and sustain their employees' capacity—their energy. Typically taken for granted, it is this greater capacity that makes it possible to get more done in less time at a higher level of engagement and with more sustainability. Fundamental to managing your energy more productively is making time to do so—regularly checking that your planned activities are aligned to your goals.

Gene O'Kelly's inspirational story of the last three months of his life (see 8.6) provides a serious wake-up call for Type-A personalities. He sought to make those last days the best of his life by maximising his ability to focus on the present, rather than the future as he always had, 'to enjoy each moment so much that time seems to actually slow down...without a care about what came next...a less cluttered awareness of each moment'.[2]

O'Kelly's impending death made him reflect on his work as CEO of KPMG USA. He had always admired and stood for 'commitment', but he now realised this was too often measured in business by how many hours you were willing to work or how much time you were prepared to take away from your family. He reflected that 'commitment' is not about time, nor reliability, nor predictability—rather, he concluded, it was about depth, effort and passion. Ultimately, it was about wanting to be in that place, not somewhere else. Commitment, he said, 'is best measured not by the *time* one is willing to *give up* but, more accurately, by the *energy* one wants to *put in*, by how present one is'.[3]

In his final weeks, O'Kelly began to think of what he called 'Perfect Moments', where 'time came close to standing still'. Moments where his heightened awareness of the present enabled him to experience things that would have been impossible in his former hustle and bustle lifestyle, when thoughts of the past and the future had strangled the present. Importantly to O'Kelly, you had to be open to a Perfect Moment in order to experience one. In his openness to Perfect Moments, O'Kelly increasingly realised the virtue of spontaneity. He also lamented that too few people asked themselves the simple question: 'Why am I doing what I am doing?'

O'Kelly recognised that he was powerless to change his imminent mortality but he had the power to make things better because he still had power over himself. The book concludes with five valuable lessons from O'Kelly's experience, told by his wife Corinne:

→ face reality
→ simplify
→ live in the moment
→ recognise perfection
→ achieve balance.

10.3 The 80/20 rule

Less is more.

—Mies van der Rohe, architect

In 1906 the Italian economist Vilfredo Pareto observed that 80 per cent of Italy's income was received by 20 per cent of the Italian population. Subsequently, management thinker Joseph Juran observed that the same principle applies for many phenomena—namely, that 80 per cent of consequences stem from 20 per cent of causes. This he named the Pareto Principle, colloquially known as the '80/20 rule'.

The 80/20 rule will never be a perfect fit to your situation. Nonetheless, it is valuable to pose the question: 'What are the 20 per cent of opportunities that are going to make 80 per cent of the impact in building my Life Capital?' Despite their importance, they'll probably not seem urgent, so some conscious 80/20 thinking is needed to ensure you don't defer these opportunities forever.

Just contemplating the 80/20 rule leads inevitably to concepts like 'learning to say no' and 'de-cluttering your life'. Golfer Tommy Armour was an 80/20 thinker:

> *Simplicity, concentration, and economy of time and effort have been the distinguishing features of the great players' methods, while others have lost their way to glory by wandering in a maze of details.*[4]

10.4 Multiplicity

Wealth Insert 3B introduced the concept of annuity-based thinking. Its key principle is that benefits that regularly recur may have a present value worth 10 or 20 times that of a one-off benefit. Annuity-based thinking is therefore a specific example of the concept of 'multiplicity'.

Due to multiplicity, minor but regular occurrences can add up to a major impact—simply because they happen so often. Ask the person in the open-plan office whose neighbour can't resist chatting to them or making social telephone calls, or the person whose team mate has to leave the office regularly for a smoke.

If you are in a customer-facing role, you may be talking to customers or prospective customers several times per day or per hour. If some action can enhance your customer interaction, there is obvious multiplicity in its impact.

If something you do several times a day adds no value or need not be done, avoiding or removing it has a multiplier effect on your available time and personal effectiveness. The same multiplicity of benefit is applicable if you can effectively delegate that task.

In thinking about multiplicity, however, it is important to seek genuine multiplicity:

→ *In building your career experience,* be mindful of the difference between one year's experience repeated three times (non-multiplicity—at the end of three years you still have only one year's experience) and three years each with different experiences (multiplicity—at the end of that time you genuinely have three years of experience). You wouldn't spend three years at university doing the same course each year. If your employer tends to think that way in order to capitalise on your vast experience in doing the same job, persuade them to think again or find a new employer. Remember George Bernard Shaw's maxim: 'Men are wise in proportion, not to their experience, but to their capacity for experience'.[5]

→ *In seeking advice,* it is more valuable to seek the input of four people with different backgrounds (multiplicity) than 15 people with similar backgrounds (non-multiplicity).

→ *In networking,* relationships of mutual respect are much more valuable than acquaintances. Legendary investment banker John Whitehead believed such relationships to be 100 times more valuable[6]—so an extra 50 acquaintances wouldn't represent real multiplicity for Whitehead. As per the 80/20 rule, it's a case of all things not having equal weighting.

Mind the multiplicity effect at meetings

If you are preparing for a meeting where difficult decisions have to be dealt with and you have a major role (for example, you're chairing the meeting), think:

1 How many people will be at this meeting whose input I can maximise, or whose respect I can earn or reinforce if I am properly prepared and they are well briefed?

2 How many people will be at this meeting whose time and input I can waste and whose respect I can lose if I am not properly prepared or they are poorly briefed?

Respect has a very high value, so think about how well you are going to prepare and consult before attending such meetings.

10.5 Rates of change—differentials

Sir Isaac Newton invented differential calculus. He was the first to scientifically define rates of change (the first differential—like the speed of a car) and rates of change in those rates of change (the second differential—like the acceleration of a car). We can take immense value from these concepts without needing to understand the detailed mathematical calculations of a Formula One engineer.

If you believe that growth in Life Capital is important, then it is good to have some perception of the growth and acceleration or deceleration of your Life Capital or your career capital and those of others. Different questions are prompted by perceptions of:

→ rapid and accelerating growth
→ rapid but slowing growth
→ slow but accelerating growth
→ positive but slow growth
→ negative growth.

In some fields, this can be highly quantified. In the business world, announcements of earnings per share ('EPS') results are eagerly anticipated. Understandably, there are vast differences in reactions to a 3 per cent growth versus 10 per cent versus 20 per cent. These numbers have some absolute significance, but they have much more when compared with last year's growth, competitors' growth and market expectations for growth. Even if muddied by 'corporate spin' and accounting standards, EPS growth rates prompt questions for management, for boards and for analysts. In the quest for corporate improvement, these questions may be more important than the numbers themselves.

In most sports, the measuring stick is far more accurate than accounting results. In swimming or track and field, comparisons with previous results and personal best results (PBs) are highly accurate, revealing growth and accelerating growth very clearly.

In 1989 Australian Glen Housman broke the longest standing world swimming record, the 1500-metres freestyle, with a time of 14 minutes 54 seconds. Unfortunately, the failure of the official timing mechanism robbed Housman's swim of world record status—despite three officials with handheld stopwatches recording his time as being inside the record. But this story isn't so much about the unlucky Housman but about the guy who was about 25 seconds slower in the same event. The young Kieren Perkins achieved a 20-second improvement in his PB. Despite knowing nothing about swimming, I immediately remarked to Tori that Housman might never get his just deserts of a world record because it was quite likely that Perkins's rate of improvement would soon take him past Housman.

As it turned out, I wasn't quite right. Housman did beat Perkins again but sadly he never achieved an official world record, missing it once by less than half a second, with Perkins coming second. I was right, however, in seeing significance in Perkins's remarkable rate of improvement. He went on to win two Olympic gold medals in the 1500 metres and set 11 world records from the 400 meters to the 1500 metres. Even though I had no knowledge about swimming, I could see Perkins's talent from his rate of improvement.

Beware your scepticism of rapid performance change

When you see someone making very rapid progress, is your first question 'What are they taking?' (if in sport), 'Who are they sleeping with?' (if in management) or 'Who have they bought?' (if in property development). Unfortunately, this is the first question asked by many people, because they are envious and sceptical of how others make rapid progress. This thinking is an important contributor to what is called 'tall poppy syndrome'. I suspect that such scepticism is justified only in a small, possibly even tiny percentage of cases. Any confirmed cases attract big press coverage, so, just like shark attacks, you feel they are more common than they are. The real disadvantage if you're automatically a sceptic is that you spend your time looking for the sinister explanation of rapid performance improvement, rather than viewing it objectively and learning whatever you can from it.

Even if you do not generally dislike tall poppies, is your ability to identify and then learn from talented people enhanced if you like them, or diminished if you dislike them? If the latter is true, you could experience real opportunity loss. For example, if your aim in the 1980s was to learn about tennis and become a better player, watching John McEnroe play was a must, regardless of how much his on-court antics infuriated you. It's no different in public life, the arts or corporate politics.

Rates of change and recruitment

Imagine you're a football coach aiming to recruit the person with exceptional talent who will help your team go forward in leaps and bounds. It seems logical that of the two seemingly equal candidates, the person who shows greater improvement in their performance probably has the greater potential. A corollary is that the person who has overcome a disadvantaged background is often a standout — at least as far as their growth in human capital (that is, learning) is concerned.

A similar concept applies in the context of social capital; this is a more important factor if you're trying to fill a senior position at a professional services firm, rather than a football team. If two applicants have seemingly equal social capital, and one was new to the country only eight years ago whereas the other started with the benefit of the right school and university networks, then the immigrant's ability to build networks is clearly higher than the person who started with a big advantage.

The dangers of statistical discrimination

In The Logic of Life, economist Tim Harford writes about the 'dangers of rational racism'.[7] He describes the experiments of Marianne Bertrand and Sendhil Mullainathan, whose research team responded to over 1000 job advertisements in the Boston Globe and Chicago Tribune with contrived CVs. To isolate the effect of having a 'black-sounding' name, they sent in four CVs: an impressive 'black' CV, an impressive 'white' one, a less impressive 'black' CV and a less impressive 'white' one. The depressing results were:

→ 'White names received 50 per cent more invitations
   to interview'
→ 'High-quality candidates were more likely to be invited for an
   interview, but only if they were white. Employers didn't seem to
   notice whether black applicants had extra skills or experience.'
   So: 'Why bother to get a degree or work experience if you are
   young, gifted and black?'

Harford describes this as 'statistical discrimination', 'when employers
use the average performance of the applicant's racial group as a piece of
information to help them decide whether to hire that applicant'. This,
he says, 'can hurt minorities in two ways: directly, by denying them
opportunities; and indirectly, by sapping the incentive they have to
study hard and aim high. The indirect effect is insidious and probably
even more serious in the long run'.

Ironically, I believe that this statistical discrimination not only
hurts the relevant minority as Harford points out, but also potentially
disadvantages the employer. It means they are missing out on those
well-qualified members of the disadvantaged group (in the above
example, black Americans), who have probably shown greater
acceleration in their career to date than an equally qualified white
American. Obviously, however, an individual's ability to build up a CV
is not the only criteria to take into account in filling specific positions
in a team.

Growth and acceleration of your career

The following concepts are potentially relevant to your career:
→ it is valuable to have some perception of whether your career
   capital is growing rapidly, growing slowly, static or declining
→ it is valuable to understand why
→ that understanding may be enhanced by comparing your career
   this year with last year, with your prior expectations, or with
   others who have the same background or who are operating in
   the same environment
→ your conclusions may relate to something about yourself or
   something about your career environment (for example, your
   employer, your professional colleagues or your team mates)
→ your career capital will be enhanced by putting the right people
   around you; for example, employing people who are smarter

than yourself. Often the right people are the ones who are growing, learning and adapting fastest.

The differentials of speed and acceleration are important, not only regarding people, their performances and their Life Capital but also regarding the environments in which they are performing or operating. The prospects are likely to be greater if you live in a growth economy and work for a growth organisation or in a growth industry, rather than if you live and work in a non-growth environment.

Note, however, that sometimes the current rate of growth may give a false impression of future prospects, especially in less mature sectors of an economy. For example, a 15 per cent per annum growth rate last year, slowing at 5 per cent per annum, will be down to nil growth in three years.

10.6 Growth curves

The principal common theme in my business life has been to work with others to build businesses. I've always looked for a healthy balance between operations in the early, middle and late stages of maturity. In a retail chain, for example, this would be a balance between stores in the planning stage and those about to be opened, those newly or recently opened, those at peak growth and performance, and the mature 'cash cows'. The same concept applies to hotels in an accommodation chain or projects in a property development business.

The longer the period of planning and/or the longer the period of negative cash flow or negative profitability before each individual start-up 'turns the corner', the more important this pipeline thinking is for the business as a whole. So it is also for our lives. You need stability in some parts of your life if you are facing major changes in others. You need nourishment from some relationships if you're giving heavily emotionally in others.

Wealth Insert 10B: S-curves and stall points

Peter Lynch's fast growers (see 7.2) reach a point of inflection after a while, becoming stalwarts and in due course slow growers.

When their figures, whether revenue, profit or market capitalisation, are plotted over that longer period, the graph is like an S-curve (see figure 10.2). It represents growth starting slowly, accelerating and ultimately flattening out.

Figure 10.2: the S-curve

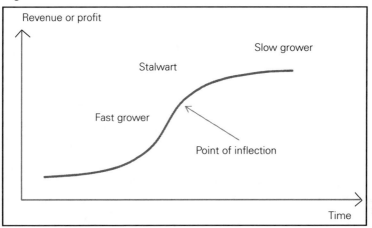

S-curves and inflection point thinking are potentially relevant in analysing sales and earnings—whether at industry, company, division or branch levels.

The ultimate significance for investors is the company's market value. A 1998 study by the Corporate Strategy board called these points 'stall points' and found that approximately 70 per cent of the companies that reach such a stall point later lose at least half of their market capitalisation—the market's recognition that they are 'ex-growth'.[8]

A 'stall point' in your life or career would be characterised by limited new experiences, responsibilities or relationships; this translates into limited investment by you in your human capital or your social capital. In this situation, your human and social capital will be declining with the passage of time, just as severely as the ex-growth companies in Wealth Insert 10B.

Your growth curve

If you are to identify and understand opportunities, understanding the growth profile of your career or Life Capital is just as important as it is for a CEO or investor to understand the growth profile of a business. Being objective about that growth profile is also important for your psychology:

→ for your resilience and self-respect; for example, if you're Edison having just found yet another way how *not* to make a light bulb while all your old mates are growing wealthy charging regular fees for their dentistry or legal services

→ keeping your feet firmly planted on the ground if you've just had extraordinary luck in a volatile profession or had a blessed life.

If you work for a long period of time in a large organisation, promotions function like steps. A colleague in a bank once told me that if you started at the bottom at age 18 and hoped to make CEO before the age of 55, you had to receive a promotion on average every 18 or 20 months throughout your career. If that's the environment you're in, the obvious key is to reduce the period between promotions to a minimum—but the real keys, apart from luck, are:

→ to minimise in each new position the length of your induction period before you are effective

→ to keep building your human and social capital and, equally importantly, others' perception of them, so you have the opportunity to apply this capital as often as possible

→ to have the resilience to handle the frequent situations where things go the wrong way for you.

You almost need a schizophrenic mindset: on the one hand, recognising the long life or career ahead of you and that there is no great rush; on the other, having some sense of urgency at the times that have a leveraged impact on you and others—like 'the first 90 days' often talked about after a leadership change. Situations with leveraged impact are the subject of Principle 19.

Over to you ...

Reflection

- Do you measure your commitment to something by the hours you put in or by the depth of your passion for it?
- At what hours of the day are you most effective? At what hours are you least effective?
- Has your progress in an important dimension stalled? If so, what do you need to do to regain momentum?
- Which of your experiences are becoming repetitive and hence contributing little to your accumulated life experience?
- Who have you recently noticed really accelerating in their personal development? What led to that acceleration and what can be learned from it?
- How do you recognise that you or one of your family or team is approaching a 'stall point'? What are the warning signs? For example, appearing enervated, not enjoying things, not learning anything new, being in the same position for a number of years. What can be done?

Action

- Imagine that your diary is always absolutely full. Analyse the potential negative impacts of operating consistently on this basis and assess their significance (appendix B2 may prompt further thoughts).
- Apply the 'A = B – C' opportunity to achieve a better allocation of your time to do the things you are passionate about. Start by checking what you are spending your time on each week, and how much of your time is under your own control.
- Allocate at least 10 minutes per day to reviewing and adjusting the alignment between your planned activities and your goals.
- Look at de-cluttering your life. Identify the things that you do not enjoy and can be eliminated (such as producing a report that no-one reads) or that you can delegate, thereby giving someone else a development opportunity.
- Use some of the time and energy you gain from de-cluttering your life to accelerate your plans in something you are passionate about—without totally refilling your diary.

Principle 11
Manage your assets and your liabilities

Your Life Capital will grow faster if you take opportunities both to grow your assets and to overcome your liabilities.

Which is more valuable: building on your assets/strengths or overcoming your liabilities/weaknesses?

This question is regularly asked of coaches, whether in sport, careers or life in general. While there are no universal answers, it is quite widely thought that the best way to achieve outstanding performance is to find your weaknesses and fix them.

11.1   Seligman's positive psychology

For decades until the late 1990s, the psychology profession focused principally on people's weaknesses and negative emotions. In 1998 US psychologist Martin Seligman resolved to bring better balance by focusing on positive psychology—the study of wellbeing, the strengths and virtues that enable us to thrive, and the positive emotions that make us more tolerant and creative and dilute or dissipate negative emotions.[1]

Among positive emotions, Seligman distinguishes between rapidly dissipating pleasures (like eating an ice-cream or watching a movie) and the more sustaining gratification received from the exercise of our strengths and virtues in rising to an occasion or meeting a challenge (such as an act of kindness or generosity).

Seligman notes Mihaly Csikszentmihalyi's concept of 'flow'—the experience of finding that while being absorbed in something challenging but well linked with your abilities, time seems to stop and you feel no emotions. Seligman sees flow as a context of immense gratification in which you are building psychological capital for the future. Americans, he says, receive much more flow at work than through leisure—especially if their work goals and rules of performance are clear, and feedback is regular and constructive.

For Seligman, strengths are psychological and moral traits, which you reveal across different situations and over time, and are distinguished from natural talents such as speed or beauty. He emphasises the importance of finding your signature strengths—those you really celebrate—and aiming to exercise them every day in your work, family and leisure time. You can thereby maximise your satisfaction and take yourself off the modern 'hedonic treadmill' of adapting rapidly to each new possession or accomplishment without receiving any lasting increase in your happiness. He notes that rich people are, on average, only slightly happier than poor people.

Seligman distinguishes between:

→ *a pleasant life* with plenty of positive feelings
→ *a good life*, where you use your signature strengths to obtain abundant gratification
→ *a meaningful life*, where you use your signature strengths in the service of something larger than you (along the lines of the importance of having meaning in your life, as discussed in 5.2).

Importantly, he defines a *full life* as combining all three.

The application of positive psychology has since been popularised among individuals and organisations by strengths movement writers and motivators like Marcus Buckingham, the author of *Go Put Your Strengths to Work*. However, whereas Seligman sees strengths as psychological or moral traits, Buckingham sees them as activities for which you have a talent or feel passionate, which make you feel strong and towards which you should target your day.

11.2 Your Life Capital is a big A = B – C opportunity

When you view your Life Capital as your life assets less your life liabilities, it is of the form A = B – C, where B and C are both large and complex. The larger they are, the greater the leverage in managing both assets and liabilities. The more complex they are, the wider the range of opportunities for increasing your Life Capital.

A few of the many dimensions of opportunity and complexity are exemplified by asking yourself the following questions:

- → What are the many assets or liabilities you could manage better?
- → For each of those assets, does this involve building on your strength (for example, if you have mathematical talent, learning more about mathematics or one of its applications such as finance) or increasing the extent to which you are able to work with that strength in your daily life? Or does it involve both?
- → For each of those liabilities, does this involve overcoming a weakness (for example, your lack of confidence in public speaking) or decreasing the frequency with which you have to depend on that weakness? Or both?
- → If you manage a weakness by decreasing the frequency with which it is relevant to your life, what are the associated opportunity costs?
- → Is something really an asset if you don't use it in your daily life? What is the opportunity cost of not using it?
- → Which liabilities can you convert into assets? (see 11.3)
- → Can you apply the same approaches to managing strengths as you do to managing weaknesses? (see 11.4)
- → Recognising your finite energy, the current personal and professional contexts of your life and the dangers of trying to focus on too many different things at once, how will you determine which assets or liabilities to prioritise? (see 11.5).

11.3 Turning your liabilities into assets or your problems into opportunities

Opportunities to convert liabilities into assets are very valuable, simultaneously increasing your assets and decreasing your liabilities, and therefore having a double impact on your Life Capital. One example is that of turning blind spots into strengths. This is particularly valuable because, as explained in 9.3, many blind spots take the form of a lollapaloser—where one of our habits causes us to repeatedly miss out on opportunities.

Before examining this further, let's see how the principle of turning losers into winners works in a financial context.

Wealth Insert 11: turning losers into winners

In his book *The Great Game of Business*, Jack Stack offers the tip 'look for the profit in problems':

> Whenever you turn a loser into a winner, you get a double bang for your buck. Say you have a problem that's costing you $500 000 a year and you figure out a solution that winds up earning you $500 000. You don't have a $500 000 winner. You have a $1m winner. When you can stop bleeding and turn it into healing, you're twice as well off as before.[2]

Actually you may even have a $1 million per annum winner—something that's much bigger!

The same applies to personal savings. If you're a student saving for a trip overseas, you will be doubly advantaged financially if you choose to babysit (a financial winner) instead of going out 'clubbing' (a financial loser). You will also be doubly disadvantaged financially if you choose 'clubbing' over babysitting—and even more so if you make that choice regularly.

Your advantage will be compounded if the kids are asleep when you arrive so you can complete your university assignment while you babysit. It will be further compounded if you are so reliable, as my daughter Emma was, that the babysitting client helps you find a professional job post-university.

A classic potential Life Capital application of turning losers into winners is achieving a transformation from pessimism into 'flexible optimism'. It's accepted that optimists have more fun and, because of their resilience, they achieve more at school, at work and at sport and enjoy better health than pessimists. Therefore, a change from pessimism to optimism, turning an ongoing loser into an ongoing winner, would be an enormous increase in your Life Capital.

Optimists seek benefit and lessons in every situation, especially from setbacks or problems. They don't let negative emotions distract them from the task at hand, continuing to focus on the big picture and communicating the confidence that they can make it.[3]

In *Learned Optimism*, Martin Seligman presents the cognitive skills a pessimist can learn to apply in order to become more of an optimist and overcome their previous helplessness in the face of disappointment. The key, Seligman says, lies in the person's habitual way of viewing the cause of bad events. Pessimists tend to see the causes of these events as being permanent, more widely based than the individual incident and caused by their own acts or shortcomings. Optimists are likely to see the opposite — temporary causes, restricted to the incident and caused by external events.

Seligman has devised a framework of thinking (which he calls ABCDE), which the pessimist can apply to achieve a major transformation:

→ identify the Adversity, your Beliefs about that adversity and your Consequent feelings
→ then, aware of these beliefs and feelings, intentionally Dispute the beliefs until you get them in more realistic perspective and are better Energised to move on.

With practice, and the increased awareness that results, this framework enables the former pessimist to adopt an optimistic stance as the circumstances demand. 'Flexible optimism' is a much stronger position to operate from than pessimism. It is also stronger than blind optimism, which lacks pessimism's major virtue — pessimism supports a more objective sense of reality, something that is particularly important in situations where the costs of failure are high.[4]

There could be few more life- or career-significant transformations than achieving a move from pessimism to 'flexible optimism' — that is unless you are a lawyer. According to Seligman, pessimists do better at law than optimists![5]

11.4 Strengths and weaknesses demand different approaches

Marcus Buckingham distinguishes a strength as something that makes you feel strong, inquisitive, optimistic and courageous — and a weakness as the opposite. Proponents of the strengths movement, like Buckingham, advocate different approaches for managing strengths and managing weaknesses.[6]

Buckingham notes that people on high performance teams report that they call upon their strengths more than 75 per cent of the time. In contrast, and a sign of enormous opportunity loss, only 17 per cent of people report that most of their typical day is spent playing to their strengths. Buckingham emphasises the importance of maximising the proportion of your week in which you are working with and invigorated by your strengths—by reshaping your job or your training and skills around your strengths. One important avenue is to have people around you who are strong in your areas of weakness. For example, if your strength is in generating ideas, and not in reviewing the detail, find someone strong in administration or project management to work with.

Buckingham views dealing with your weaknesses as being just as important as building your strengths. However, he notes that your progress in working with your weaknesses or aiming to overcome them will be slow and will drain you. He therefore presents a strong case for working around your weaknesses—understanding them so you can recognise and avoid or minimise them and stop them infecting your week. As one approach, he suggests that if there is an activity that drains you, stop doing it and see if anyone notices or cares.

11.5   Rationing your energy

As discussed in 10.2 your energy is one of your most limited resources and needs to be invested carefully. While there can be no perfect science to selecting which of the myriad options for enhancing your Life Capital to prioritise, it seems logical to adopt a loose 80/20 approach—to look for the small number of options that have the greatest expected impact per the expected energy required.

A good starting point would be to allocate the alternatives as shown in table 11.1, showing the expected impact (low, high) and the expected energy required (low, high). The next step would be to first select those alternatives with a high impact and low energy requirement—whether they involve working on assets or on liabilities—akin to the discussion of low-hanging juicy fruit in 4.2 and 4.3.

Table 11.1: expected impact/expected energy required

	Low impact	High impact
Low expected energy required		Low-hanging juicy fruit
High expected energy required		Higher juicy fruit

In order to populate this matrix, you'll need to think through a number of searching questions. The answers will be based on common sense, experience and self-awareness, and can only be roughly quantified.

→ What are the full dimensions of the upside of an opportunity? Unless you think deeply about an opportunity, it is easy to underestimate its dimensions. Taking the example of constructive feedback we discussed in 3.2, the benefits were shown to go well beyond the initial impact of improved performance in the period immediately ahead, with additional benefits being derived from the permanent rather than just one-off nature of performance improvements. A significant impact was also made on your relationship with the person who offered the feedback, and the various improvements that could then arise from the improved relationship. In addition, there was a further dimension—the impact of success or failure on your empowerment to tackle other opportunities.

→ What is the probability of achieving the full upside? What can I do to enhance that probability by engaging others or researching it deeply to make it more of a downstream than upstream swim?

→ What is the probability of failure and what are the full dimensions of the downside? How then do I minimise that downside, other than by giving up easily and thereby increasing the probability of failure?

11.6 High-impact changes that also demand high energy

Having pursued all the high-impact, low-energy opportunities, the high-impact, high-energy quadrant begs serious investigation. Not pursuing those opportunities risks big opportunity loss, while pursuing them risks a large investment of energy and substantial risk of failure.

Two classic examples are beating an addiction to smoking or overcoming obesity from poor long-term eating, drinking and non-exercising habits. Both examples are linked to the issues surrounding behavioural change in heart patients, which we discussed in 4.1 and 4.2. The first heart patient story was notable for the very high proportion of patients who, despite the increased risk of death, failed to sustain behavioural change. The second noted a significant increase in success when the patients were supported by Dr Ornish's one-year program.

When, how and with whose support you tackle the high-impact, high-energy-demand opportunities will affect your chances of success, and therefore the merits of trying in the first place. In assessing the upside, it is important to recognise that these sorts of opportunities impact your empowerment to meet and overcome other challenges. For example, if you succeed in overcoming obesity or a nicotine addiction, the impact on your self-esteem and self-confidence has many dimensions. It may, for example, transform your chances of success in the next high-impact, high-energy opportunity you undertake.

Because these high-risk opportunities demand such high energy, they are best tackled one at a time and preferably in conjunction with other opportunities that play better to your strengths. You are thereby more likely to find flow and the related building of psychological capital (described in 11.1) to balance the drain of your higher risk opportunity.

11.7   Reinventing yourself

Self-awareness, listening to others and having an open mind will bring many opportunities to build your career capital, without having to reinvent yourself as extensively as Al Gore or as often as Madonna. However, you shouldn't automatically shy away from the invigoration of self-reinvention opportunities—regardless of your age.

Perhaps you are inspired by film producer Mel Brooks's very successful self-reinvention as a Broadway songwriter at age 75. My family, of all ages, were inspired by our late friend Alan Waddell's self-reinvention. After the death of his wife, Marge, Alan began walking the streets of Sydney. In the last six years of his life, from the age of 88 to 94, he walked every street in 284 suburbs. He gave his first ever public speech (reputedly the challenge many people fear most) at 90 and became an international celebrity, regular TV guest, public speaker and inspiration to many—young and old—especially in encouraging people to do more walking. His website <www.walksydneystreets.net>, still maintained by his sons, has to be seen to be believed.

Over to you ...

Reflection

- When did you last experience flow?
- Do you find lasting increases in happiness from new possessions or accomplishments? If so, what type of possessions or accomplishments?
- What significant asset of yours do you not use in your daily life? What is the opportunity cost of not using it?
- Are you generally open to opportunities to add to your Life Capital by taking on new things?
- Which of your major assets do you most risk overworking and converting into a liability, either generally or in specific circumstances?

Actions

- Identify something you feel has been holding you back. Analyse how it would benefit you to remove that brake and how significant these benefits are (appendix B4 may prompt further thoughts). If the benefits are large enough, see what you can do to make the positive change. See what you learn from the process and how you feel about it.
- Find and complete an internet test of optimism/pessimism or some other quality you think is worthy of exploration.
- Add one thing to your skill set that you have not felt comfortable doing before, or have put off learning. If it is a group activity, such as dancing, playing cards, singing in a group or joining a book club, identify the social interactions that flow from this new activity.
- Keep a record of the proportion of time your current job uses your strengths and develop a strategy to increase that proportion.

Spend a short period of time each Sunday night reviewing the week ahead and thinking how you can rearrange your activities so you spend more time working with your strengths.
- Think of one of your friends or colleagues who has reinvented themselves. Contemplate with an open mind your own reinvention and review any learnings.

Principle 12
Conversations
and opportunities

Any engaged conversation offers you multiple potential benefits, most fundamentally the opportunity to leverage others' Life Capital.

The leverage in most real-life systems is not obvious to most of the actors in those systems.

—Peter Senge[1]

A communication that has a clear objective, such as arranging a meeting, conveying information or making a decision, can arguably be considered a success if that objective is achieved efficiently. A seemingly successful outcome may, however, leave many other opportunities unrealised. These lost opportunities may have emerged through face-to-face rather than email contact, a little more planning or a little less rush. Deeper engagement may have offered to all participants the chance to raise other issues, to give or receive feedback on ideas or to enhance their relationships.

12.1 Leveraging conversations

Conversations offer a significant opportunity to leverage (see Wealth Insert 12A) others' generosity with their Life Capital—their ideas, contacts, market knowledge and experiences, their judgement...and their knowledge of you.

In this context there are two concepts of leverage at work:

→ multiplicity of issues

→ leverage off another person's Life Capital.

Wealth Insert 12A: the power of leverage

The simplest and most common form of investment leverage arises when an investor is able to increase the returns on their own capital by accessing others' capital. The greater the access to others' capital, the greater the leverage.

The most familiar scenario is when an investor with $500000 capital borrows $500000 from a banker to buy a $1 million investment property. Thereby, the return on the investor's $500000 investment is leveraged 2:1. If the property increases in capital value by 40 per cent over five years, the value of the investor's $500000 increases by 80 per cent—assuming the rental income has covered the bank interest charges. If the property drops 20 per cent in capital value, the value of the investor's $500000 drops by 40 per cent.

Money managers work this principle to the full, with their revenue opportunity (and hence also the capital value of their businesses) heavily linked to the amount of money they manage on behalf of others. Many increase that leverage (with no or minimal risk) by charging additional fees for performance over an agreed benchmark level. One outcome of this highly leveraged revenue opportunity was that in 2006 three hedge fund founders each earned more than US$1 billion.

As in borrowing, the greater your Life Capital, the greater your ability to leverage off others' Life Capital because of your greater ability to reciprocate. Sometimes you don't need to be able to reciprocate because you're already paying a fee, a classic example being brokerage on stock purchases (see Wealth Insert 12B).

Wealth Insert 12B: a leveraged conversation with a broker

In *One Up on Wall Street*, Peter Lynch ponders what you get for being the client of a full-service broker instead of a discount house. He asks:

> Why is it that people who wouldn't dream of paying for gas at the full-service pump without getting the oil checked and the windows washed demand nothing from the full-service broker? Well maybe they call him or her a couple of times a week to ask 'How are my stocks doing?' or 'How good is this market?'—but figuring the up-to-the-minute value of a portfolio doesn't count as investment research. I realise the broker may also serve as a parental figure, market forecaster, and human tranquiliser during unfavourable price swings. None of this actually helps you pick good companies.[2]

Lynch lists the vast information sources available to a full-service broker, which are potentially available to you as a full-service client—if you choose to ask. He then presents two takes of a client's conversation with a broker. The first is nothing more than the broker recommending the stock as a special situation, the client asking a rhetorical question in response and then deciding to buy it.

The second take is qualified by the introduction 'if you use a broker as an advisor (a foolhardy practice generally, but sometimes worthwhile)'. It then demonstrates an appropriately leveraged conversation with the broker—starting with asking the broker to give you a two-minute speech on the recommended stock. He notes that you might have to prompt the broker with questions like how the stock would be classified (for example, cyclical, fast grower and so on—see Wealth Insert 7). By asking appropriate questions in the ensuing conversation, the client then requests to be sent a range of relevant reports and information, and sets himself up to call the broker back to discuss them.

Although Lynch's story is from a bygone era, when there were full-service gas stations and no low-commission internet stock trading, it aptly demonstrates the principle of leveraging a conversation. By having such conversations with a broker, and noting the subsequent performance of the companies discussed, it soon becomes evident whether the broker is one whose advice is well founded and how much you should listen in future.

You might rightly question whether you would have the same pull with a broker as a legend like Peter Lynch. You may have little or none—at least not until the thinking broker realises they might also learn something from your intelligent questions. You may not believe that this is possible but I do. The foundations of my belief lie in Wealth Inserts 23A and 23B.

12.2   Leveraged conversations and job search

These days, most people change jobs on average every three to five years. While premium opportunities emerge unsolicited for some lucky few, most people carry out at least five to 10 job searches in a career. The career upside is enormous if you can achieve the compound benefits of an average 15 per cent better 'job fit' each time—perhaps also with commensurately higher remuneration. This is a realistic goal if you commit to a disciplined process each time, by:

→ understanding your own priorities and objectives, including family and work–life balance issues
→ generating a number of opportunities that potentially suit you
→ modifying some of those opportunities to better suit you
→ fully understanding the alternatives and deciding which is best
→ effectively negotiating the basis and expectations of your employment.

Let's look at this example. John, an experienced Wall Street mergers and acquisitions adviser, is looking for a new job in the financial markets. His mate and former colleague Bill moved two years ago to work for a private equity manager. While phoning Bill is an obvious next step, John is concerned about taking up too much of Bill's time. He knows Bill is busy on a couple of new deals and has been travelling a lot for meetings with portfolio companies. He phones Bill:

Take 1: non-engaged and minimal leverage

'Hey Bill. I've decided its time to look for a new job, maybe a move into private equity, and was wondering if there's anything on offer down at your shop.'

'I'm not aware of anything right now, John, but I'll keep on the lookout. I've been working round the clock and Jane and I and the kids are off to Acapulco tomorrow for a week. I'll see if we've got anything going here when I get back.'

Take 2: fully engaged and fully leveraged

'Hey Bill. I've decided it's time to look for a new job, maybe a move into private equity. It would be great if you could spare me an hour or so to really chew this over—any dimensions on this you can think of. From my point of view, the sooner I get your input the better as I'm about to fire up this search. You know this territory and the players so well that I'd really value it.'

'Great. Don't know whether I can be of help but you never know. Let's make it breakfast on Saturday at the Grande so we're not rushed. Send me an email with your CV so I can think about it a bit beforehand. If you can add a couple of paragraphs about what you're looking for, that might help to get us focused.'

John and Bill meet at the Grande. After a chat about the weekend football:

'John, your CV's great and private equity is a big growth area, so there should be lots of opportunities worth chasing. But before we get to them, let's focus a bit on your current job.'

'It's going very well but I just get that feeling it's time for a change. I've been in the same position for three years and something's urging me to see what other opportunities are out there.'

'At least your current job takes away the time pressure for finding something new, and provides a strong benchmark for any new opportunities.'

'I'd like to have a number of choices—and preferably at the same time!'

Bill introduces his well-tested theory on job searches: 'You've hit the nail on the head! The way I see it, if you can have five jobs to choose from rather than just one, the fit of the ultimate job is likely to be

10 to 50 per cent better, perhaps more — and maybe the remuneration as well. You'll have a far better idea what you're worth and be better placed to negotiate.'

'It's not much different from the big premiums on the contested takeover bids (see Wealth Insert 12C) I work on seven days a week — the more competition for the prize the better — only in this case I want to be the prize!'

'There is one important difference, John. Everyone hears about the public companies that get takeover bids. In your case, you've somehow got to find out who the logical bidders are and let them know that you're available and interested.'

From this unorthodox start, their chat has many dimensions. John elicits from Bill a whole range of ideas of potential employers and they examine some possible changes in direction for John — including some thoughts about job opportunities in overseas markets. Bill also comes up with some ideas on what new experiences might complement John's previous work.

John remembers reading that more people find their jobs through people they see occasionally, rather than the people they see often, because the latter generally operate in much the same information pool as they do.

This prompts John to ask Bill the obvious question about who else he should be talking to (potential employers, other contacts of Bill's and head-hunters). These questions prompt a few ideas from Bill and he notes a few specific introductions he is happy to make for John — at his own firm, at another private equity firm and to a close head-hunter contact. He reminds John that when you're searching for a job, the head-hunters are the gatekeepers. He even suggests a couple of contacts at some hedge funds, just to give Bill a broader perspective on the options.

It's been a very productive start but John senses that Bill's good for more: 'Have you got any other advice?'

'Just a few suggestions I've marked on your CV. You come over really well from both your CV and your presentation. It's clear what you stand for and what you're looking for. You've obviously reflected on those qualities quite deeply. There are also a couple of books you might find relevant. I found them valuable to test my thinking when I made the move to private equity. One helped me clarify my preference for private equity; the other gave me some ideas about how to craft and negotiate the actual role and expectations to suit my sweet spots. I'll email you the titles.'

'Bill, thanks for all those thoughts. It's been particularly helpful. One last request: would you be happy to be a referee for me?'

'Delighted! No doubt you'll let me know where you're tossing your hat in the ring so I can anticipate a call. Let's have a chat about the specific targets at that stage. It might be worth asking Fred too. He's told me a couple of times how highly he regards your work.'

John leaves with pages of notes, confident that he has made a great start. Across a number of dimensions he has heavily leveraged Bill's Life Capital.

Bill has a few introductory calls to make on John's behalf and is confident that his time with John has not been wasted. He feels good about being able to help his old friend. John's command of the situation was impressive and objective, so Bill is very comfortable being a referee. The more he reflects on it, the more he realises how well John has milked their chat for everything he can — and Bill is delighted that he has!

Wealth Insert 12C: contested takeover bids bring bigger premiums

Most takeover bids for public companies are made at a premium of around 30 per cent to the share price prior to the bid announcement. Pitched there, they have a reasonable chance of being recommended to shareholders by the target company's board — 'in the absence of a higher offer'. Many of these bids then proceed smoothly from recommendation to successful completion at that offer price or a slightly higher price.

In some hotly contested situations, one or more counter bidders emerges and the ultimate price for the takeover is a premium of (say) 50 to 100 per cent over the pre-bid average price, sometimes more. To achieve these premiums it is essential that the target company's strategic value is well understood by the potential bidders.

Translating this to a job search, it is vital that your potential employees understand what you've got to offer, and if you're going to communicate that effectively, you have to know and understand your assets.

12.3   Negotiating a new job in a new company

Understanding and negotiating the terms and expectations of any new job are multi-dimensional challenges, which, like a job search, offer the opportunity for leverage through conversation. The dimensions to understand or negotiate might include:

→ The business
  - strategic and competitive position
  - management depth and reputation
  - financial position and performance
  - approach to incentives, performance reviews and feedback
  - approach to induction and training
  - culture of workplace
  - legendary stories about the business

→ The role
  - job description, resources and support staff, responsibilities and expectations
  - travel requirements
  - experience of previous people in the role and where they have progressed to
  - any preconditions to ensure you're set up for success

→ Terms and conditions
  - contractual financial terms (base, short- and long-term incentives, performance hurdles, leave, travel and other conditions and benefits)
  - flexibility of salary packaging
  - induction and training
  - performance reviews and feedback.

The significance of this list lies not in the specific items but in its multiple dimensions.

After two months of searching and scores of conversations, John has fulfilled his objective of receiving a few, almost concurrent, job offers. He has identified the job he likes most, offering interesting new horizons and a strong corporate culture, but it's a departure from Wall Street.

He calls Bill:

Take 1: non-engaged and no leverage

'Hey Bill, I've just signed a great deal at Enron. They'll be paying me a squillion base, a potential bonus of a squillion squared and a big load of options fully vesting after three years' service! I'd like to have a celebratory breakfast at the Grande on Saturday. How are you placed?'

'Great news! Saturday's good for me. See you there at 7.30. Sounds like it's your shout!'

Take 2: fully engaged and fully leveraged

'Hey, Bill, I'm almost ready to deal on a new job. It's in Houston. In some respects it's almost too good to be true. I'd just like to talk it through with you to check if I'm missing something I should check out further or cover off in the final negotiations. Any chance of catching you tonight for a short while?'

'Sounds good—see you at the Grande at 6 pm. What's the position?'

'Leading the acquisitions team at Enron.'

'Interesting!'

'My lawyer's reviewed the contract and suggested a few changes. I've met with most of the executive team, and they've been very open and welcomed my questions. I've even passed the psyche tests. I've covered off most bases. Now I'm digging deeper into the reputation and success factors for the whole business and whether my role will be set up for success or for failure. If the latter, then any performance-based incentives could be very illusory. That's where I thought your industry knowledge and contacts would be valuable.'

'Would you like me to do some soundings with a few analysts?'

'If you've got time, that could be particularly valuable. So far I've studied the numerous analysts' reports and they were pretty positive "buys", despite the recent one-third decline in the share price. I also spoke to one analyst who told me about a recent conference call on Enron's quarterly results. Apparently, a hedge fund manager asked Jeff Skilling for Enron's balance sheet, commenting that Enron was the only financial institution that couldn't produce a balance sheet or cash flow statement with its earnings statement. Everyone then heard Skilling call him an "asshole" under his breath. I want to understand what's behind it.'

'It's a surprising signal, especially from a CEO who's been rated as America's second-best CEO and talks about his company becoming the highest market cap company in the world.'

John has focused this conversation with Bill on his immediate needs and leveraged Bill's career capital.

John and Bill meet at 6 pm, by which time they have both made a few soundings with people in the financial services and energy sectors who have dealt with Enron. John has done more searching on the internet. It appears there is a lot more scepticism about Enron's business model and fundamentals than expected, and this has come through in brokers' reports. Few, it seems, want to shout it from the rooftops but there is increasing disquiet, even disbelief, about Enron's accounting. Some feel their results are defying gravity, given the prevailing conditions in a number of their markets.

All the soundings suggest caution at investing capital, let alone your career, in an organisation where nobody seems to really understand how it makes money and the CEO becomes so upset when asked reasonable questions about financial statements.

12.4   Return on your investment

Earlier in this chapter, I asserted that while making five to 10 job searches in a career, it's quite realistic to target an average 15 per cent better 'job fit' on each change of jobs (and maybe commensurate remuneration increases) if, each time, you commit to a disciplined process that leads to multiple opportunities you understand well and from which you can choose. While I have no firm data to support this assertion, it just feels reasonable. But is it worth the trouble?

Many of the steps involved in a disciplined job search warrant a significant commitment of time and energy, which may be difficult if you are deeply consumed by your current responsibilities. However, this commitment pales in comparison with the 2000 hours you are likely to spend in that job each year—or the 5000 to 10000 hours of work until you next change jobs!

If effective conversations help you to find a better job fit sooner and to be better set up for challenge, pleasure and success in that new role, then the return on investment is enormous. The return is even greater if those conversations and other information sources also help you negotiate competitive remuneration with realistic performance criteria. And the more you learn about your employer in advance, the more able you are to hit the ground running.

Over to you ...

Reflection

- Think of a conversation that you believe you leveraged well. How do you feel the others involved found that same conversation? In what other ways could you have leveraged it better? What caused you to miss those opportunities? Was it brought to a premature conclusion, and if so, why? Is that a habit of yours or someone else's?
- Reflect similarly on a conversation that you or others did not leverage well.

Actions

- Analyse the benefits to you of being more engaged in your conversations and leveraging them better, and the significance of these benefits (appendix B10 may prompt further thoughts).
- Talk with friends or selected acquaintances about your next significant step or decision in life—a big trip, job change, buying a house, getting married. Test your ability to leverage those conversations for ideas, wisdom, introductions, offers of follow-up conversations, and to keep the conversation going through open rather than closed questions. Watch for any dimensions you would never have anticipated (serendipity). Look for the opportunity to reciprocate—at the time or later.
- Select some conversations in which you decide not to be the person who cuts off the conversation and see what happens. With each conversation, aim to get the most leverage you can from it—in as many directions as possible.

Principle 13
Free options

Engaged conversations lead to many opportunities. These free options cost you nothing other than your time and energy, but they may be very valuable.

I always feel that I have to talk to people: one call leads to another, which leads to the next opportunity.

—Richard Branson[1]

I am regularly amazed at the opportunities that emerge from conversations. Other than the time and energy spent conversing, they are 'free options'.

Some opportunities you will choose not to pursue further (no prize and no cost). Some you pursue will lead nowhere (again no prize but probably some cost). Metaphorically, some of these free options will show net rewards in the $5 to $500 range, some in the $500 to $50 000 range, and some in the $50 000 to $1 million range and perhaps far beyond.

Sometimes these free options emerge as the result of a conscious search or line of questioning, such as where you have the opportunity to meet with someone who has previously made the journey you are about to take. Sometimes they emerge from vigorous debate. Often, however, they are unsolicited or emerge tangentially. They come in many forms, some of the more significant being ideas options (13.1), people options (13.2), people options already on your team (13.3), self-awareness options (13.4) and inspiration or motivation options (13.5).

13.1   Ideas options

Conversation is the greatest idea generator known to man.

—Rudolf Flesch[2]

Serendipitously, often the best idea you take from a conversation won't be the one you were looking for. Perhaps you explore a current work challenge and come away with a new career vision; you discuss someone else's problems and solve one of your own; you seek advice on an investment proposal and come away with a new book that influences your investment thinking. Sometimes the idea will take the form of 'this won't work because …' or 'your proposed business model is unsound because …', saving you from following one of life's many false trails.

The chance of a valuable idea emerging from an engaged conversation is material because ideas take so many forms, including the following.

A vision

Some people see things as they are and ask why. Other people see things as they could be and ask why not?

—George Bernard Shaw

A vision, one of the hardest things to find, is arguably pre-eminent among ideas because it is a prerequisite for so much else that is positive.

An opportunity

A great holiday idea or a source of funds for your community project.

An interpretation or structuring of knowledge to fit your immediate needs

While technology offers instantaneous access to factual knowledge, a targeted conversation is often the most efficient bridge to your specific needs.

An alternative interpretation

Two people watching events unfold often interpret them differently. If something unusual worries you, compare notes with someone else who witnessed it. Their interpretation may be helpful in clarifying whether your concerns are signals of a material problem. For example, as a parent, did you notice a significant change in the confidence or behaviour of your child? Did your partner also notice it? What in their view was its significance? Or, in business, did events you witnessed suggest a genuine change in the commitment, confidence or behaviour of the CEO? If so, what was its significance? Did others notice it and how did they interpret it?

Other people's views will be more valuable to you the less you have influenced them by presenting your own interpretation first. The importance of such independence is explored further in 23.1.

A problem or a question

Never underestimate the value of a chat if all you have come away with is an awareness of a challenging problem or question. Philosopher Mortimer Adler viewed curious young children as a wonderful source of profound questions. This curiosity, he said, is later dulled by rote learning for school or discouraged by parents' poor handling of their questions—giving no answer when there is one, being irritated when baffled or demanding that they stop asking questions. Adler lamented that by adulthood their curiosity deteriorates, becoming more focused on facts rather than on understanding why.[3]

Fortunately, not every adult is so afflicted. Ideas generators retain the quality of their curiosity and their ability to identify problems or questions. At a conference two years ago, Goren Roos, a founder of the modern field of intellectual capital, lamented the education system's focus on teaching students to *solve* problems while ignoring their ability to *identify* problems. He then described a three-hour exam he sets where students are given piles of papers related to a company and the sole exam question is: 'What is the problem?'

A valuable challenge to your fundamental assumptions, values or models

Implicitly or explicitly, you run your life on a set of fundamental assumptions, values and models. Unexpected events are a good reason for challenging these fundamental ideas; however, you may be so wedded to them that you instead try to solve problems at the margin and perhaps end up 'beating your head against a brick wall'. Getting someone else's helicopter view might help challenge your assumptions, values or models more effectively than you can alone, and help to open up your mind to opportunity.

Just as there are many forms of ideas, so there are many different people who may be sources of ideas:

Team mates or peers

They often challenge you with 'Why this way? What if you ...?'

Clients

Listening to clients discuss their own issues or experts' views on industry developments is a regular ideas prompter for professional advisers.

Others who have tried before, whether they succeeded or not:

In 1984 a young American lawyer asked Richard Branson whether he was interested in financing or operating an airline on the Gatwick (London) to New York route vacated by the 1982 collapse of Sir Freddie Laker's low-cost airline Laker Airways. In learning about aviation, and deciding whether to proceed in setting up Virgin Atlantic, Branson consulted

Laker, whose advice was wide-ranging and valuable—he discussed issues from market positioning and attracting customers to competitive issues with British Airways and even stress and medical issues. Years later, Branson continued to keep in close contact with Laker during his competitive issues and litigation with British Airways.

Laker advised Branson not to merely set up a no-frills economy service such as Laker Airways, which had been too vulnerable to competitors' cost-cutting—advice Branson heeded. This same advice would not have been as helpful to Michael O'Leary, who in the early 1990s was invited to step up as CEO of the then unprofitable Ryanair. It would only have confirmed O'Leary's initial reaction that Ryanair should be shut down. However, O'Leary kept an open mind and, at owner Tony Ryan's suggestion, went to Dallas to visit the legendary Herb Kelleher, who had built Southwest into the world's largest low-fare carrier and the most successful US airline. Lessons learned from Kelleher and Southwest gave O'Leary the vision and some of the ideas he has since applied in building Ryanair into Europe's biggest discount airline, and one of the world's largest airlines by market capitalisation.

Those with a big ego

Pancho Gonzalez was my hero because his face was on my Spalding tennis racquets. John Newcombe described the fiery Gonzalez as an angry, hard man who 'would have eaten renowned bad guys John McEnroe, Jimmy Connors and Ilie Nastase for breakfast'. Newk cherished his relationship with Gonzalez:

> Like me, he was a great studier of other players and would spend hours observing his rivals' technique in their matches, working out ways to beat them. Whenever Rosewall and Laver played we'd often sit together in the stands and I'd ask Pancho questions about these guys and their tactics. With his enormous ego, Pancho loved being the master…and this made his encyclopaedic knowledge available to me.[4]

Someone from the outside

People who aren't blinded by the same organisational or contextual noise as you are may bring new perspectives or new options.

Those you know have the relevant knowledge

Life is generally an open-book exam. Fortunately, you don't have to remember the information in the street directory, the phone book or your diary. All you have to remember is the nature of their contents and where you left them.

Similarly, in family, work or other relationships, it's not just what you know; it's who you know, what they know and what you know about their knowledge. You don't have to remember everything, you just need to know who else has the information and how to communicate with them. In my case, this could be the time the plane leaves for the family trip (my wife), how to work the CD or video recorder (my son), where a family photograph or important document is (my wife), what concerts are coming up (my daughter) and who sang that song (1960s—me, 1970s—my wife, anything thereafter our kids). Now I realise why Tori regularly gets annoyed with me and calls me '20 questions'!

This aspect of 'how people remember things in relationships and groups' was named 'transactive memory' and developed by psychologist Daniel Wegner and his colleagues. You really learn how valuable transactive memory can be when the person you rely on for information is scuba-diving in the Pacific or climbing in the Himalayas!

If you don't know who knows the answer, there are some people you suspect will—simply because they seem to know just about everything. They're called 'mavens' and you'll meet them in 13.2.

Because you have confidence that someone else already knows or will learn something, you switch off from having to learn it. You inevitably become a specialist in certain categories of information; so do others, and they form a part of your transactive memory.

An achievable goal—one creative conversation per day

Ken Hudson, founder of the Ideas Centre, believes that 'every business manager or leader should aim to have one creative conversation per day, during which they must place an emphasis on being positive'. He defines a creative conversation as one in which 'the creative potential of both the producer and receiver of an idea is fully realised'.[5]

Regardless of your field or passion, if you seek creative conversations and keep asking yourself about their significance, your own body of knowledge and understanding will grow and empower you even more to find and develop the next conversation.

We revisit ideas options on a more leveraged basis in Principle 18.

13.2   People options

In the 21st century, you are more than ever dependent on others. You need to have ways to spot the right potential partners—the ones who can enrich your life and you theirs, and with whom you want to build relationships. Conversations offer the opportunity to observe others—how they think, participate, contribute, negotiate and empathise. These observations might alert you not to deal with them again. More positively, however, they can be the basis for significant future opportunity if you spot:

→ *Someone whose company you've enjoyed or found inspiring:* the essence of life!

→ *Someone with exceptional talent:* who you're brave enough to play with or to employ.

→ *A maven:* a keen gatherer of information who is happy to share or trade knowledge on a variety of subjects.

→ *A connector:* a person who is comfortable in quite varied worlds—cultural, professional, social, political, sporting or financial—and naturally introduces people from those worlds.

→ *Someone with complementary skills or thoughts* with whom you can collaborate (the benefits of collaboration and cross-fertilisation are covered in Principle 18).

→ *An ally:* who might add greater legitimacy, resources or contacts to your cause.

→ *An ideas generator; a maverick or a person who can solve a particular problem.* My coaching colleague Sandra Yates has a simple tip for spotting ideas generators: look for people who can talk about abstract ideas, who can describe a gap and can imagine what might go there.

→ *A devil's advocate:* to constructively challenge your ideas—derived from the former role in the Roman Catholic Church of the Promoter of the Faith. The role, abolished by Pope John Paul in 1983 after almost 400 years, was to take a sceptical view of a candidate for sainthood, to look for holes in evidence and to argue against their candidacy. People in high places sometimes find it quite difficult to locate a suitable devil's advocate.

→ *A great leader or boss:* these people can be very important in your life, so seek out good ones.

→ *A great adviser:* whether a mentor, coach, investment adviser, tax adviser, doctor, psychiatrist, personal trainer or other confidant you can choose to consult or who can celebrate your successes and listen in the tough times. They are all potentially important parts of your Life Capital.

My favourite story of a mentor/coach is that of Brother Colm O'Connell, who travelled from Ireland to teach geography at St Patrick's High School, 2400 metres above sea level in Iten, Kenya, over 30 years ago. With only limited prior exposure to athletics, he soon became responsible for the school's athletics program, and more than 100 of his athletes have since become world class. Great mentors and coaches like O'Connell think holistically and long term. When asked about the Kenyan athletes who come from nowhere, win something big and then disappear, he replied that culturally the men are the breadwinners and if they win quickly, they're satisfied and their ambition, interest and performances drop—even in their early twenties. Hence he encourages his athletes to focus on track events (rather than road races) where they are less likely to become rich overnight and so gain a 'greater opportunity to develop physically, mentally, financially'.[6]

→ *A role model:* as Peter Montgomery, vice president of the Australian Olympic Committee, has said: 'The role model provides the vehicle for the personal visualisation of the possibility of high achievement by young people in all societies. This mechanism is one of the great benefits of sport—particularly the Olympic Games'.[7] We've seen this in many sports, but my favourites are the two fathers of African distance running, Ethiopian Abebe Bikila and Kenyan Kip Keino. Bikila, the first African Olympic gold medallist, won the marathon in 1960 in Rome, running in bare feet, and again in 1964 in Tokyo, 40 days after the removal of his appendix. Keino won both gold and silver middle-distance medals at Mexico City in 1968, despite suffering from gallstones and running against doctor's orders. Keino won gold and silver again at Munich in 1972. He went on to found and run a farm orphanage in Kenya, and later to become president of the Kenyan Olympic Committee. Keino's 80-hectare farm is the home from time to time of up to 100 orphans, mainly girls, and dozens of international athletes who visit to train, many from other African countries. Ever since the achievements of Bikila and Keino, all the great middle-distance races seem to have been dominated by African runners, especially Kenyans and Ethiopians.

The significant impact of role models on those who try to emulate them is obvious. Often just as significant, but more subtly so, is the influence of role models on the expectations of the families and friends of the aspirant. Brother O'Connell's observations of female Kenyan runners reflect this. Kenyan girls, he says, mature young and, following cultural norms and social pressures, talk about marriage when they're about 20. Hence, thinking that they should make their money by 20, they run too many races and become burned out—especially those involved in road racing. He aims to keep these athletes in education (perhaps including US colleges) long enough for them to mature more broadly—in their running, in their personality and personal presentation, in how they promote their sport and what they put back into it, and in how they handle their affairs. O'Connell says it's becoming easier for young women to explain to their parents why they're not getting married soon:

> As they've seen some role models go ahead ... make money, build houses, build camps, have farms, the parents are gradually beginning to realise 'My daughter may be more valuable to me as an athlete than in the form of a dowry from her husband'.

One wonderful career role model for both men and women is Colleen Barrett, who started as an executive assistant at a law firm. When her boss Herb Kelleher moved to start up Southwest Airlines in 1978, he took her with him as his first employee and she became corporate secretary. After senior roles in both administration and customer service, she became president of the company from 2001 to 2008. To me, the most interesting part of Barrett's story is her aim as a young woman to be 'the best damn secretary who ever walked the face of the earth'.[8]

Her potentially achievable (but obviously not measurable) aim resulted in her performing and developing so well that interesting career options inevitably arose. Her story is not only an inspiration to executive assistants with higher aspirations, it is also a healthy reminder to sceptics who think executive assistants or equivalents can't make it to the top.

Role models show you what can be done and inspire you to visualise yourself doing something similar. For example, until 1954 everyone thought the four-minute mile was not humanly possible. However, after Roger Bannister role-modelled the four-minute mile, 45 other athletes achieved it in the next 18 months.

→ *An anti-role model:* providing the perfect example of 'what not to do'. The very successful coach of the football team I support, the Sydney Swans, is Paul Roos. When he finished his playing career, he made a list of what he liked about coaches and what he didn't like. He knew he could learn from anti-role models, just as he could from his role models. He takes the list out from time to time to remind himself of the basics.[9]

Exercising your 'free people options' effectively

Imagine you're at a lunch, sharing a table of 10. You're well acquainted with the host and two other guests. If you're well engaged with the conversation, you earn the option to ring any of the nine participants later. It's likely that one (or more) of your six new acquaintances has attributes you admire or find of interest.

You're unlikely to spot those attributes if you do all the talking and don't have your mind open and alert to the opportunity. People options often favour the good listeners, who are genuinely interested in hearing what others have to say and weighing up what they hear. They will typically be more alert to the experience, flair, depth or imagination of the people they meet.

In busy lives, the hardest step can be to take the time to call the person who impressed or excited you—whether to pursue a subject they raised, to let them know your interest in what they said, to catch up for a coffee to explore mutual interests, to invite them to the next lunch you are organising, to offer them a job…the opportunities are endless.

Even if you decide not to phone, it's valuable to keep an eye out for the people it would be most interesting and rewarding to develop a relationship with—and to be clear on why. It's an instructive blend of speed-dating and window-shopping.

In many situations, especially challenging ones such as a negotiation, a presentation of a proposal or a sales pitch, you need to focus on your own role and immediate responsibilities. Thus absorbed, you can easily miss the people option—the opportunity to spot someone who is doing something extremely well, someone you can learn from or a relationship you can build on in future. On subsequent reflection, even when an outcome is disappointing, you might realise that someone on the other side impressed you. Perhaps your toughest critic on the day challenged you so well that you reflect, 'Next time I want them on my side!'

It was in this way that I identified an important business partner, the late Geoff Lee, who was 25 years my senior. When I put an investment proposal to a company of which Geoff was the major shareholder, his questions were particularly searching. Although I left with a rejection, a number of things about Geoff impressed me. I realised he was a person I could learn a lot from, especially as we had totally different backgrounds and different networks. A year later, when I wanted to launch a new company, I approached Geoff for his expertise and his capital. We remained colleagues for over 20 years, and the group we started was ultimately bought out by private equity interests for over $2 billion.

We come back to people options on a more leveraged basis in Principle 14.

13.3   People options already on your team

It is more convenient to assume that reality is similar to our preconceived ideas than to freshly observe what we have before our eyes.

—Robert Fritz[10]

All too often you don't notice the special qualities of people who are already on your team. Perhaps you've taken them for granted or not noticed how they have grown personally or professionally.

As Kenneth Blanchard and Spencer Johnson so effectively communicated in their 1982 book *The One Minute Manager*, it takes only one minute (and often less) to notice someone doing something special and to give them due recognition. The two authors also emphasised the importance of telling that person specifically what they did correctly or well. This is a two-way event. The other person will feel valued and be clear on the reasons why. Your recognition of their contribution signals to you that this is someone you can rely on, and that they've got talent you'd best nurture. In order to lead effectively, you need to have (and show) confidence that those you're leading can do their bit. You won't achieve this unless you've watched and recognised them performing well.

In the 1950s, US psychologists Joseph Luft and Harry Ingham developed a simple tool for illustrating and improving self-awareness and increasing mutual understanding in a group. As table 13.1 illustrates, their Johari Window separates an individual's qualities into four quartiles.

Table 13.1: the Johari Window

Individual's personal qualities	Known by self	Unknown by self
Known by others	Q1. Open self	Q2. Blind self
Unknown by others	Q3. Hidden self	Q4. Unknown self

Some of the simpler principles for applying the Johari Window concept are:

→ in groups, the aim should be to expand each person's open self (Quadrant 1), because people are most effective when working in this area

→ feedback can reduce your blind self (Quadrant 2), expand your open self and thereby make you more effective

→ revelation of the less personal parts of your hidden self (Quadrant 3) expands your open self and can lead to more effective working relationships

→ the unknown self (Quadrant 4) is generally larger in younger people or those with a narrow experience curve—such as those who have worked in one job for 10 years, which has effectively equalled 10 times the same one year's experience. Hidden in this quadrant could be conditioned behaviours from childhood, repressed feelings or abilities that have either never been tested or been tested in the wrong circumstances.

Abilities hidden in Quadrant 4

Most people are born with talent but the majority of people don't know about their talent.

—Gennadi Touretski[11]

The great linguistic and academic abilities of one of my friends had been hidden all her life by dyslexia. Once the problem was identified and remediated, by her wearing coloured spectacles, she achieved remarkable results. Unfortunately, she was then almost 50 years old. The enormous waste and frustration implicit in her story are being replicated everywhere, every day. Our challenge as parents, friends and colleagues is to do our very best to ensure that others discover their talents, so they are not left unidentified in Quadrant 4.

Helen Lynch, one of my former colleagues, talks of dream-makers —those who do their best to identify your capabilities, to encourage you to set high goals and to reach them. She contrasts them with dreambreakers, who discourage you.

The importance of dreammakers is underlined by strong forces that can take you in the other direction. These forces start early in your childhood when, for your safety and survival, you are regularly given limits—what you can't do or can't have rather than what you can. Being taught about limits is very easy to extend to concepts of your own limitations. From time to time, we all need a healthy reminder of Henry Ford's words: 'If you think you can't you're right; if you think you can you're right'.

The Quadrant 3 trap

As we all know, it's easy to take for granted or not notice the qualities and interests of those you've been closest to longest—especially your partner.

Flying over the north-west coast of Western Australia, one of the most remote spots in the world, I was in a small plane with only the pilot and Tori onboard. Tori was in the front seat next to the pilot; they had two-way earphones and I had only one-way. I could hear, but couldn't butt into, the fascinating conversation they were having regarding the region. Unbeknownst to me, Tori had read vast amounts about this part of the country over the years—both fiction and non-fiction. It reminded me, if I needed it, what an interesting and interested woman she is. Then I realised how little we talked about the things we both read, probably because, other than newspapers, they are so entirely different. This enforced listening to my wife's conversation provided me with a free but valuable self-awareness option and an additional opportunity for our relationship.

Fortunately, we didn't have to go as far as the bloke in Rupert Holmes's hit song 'Escape (The Pina Colada Song)'—exchanging letters in the personal columns and meeting his correspondent at a bar, only to discover it was his partner and that they shared many interests, until then hidden away in their third Johari quadrants.

13.4   Self-awareness options

The first rule is to not fool yourself and you are the easiest person to fool.

—Richard Feynman

The greater your self-awareness, the lesser your blind self and your unknown self. They may also be reduced by learnings received from conversations with others, from:

→ their direct feedback
→ your feelings and reactions to them, and the context or conversation—especially when you are outside your comfort zone
→ your observations of them and comparisons you might draw with yourself.

The Western world's first great traveller-historian was Herodotus (5th century BC). The Histories, his writings now presented in nine books, tell of the achievements of the people he met in his vast travels. According to Ryszard Kapuscinski, Poland's most celebrated foreign correspondent whose work was significantly influenced by his study of Herodotus, the most important discovery made by Herodotus was that there are many worlds, each different, each important. Herodotus appreciated them as mirrors in which he could see and better understand his own world. As Kapuscinski wrote: 'we cannot define our own identity until having confronted that of others, as comparison'.[12]

Even though travel is so much easier today, we don't need to travel as far and wide as Herodotus to 'define our own identity'. We find his 'mirrors' all around us—people of different gender, ethnicity, religious beliefs, political leanings, nationality, age or profession. Even in business, it's amazing what a great mirror it can be for a big-company executive to have lunch with a group of entrepreneurs or a group from the not-for-profit sector—and reciprocally so. Opportunities abound, if you wish to grab them. Many opportunities, often the best ones, will take you outside your comfort zone—perhaps with people you are unfamiliar with, and perhaps in unfamiliar settings.

The most significant learnings often come from well outside your comfort zone; for example, receiving:

→ a blunt knock-back or bored reaction from a person who has no interest in something you're passionate about
→ the disrespect of a Gen Y person for things you take as unquestioned norms
→ a hard-working social worker who thinks your beloved employer Goldman Sachs is a department store[13]
→ a disarmingly simple question or uninhibited observation from a curious child.

In addition to asking magnificent questions, the young also have a remarkable capacity to give you the courage to stand up for what matters. Their presence alone reminds you what you are standing up for. In a story that I am confident would have been replicated in many brutal regimes around the world, a 41-year-old opposition leader at the time of the collapse of the Ceausescu regime in Romania said it was his 13-year-old daughter who insisted he attend, despite his fear, protests at which dozens of teenagers and college students were killed. 'What is most interesting is that we learned not to be afraid from our children. Most were aged 13 to 20.'[14]

While strangers and people with different backgrounds play a major role in our self-awareness, those closest to you—your kids, your partner or your old mates—are best placed to give you the occasional roastings essential to ensure that, when things go too much to your head, your feet are rapidly replanted on the ground. Regular grounding is especially important if you hold powerful and responsible positions.

13.5   Inspiration or motivation options

To know that these talented women didn't enter the world as
finished products—confident, successful, glamorous—is to under-
stand that it's within our grasp to reach loftier levels than we might
have dreamed of.

—Ellyn Spragins [15]

In 3.2, I presented the immense value of constructive feedback. One
aspect of this is the situation where you are told that you are capable of
achieving much more than you think you can or are currently doing.
This news is particularly motivating if it comes from someone you really
respect, like Helen Lynch's dreammakers in 13.3.

It's one thing being inspired about what you can do with your life; it's
something else being inspired about love of life.

The most important inspiration of all: love of life

Among the many people I have met, the most inspirational in their
love of life have been organ transplant recipients. My late friend Mark
Cocks, who had two kidney transplants, devoted the last 20 years of his
life to promoting organ donation. Every two years, a World Transplant
Games is held and one of its objectives is to promote organ donation.
The games in Sydney, organised by Mark, were the largest held at
our Olympic facilities before the 2000 Olympics. Tori organised the
volunteers so I attended some of the sports and a number of the parties,
including the opening and closing ceremonies. Transplant recipients
are individually inspirational in their love of live, but you should see
them when they get together! When the band started playing, 2000
people got up to dance spontaneously—even people less coordinated
than me. They loved it. More than anything, they appreciated that they
were alive and could dance.

13.6   The value of options

One of my core themes is that engaged conversation will lead you to
many options, which, although free, are potentially of substantial value
to you. You may receive many more options than your time, energy or
capital allow you to pursue. Hence, it is important to at least roughly
assess the value to you of options as they emerge.

Wealth Insert 13: the value of options

In financial markets, the range of types of options is almost unlimited. One basic version is an option to acquire a share in a company listed on the stock exchange. The option holder has the right but not the obligation (that is, the option) to buy the underlying share from the seller or issuer of the option at an agreed price (the strike price), either at any time over an agreed period (the exercise period) or at specified dates (the exercise dates). When the strike price is below the price of the underlying share, the option is described as being 'in the money'; when it is above, the option is 'out of the money'.

All the widely used methods of valuing options are rather technical. None is universally preferred because they all make simplifying assumptions regarding the movement of the price of the underlying share. However, regardless of the valuation method adopted, the value of an option to buy a share has two inherent sources of value:

- *The extent to which it is currently in the money.* Most significantly, this component of the option value will move much more in percentage terms than the value of the share. For example, an option to acquire for $3.75 a share that is currently trading at $4 is 25 cents in the money. If the share price jumps just 12.5 per cent to $4.50, the option will be 75 cents in the money—a trebling. This highly leveraged return is another example of the opportunity offered by the difference in two large numbers (see Wealth Insert 10A).
- *The potential for change in the extent to which it is in the money.* This component will be greater the more volatile the price of the underlying share, the longer the exercise period remaining and the greater the range of circumstances in which the option can be exercised.

When you hold an option over a share in a listed company, there is nothing you can do to enhance the value of the underlying share — unless, of course, you are one of the senior executives.

This is not the case with the free options you are offered in life. Their value to you will be quite different from their value to someone else.

They are more akin to an option over a block of development land; you can enhance or diminish their value, depending upon your knowledge, vision and plans. If you have an option over a job or an option over meeting someone, whether an industry leader or a blind date, you can plan how to maximise it and then determine whether you will exercise that option.

Options generally have higher values at times of uncertainty; in the stock market, that means times of high volatility of stock prices, whereas in real life that means times of significant change or big decisions. The more change and the more decisions, the greater the value of relevant options and the greater the importance of having multiple options.

This is a variation on the theme of qualified deal flow (see Wealth Insert 19C) — the concept that, for example, if you are looking to change jobs, the greater the number of job options available to you at decision time, the better. The longer your option exercise period for each job, the better, as it gives you more time:

→ to understand the potential of the job and build value into it through your vision or through other related options that emerge (for example, identifying someone who could become a key part of your team if you take that job)

→ to line up other alternative jobs to compete for your selection.

You thereby maximise both the number of options at the point of decision and the values of the individual options. The accumulation of multiple options by the time of decision involves planning, luck and the ability to spot options, capture them and develop them.

It is possible and valuable to expand your ability at spotting options. A good starting point is the exercise of focusing for a few days on immediately writing down in a notebook every opportunity you spot. You'll find it analogous to carrying a camera and consequently noticing things in nature or society you otherwise would not have observed. The discipline of writing down ideas or opportunities in a notebook is, as you'll see in 22.7, good enough for Richard Branson, as it was also for Leonardo da Vinci.

Any option ultimately leads to a decision whether to exercise it or not. A decision to exercise an option will generally lead to an investment of your time, energy and/or money. It may have to be done to the exclusion of other options, which then lapse for you. In this context, the decision-making principles and techniques of Principles 19 to 23 come to the fore, not least the ability to say 'No' (see 22.8).

13.7   The tradeability of options

On the stock market, you can sell an option if you don't want to exercise it. In life, many options are not tradeable, but there are a lot more tradeable ones than you might think there are. It is important to identify which life options are tradeable.

An option you do not wish to pursue may nevertheless be of substantial interest and value to someone else you know, and may thus be 'tradeable'. For example, you are called by the CEO of a football club testing your interest in coaching their top team—a great opportunity. While you unfortunately can't do it because of conflicting obligations, that option is potentially tradeable. Who else do you know who might be appropriate and would value the opportunity? By suggesting them to the club, you find some extra meaning in your day. You may also earn substantial 'brownie points' from them and/or the club.

If you seek, wherever possible, to pass on to others valuable options you do not wish to exercise, you will ultimately be a major beneficiary:

→ through the extra meaning in your life
→ through the rule of reciprocation, to which every human society subscribes
→ through understanding better others' objectives or priorities
→ through the people in your networks having more Life Capital as a result of the opportunities you introduce to them.

Over to you...

Reflection

- Have many free options come your way from conversations in the past week? What forms did they take—ideas and visions, job opportunities, introductions to special people, open-ended invitations, better awareness of the people around you, self-awareness, inspiration or motivation? What led to them? Have you prioritised them or done anything about them? If not, why not?
- Is there any particular aspect of your life (perhaps one going through significant change or where you have decisions coming up) in which you would currently welcome a range of free options—client introductions, self-awareness, job opportunities, ideas for your next holiday, investment ideas...?

- Are you typically a dreammaker or a dreambreaker?
- How well do you know the people already on your team? How well do they know you? In terms of the Johari Window concept, what can you do to increase your open self, and that of others, so you work most effectively together?

Action

- For the next week, take a note of any free options coming your way from conversations. After a few days, try experiments to increase the flow of free options. Prioritise the options and decide what you are going to do about them. Consider whether there are any you do not wish to pursue but should pass on to others.
- Next time you're out with a group, some of whom you have not previously met, ask yourself who you would most like to meet again and why. Decide whether to call them or not.

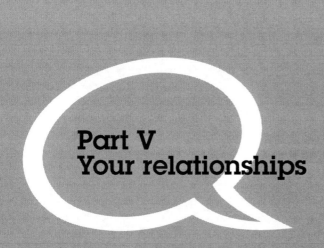

Part V
Your relationships

Your social capital is made up of:

- → your relationships and networks—family, social and professional
- → the institutions and norms in your community and society.

Your conversations—the interplay of your human capital with your social capital—are fundamental drivers of the growth of all aspects of your Life Capital.

The two principles in part V focus on making investments in your relationships with others:

- → *Principle 14:* Many opportunities for using your human capital depend on your social capital. Strategic investment in your social capital, especially in your networks, will be well rewarded.
- → *Principle 15:* Every conversation has a context in a relationship, as another step in building that relationship and having an impact on its future. Reciprocity builds relationships.

Principle 14
Networks and
networking

Many opportunities for using your human capital depend on your social capital. Strategic investment in your social capital, especially in your networks, will be well rewarded.

Your extended family represents a form of social capital, as do your Sunday school class, the people you meet regularly on your commuter train, your college classmates, the neighbourhood association to which you belong, the civic organisations of which you are a member, the internet chat group in which you participate, and the network of professionals recorded in your address book.

—Robert Putnam and Kristin Goss[1]

Networking is an important form of strategic investment in your social capital. Your networking is likely to be more rewarding to you and to those you engage with if you have a good understanding of the networks you are capable of accessing and what makes them valuable to you.

14.1 Family

Some people thought 1873 was a significant year in the history of the world because it marked the death of the last person reputed to know everything there was to be known—British philosopher and political economist John Stuart Mill. At preschool age, Mill was taught Latin and Greek by his philosopher/historian father. As an older child, he was invited to critically discuss drafts of his father's manuscripts with his father and Jeremy Bentham, the father of utilitarianism.

In a 1988 paper, James Coleman of the University of Chicago suggested that the central difference in the development of Mill's human capital was not genetic, nor because of his father's learning, but because of the time and effort spent by his father with him on intellectual matters—an example of the role of social capital in the family in the creation of human capital in the next generation.[2] Coleman cited another example, but at the other extreme of parents' education—the purchase by Asian immigrant families in one US public school district of two copies of each text, the second copy being for the mother to study so she could help the child learn.

On the basis of a random sample of 4000 school students, Coleman concluded that the stronger the relations between the children and their parents, the more the children benefited from their parents' human capital. As Coleman put it, 'Social capital in the family is a resource for education of the family's children, just as is financial and human capital'.

One part of Coleman's methodology attracted my attention. He used the number of siblings as a measure of social capital in the family. Surprisingly, the presence of more siblings represented to Coleman a dilution of adult attention to the child, and therefore lower social capital in their family background. In addition, Coleman noted that younger siblings and children in larger families produced weaker measures of achievement and IQ.

Using Coleman's measures it would seem that I was particularly disadvantaged by having four older siblings and, even worse, having to share the remainder of my parents' attention with my twin sister, Anne. I find Coleman's approach, measure and results interesting and surprising. I generally found my siblings to be valuable additional sources of attention, and not necessarily diluters of parental attention. They also provided a richer source of interests, viewpoints and experiences for me to debate or observe and learn from.

I share Rudolf Flesch's view:

> If you want to shut out noise and interruptions, you'd better go someplace else. But if you want to pool quickly the viewpoints of various ages and sexes, stay right at home. The basis of clear thinking is the realisation that we think with our experience. The family — a mixed assortment of all kinds and degrees of experience — is the place to learn this once and for all. [3]

Thus an environment of multiple siblings can be wonderful for human development — not just intellectually, but also emotionally, physically and spiritually.

Family influence on your social networks

The family environment is also a child's first experience of social networks. Before going to school, family is the principal source of a child's networks. Social capital grows from that already established by the child's parents and older siblings — so for social networking, in my view, the more siblings the better. When a child starts school, they begin to establish their own networks outside the family — school friends. The child soon finds their parents getting in on the act and establishing close friendships with their school friends' parents.

Parents don't find just their kids useful for networking — there's also the family dog. Who better to introduce them to other interesting people? If you're a regular dog walker, you'll understand. One of our dogs, Hali — black, with a wagging tail and wild eyes that always look people in the eye — loves chasing balls and always carries her ball to the nearest group of people at the park and drops it next to the youngest child, ready for an extended game of throw and chase. Hali is a networker extraordinaire and, leveraging off her personality, Tori or I can meet anyone in the park. Unfortunately, I can't say the same of her companion, Banff. So, if you're serious about networking, find a dog with an outgoing personality!

So, your social networking begins at home and, even though your networking sources diversify over the years, your family always has a major role to play in it.

14.2   Social networks

Social networks are important in all our lives, often for finding jobs, more often for finding a helping hand, companionship, or a shoulder to cry on.

—Claude Fischer[4]

Experts categorise social capital and social networks in a number of ways. Probably the most important distinction is that between:

→ bonding (exclusive) social capital—groups and networks that tend to look for new members with backgrounds similar to those of existing members

→ bridging (inclusive) social capital—groups and networks with diverse memberships, which thereby enhance relationships across social, ethnic, religious or family backgrounds.

You are more likely to receive moral support from your bonding networks than your bridging networks; however, bonding networks are more likely to have negative effects on those outside the network—commonly cited extreme examples being the Ku Klux Klan and the Mafia.

The selection criteria in bonding networks do not have to be as exclusive as those of the KKK or the Mafia to nevertheless produce extreme results. Nobel Laureate Thomas Schelling demonstrated that if everyone has a very small preference not to have too many people unlike them living in their city neighbourhood (a form of preference for bonding capital over bridging capital), then neighbourhoods will tend to move from reasonable diversity to significant segregation.[5]

For most of us, bonding networks are more natural territory. We tend to be drawn to people who are similar to us because their qualities reaffirm the validity of our own. However, bridging networks can expose you to more opportunities than bonding networks. This is exemplified by:

→ people being more likely to find jobs through people they see occasionally, rather than through those they see often, because the former presumably move in different circles from them (elaborated on in 14.5)

→ the entrepreneurial success of those members of minority groups who live near but not in their groups' ghettos, and provide a bridge to the outside world and services in either direction.[6]

Bonding network pressures in disadvantaged communities

In some situations, those who seek to capitalise on the opportunities offered by bridging networks risk giving the impression to those in their bonding network that they are looking for an escape route, and therefore can't be trusted. This is an element of the US 'acting white' debate — the concept that black children are discouraged from studying hard in order to avoid being deemed by some in their own community to be building an escape route. In his keynote address to the 2004 Democratic National Convention, Barack Obama referred to 'the slander that says a black youth with a book is acting white'.

Professor Roland G Fryer of Harvard's American Inequality Lab surveyed 90 000 students from grades 7 to 12 in 175 US schools. He found clear evidence of acting white in integrated schools, but not in predominantly black schools. The effect was even more marked with Hispanics. Variants on acting white have been identified in other disadvantaged groups around the world; Fryer cites the Italian immigrants in Boston's West End to the New Zealand Maori, the Burakumin outcasts in Japan and the British working class.[7]

According to Fryer, social groups have long sought to preserve their identity, especially when their internal cohesion is threatened. Groups that risk losing their most successful members to outsiders will seek to prevent the outflow, with the penalties to those who differentiate themselves increasing as the threat to the group's cohesion increases.

In respect of integrated schools, Fryer concluded:

> As long as distressed communities provide minorities with their identities, the social costs of breaking free will remain high. To increase the likelihood that more can do so, society must find ways for these high achievers to thrive in settings where adverse social pressures are less intense. The integrated school, by itself, apparently cannot achieve this end.

It takes courage to be different, especially in a tight bonding network. However, those role models who have such courage encourage and permit others to do the same.

14.3   Business and professional networks

Whether you work in a large organisation, the arts or sport, your professional networks are likely to be one of your major sources of valuable contacts, important information, advice and feedback, as well as early news of opportunities or potential problems. Insights from your contacts help you to clarify your plans, build up your body of knowledge in your chosen field and plan your approach to problems. Your networks fall into two categories: those within your organisation and those outside.

Internal networks

In most positions, you need strong internal networks just to do your job. For many years prior to writing his 1998 book *How to be a Star at Work*, Robert Kelley had been asking people the same question: what percentage of the knowledge you need to do your job is stored in your own mind? Between 1986 and 1997, across a wide variety of companies, the answer dropped from typically 75 per cent to between 15 and 20 per cent. Thus it seems that people's dependence on accessing group knowledge and expertise through their transactive memory (described in 13.1) has become very high.[8]

But what if you aspire to having some real influence on the direction of your business, or to enjoy genuine prospects for advancement? Then you need networks for more than just transactive memory. You need peer networks, as well as downwards and upwards networks, preferably two levels below and two levels above your own. Given today's high rates of management turnover, it is dangerous to focus on just one level and you need to be comfortable dealing with those who are two levels above you. Never assume that it's almost impossible to access your boss's boss. If they are doing their job, they should be aiming to build some rapport with you and your peers, so they have more than just one source of information regarding how things are going in your area.

If you work in a knowledge economy services organisation, your company's most valuable assets are its internal networks and intellectual capital. The sooner you learn to capitalise on these assets, the more effective you'll be in developing your team, servicing your clients and attracting new ones — your three main roles. In this vein, the McKinsey management consultancy firm informally encourages associates to 'build their own McKinsey': 'to seek out the subordinates, peers and partners to whom they naturally gravitate because of mutual chemistry, interests and goals'.[9] The aim is to help develop associates' potential, both professionally and personally. Co-mentoring is also encouraged, so that young professionals take some responsibility for their own development while also building better team skills.

External networks

Your influence in your own organisation often depends on your ability to bring fresh insight, something you are less likely to achieve if your networks are mainly internal. You don't need Bill Clinton's networking skills or his golden Rolodex. Nor, as Gene O'Kelly acknowledged in his last 100 days, do you need 1000 people in your outer circle (see 8.6). But you do need a network of outsiders to invigorate you, challenge you, alert you to opportunities, encourage you to think across disciplines and keep you in touch with the outside world.

I sometimes ponder networks in which I would like to have been involved. One such network would be the Graham group meetings, initiated by Warren Buffett in the late 1960s in honour of Benjamin Graham, his professor and mentor. Graham was present, as well as a core of disciples like Buffett, plus other invited guests (later including Bill Gates).[10] It would be intriguing to hear that group discussing today's issues, such as the worldwide stock market bloodbath, banking rescues and interest rate drops. It would also be insightful to hear their ideas and compare them with those of the G8 and G20 meetings.

Equally, it would be fascinating to have been part of the UK National Council of Civil Liberties meetings in the late 1930s, as they sought to protect civil liberties and promote human rights in the then pre–World War II context of fascism in Europe. I would have been sitting with the likes of EM Forster, AA Milne, HG Wells, JB Priestley, Harold Laski and others from the intellectual left.

You will perhaps have read *Guns of Navarone, Winnie the Pooh* and *The Time Machine*, or seen *An Inspector Calls*, but have probably not read Harold Laski's *The Rights of Man*. Until I read this wonderful little monograph about 20 years ago, I questioned the merits of democracy because of its apparent inefficiencies, but I never have since reading Laski.

Where would you like to be a fly on the wall?

Differences between men's and women's networks

According to Linda Babcock and Sara Laschever in *Women Don't Ask: Negotiation and the Gender Divide*, sociologists distinguish 'instrumental networks' (those based on exchanges of advice, information and help) from 'friendship networks' (those with a more social function).

Babcock and Laschever believe that workplace networks are typically somewhat gender-divided, and that there are significant differences between men's and women's networks. In particular, all men's networks, both instrumental and friendship, are predominantly male, whereas women's instrumental networks are both male and female, and their friendship networks are predominantly female. As a result, women's ties to the men in their instrumental networks lack reinforcing friendships or personal ties, and hence are less strong and less valuable. In contrast, men's instrumental networks are potentially reinforced by their friendship ties.

According to research carried out by Boris Groysberg of more than 1000 analysts in male-dominated Wall Street,[11] women are better than men at building external networks because they have to, in order to make up for their weaker internal networks. Consequently, they build stronger relationships with clients and outside sources of information, and over time their personal franchises are different from those of men. A man's internal networks cannot be transferred to the next employer (unless a whole team moves), whereas a woman's external networks can be transferred. One of the results perceived by Groysberg was that female analysts who switched jobs performed much better than their male peers. Another factor in this outperformance on change of job was deeper thought by the women about the culture of the organisations they were considering joining.

14.4   Online networks

The magical thing about this network is not just that it collapses distance and makes everyone your neighbour. It also dramatically increases the number of brilliant minds we can have working together on the same problem—and that scales up the rate of innovation to a staggering degree... these advances are triggering a revolution in what human beings can do for one another... For a few hours every week, you can use the growing power of the internet to get informed, find others with the same interests, see the barriers and find ways to cut through them.

—Bill Gates[12]

In recent years, the world wide web has been transformed from principally a source of information to a platform for creativity (through user-generated content) and community (through sharing and collaboration). Using software development nomenclature, the information-source era of the web was Web 1.0. Terms like participatory Web or Web 2.0 are common to describe the more recent vast extension of Web applications—viral advertising, user-generated uploading and downloading of videos to YouTube, blogs on MySpace and Facebook, photographs on Flickr, buying and selling on eBay, sharing life goals on 43 Things, voice and video transmissions through Skype, and all forms of emails, blogs, wikis and on-line games. This evolution has led to quantum increases in social interactions on the net, especially from email and internet content.

The next evolutionary stage, Web 3.0, is widely predicted to be the intelligent or semantic web, where software and technology will provide the artificial intelligence to make sense of internet content, and thereby deliver it to users in an ordered, meaningful, quasi-human way. While views on the form and timing of Web 3.0 range widely, the early signs of Web 3.0 are already occurring in social and business networks, and current indications are that it will emerge over the next five years.

New York blogger and thinker Seth Godin envisages a Web 4.0, which will be about 'making connections, about serendipity and about the network taking initiative'. His blog, Web4, which speculates that Web 4.0 may arrive before Web 3.0, cites a number of thought-provoking Web 4.0 examples, such as:

→ 'I'm typing an email to someone, and we're brainstorming about doing a business development deal with Apple. A little window pops up and lets me know that David over in my Tucson office is already having a similar conversation with Apple and perhaps we should coordinate.'

→ 'Google watches what I search. It watches what other people like me search for. Every day, it shows me things I ought to be searching for that I'm not. And it introduces me to people who are searching for what I'm searching for.'

Online social networking

Online social networking sites have changed the way many people — and not exclusively the young — maintain their social networks or just hang out. Although these sites are not a complete substitute for personal connections, they are a valuable means of initiating personal contact or keeping in touch between face-to-face conversations. Having no geographical boundaries, online social networking sites are accelerating the development of young people as citizens of the world, and increasing their ability to maintain strong ties with many people over great distances.

Stories abound of the dangers of social networking websites, especially for those who reveal too much on their site — like the London girl who posted a 'trash the house' party message on her MySpace page and ended up with 200 uninvited guests, resulting in £20 000 damage to her parents' house, or the employers who see little resemblance between the person they've interviewed and are about to employ and the character of the person they see when they check that person's website. As these stories spread, people are becoming more circumspect about what they post or allow to be posted on their sites.

Employers' views of social networking sites vary from banning (as a time waster or security risk) at one extreme, to encouragement and sponsorship (as a valuable professional networking tool) at the other. Online social networking has been of greatest value to employers in finding new employees.

In 2008, Facebook and MySpace were the most frequented social networks on the internet, accounting for almost 90 per cent of network sites visited by US residents in September 2008. Visits to Facebook increased by 50 per cent over the year to August 2008.[13]

Online social networking is now mainstream and a major cultural force in the web-connected world. This was well recognised by *Time* Magazine in December 2006, when it cited Web 2.0 as 'a massive social experiment' and named 'You' as the Person of the Year in 2006—for 'seizing the reins of the global media, for founding and framing the new digital democracy, for working for nothing and beating the pros at their own game'.[14]

In *Wikinomics*, authors Tapscott and Williams emphasise the fact that more and more of today's successful web companies empower their customers to create content rather than trying to control them. Reciprocally, their customers trust them. For many (they instance Flickr, 43 Things and blog search engine Technorati), customers are 'the lifeblood of the business'.[15]

Online professional networking

The line between social and business networks is blurred in such sites as:

→ blogs and forums—maintained by one party but encouraging contributions and discussions from others

→ wikis—designed so any users can contribute or modify content

→ social networking sites for specific professional groups

→ broadly based professional social networks like LinkedIn and Xing.

Culturally American, LinkedIn is the web's market-leading business-oriented social networking site. Mainly focused on career advancement, and available only in English and Spanish, it signed up its 10 millionth user in April 2007. Some 18 months later, that figure had trebled as record numbers of professionals updated their profiles, in case they lost their jobs in the financial meltdown of late 2008.

Xing operates in 16 languages and is more generally about networking than LinkedIn. According to *The Economist*, if Xing 'plays its cards right, it could become the European alternative that takes more account of cultural differences in the way business is done'.[16]

At the purely business networking end are sites like the Eli Lily–initiated InnoCentive, an open community of 'Seekers' (businesses that have a difficult problem to solve and are willing to offer an open prize for its best solution) and 'Solvers' (individuals who are willing to apply their expertise to solve real-world problems for a prize). In one example, Procter & Gamble's problem was to create a detergent that would reveal when the right amount of soap was in the sink—the Solver on InnoCentive, an Italian chemist working from her home laboratory, won a US$30 000 prize. In another example, non-profit Prize4Life posted a US$1 million prize in 2006 for identifying a biomarker for amyotrophic lateral sclerosis (Lou Gehrig's disease).[17]

To Jeff Howe, author of *Crowdsourcing: Why the Power of the Crowd is Driving the Future of Business*, InnoCentive is a prime example of his subject. Howe thinks crowdsourcing has the potential to 'form a sort of meritocracy, since it allows anyone to solve a scientific conundrum or create a television show, irrespective of age, education or profession ... Crowdsourcing liberates office slaves to pursue whatever most interests them, and in their spare time'.[18]

Other purely commercial applications of online networking include companies seeking user or customer input for branding and product development, design or testing.

Business-oriented networking tools enable people living and working in diverse locations to communicate and collaborate. According to Tapscott and Williams in *Wikinomics*, as these tools improve, workplaces 'will become smaller and teams will be more distributed, with participants drawn from all over the globe'. They note that already more than 40 per cent of IBM's employees work from home or on the road. However, they acknowledge that the proximity, familiarity, trust, body language, tacit learning and fruitful conversation of the traditional face-to-face office will never be fully replaced.[19]

14.5   Value of networks

Some people argue that an individual's social networks may sometimes be a more important determinant of their success than their human capital. This may be the case from time to time but, in general, I believe the different values of ties in your network depend on your ability to capitalise on them—in other words, your human capital. Also, the values of your ties depend significantly on your prior investment in them—also a function of your human capital.

Although it is impossible to accurately value social networks, there are some principles or tools at hand to help.

→ *Social network analysis* is the study of the shape of networks, with the objective of determining the network's usefulness to individuals in it (that is, its contribution to an individual's social capital). The network is drawn up using nodes (the people in the network) and ties (the relationships between those people). The shape of a social network influences its usefulness to the individuals in it.

One of the applications of social network analysis is the voting in Google's PageRank search engine. Another is the concept of 'weak ties'.

→ *Granovetter's principle of the 'strength of weak ties'* was developed by Mark Granovetter from his work on how people find new jobs. He showed that you are more likely to find your new job through people you see occasionally than through those you see often, because the latter generally occupy the same environment as you, whereas the former occupy a different world and so are much more likely to know something that you don't.[20] Thus weak ties (that is, looking well beyond your closest networks to your wider friends and acquaintances) can be important in finding both information and opportunities. More open but smaller networks, with many weak ties, are more likely to introduce new ideas than closed networks. So, when you're discussing your challenge or opportunity with a friend, always add the question: 'Who else should I be talking to about this—maybe someone that you know well but who I've never met, or perhaps don't know as well?' If you're pondering whether to go to that old school reunion, make a point of doing so because those people you once knew so well could now be living and working in diverse and interesting areas.

Other important characteristics of weak ties are that they don't take as much energy to maintain, so you can have much more of them and they can be with people from extremely wide-ranging backgrounds.

→ *Metcalfe's Law* is derived from Robert Metcalfe's proposal in around 1980 that the value of a network of devices that communicate compatibly (such as fax machines or telephones) is proportional to the square of the number of devices in the network. His original proposition has been modified by others and used in a much wider range of contexts. Its original purpose was to show that, because the value of the network grew in proportion to the square of the number of users, there would be a point of crossover (that is, of critical mass) at which the value of the network would equal (and thereafter exceed) the cost of installation of the devices (that is, the cost of building the network).

Metcalfe's Law has limitations in its applications, especially once the size of the network begins to significantly reduce connectivity or trust. This is particularly relevant to social networks, where the value of the network begins to decline once the network membership grows too large. Nevertheless, Metcalfe's Law provides a reminder that many networks, especially smaller ones, increase in value at a rate more than proportional to the number of members in the network.

→ *Dunbar's number* (also known as the Rule of 150) dates from 1993, when anthropologist Robin Dunbar estimated that 150 is the largest number of people that a human can have a real social relationship with — including trusting them and having sufficient knowledge about them, including how to relate to them. Dunbar arrived at the figure of 150 by studying the size of the neocortex in humans and other primates (the part of the brain responsible for higher functions such as perception, conscious thought and language), relative to the total size of the brain. He also noted that the average size of villages in a number of hunter-gatherer societies around the world was 150 people.

Some argued that on the basis of Dunbar's work, the value of an integrated social network is optimised up to around 150 people and thereafter becomes less effective and is better broken up into subsidiary interconnected networks. Gore Associates, the company that created Gore-Tex, reached the same conclusion by trial and error. Having found that plants dropped in efficiency once they had more than 150 employees, they then put only 150 parking spots at each plant; when that car park is full, it's time to build another plant.[21]

You are more likely to be able to achieve frequency of interaction in smaller networks, and thereby the level of trust necessary to achieve generalised reciprocity. Such a network is more efficient than a larger but distrustful one since, as Robert Putnam and Kristin Goss point out, people in a smaller network will do something without expecting anything immediate in return because they know that later you or someone else will reciprocate their goodwill.[22]

→ *Whitehead's ratio* appeared in John Whitehead's list of advice to Goldman Sachs's new-business people. Developed before Mark Granovetter had come up with his 'strength of weak ties' principle, the list included the notion that 'the respect of one man is worth more than acquaintance with 100'. Maybe the 'strength of weak ties' isn't as applicable in investment banking transactions as it is when you're seeking a job.

14.6   Networking

The networks of top performers are not random; they are carefully chosen, with each person being included because of a particular expertise or excellence. These networks traffic expertise and information back and forth in an artful, ongoing give-and-take. Each member of a network represents available extension of knowledge and expertise, accessible with a single phone-call.

—Daniel Goleman[23]

As discussed in 14.1, networking begins at home when you are a child and is always influenced by your family and home. It can be influenced by where your home is, as exemplified by:

→ the relatively greater serendipity of the average city dweller versus those living in rural areas (see 22.7)

→ a decision by a member of an ethnic group to increase their opportunities by living on the fringe of a ghetto rather than in it (discussed in 14.2)

→ the relatively greater comfort most people feel living among people of similar success and means.

Like so many other things, you acquire some networking skills in your childhood and your experiences refine them; you try something new, observe the outcome and you learn something. Learning to network well can be a slow process, unless you are fortunate enough to have the opportunity to watch someone who's really effective.

You'll probably notice that such people are great questioners and listeners, and they go to the trouble of keeping records. This reflects their appreciation that effective networking is not a one-way, take-only relationship, nor a case of give one in order to get one. They demonstrate a mindset of wanting to understand others, and to assist them by finding opportunities or solutions for them—a mindset that will often be reciprocated.

They probably also think somewhat strategically about their existing networks: which ones they enjoy most or energise them most; which ones they can influence positively; which ones are most relevant to their own lives and goals—and therefore which ones merit the biggest share of their time, energy or attention. They probably also ask themselves how effectively they are both investing into and using their principal networks.

Networks come in so many forms, ranging from formal clubs or professional associations to informal clubs like a book club, share club or babysitting club. The choice is vast and the effective networker knows where to draw lines so their attention and energy is soundly and pleasantly invested.

Although most people have a strong preference for working with people who think like they do, the benefits of leveraging diversity of background, culture, experience and knowledge are enormous. According to Daniel Goleman, the ability to do so 'revolves around three skills: getting on well with people of diverse backgrounds, appreciating the unique ways others may operate, and seizing whatever business opportunities these unique approaches might offer'.[24]

With such benefits in mind, it is valuable to apply the discipline of having a diversity filter when selecting which networks to invest in. Otherwise you risk having multiple versions of the same experience, and narrowing your sources of information and energy. Diverse networks help you to remain grounded. For example, if you're a business person, your links into the charitable or public sectors will prompt you to ask questions in business that would not otherwise occur to you—and vice versa if you work in the charitable or public sectors but have links in business.

The benefits of leveraging diversity are discussed in greater detail in Principle 18.

Over to you ...

Reflection

- How does your family build your human capital? How does it build your social capital?
- Does your family cause you to hold back on developing your human or social capital? If so, how or why? What if anything can you constructively change? Reciprocally, how do you build or hinder the growth of the human and social capital of the members of your family?
- How would you describe your internal networks at work? How would you describe your external networks? For example, bridging versus bonding, instrumental verus friendship, deep versus shallow, wide and diverse versus narrow, online versus face-to-face. Do you use those networks enough? Do you invest enough in them? What could make them more valuable to you?
- What can you learn from the different ways that men and women network?
- Does your personal website appropriately reflect your personal 'brand'?
- How can online social networking be of value in your personal mission?

Action

- Develop a plan for enhancing your networking skills, prioritising the skills most relevant to your personal mission and which you believe you can improve most.
- Develop a plan for enhancing your networks in a context aligned to your passions, your values and your personal mission.
- If any of your networks are in conflict with your values or holding you back from your passions or your personal mission, plan how you might deal with that.
- Identify a networker you admire. Talk to them about networking or observe and learn from them.

Principle 15
Conversations and relationships

Every conversation has a context
in a relationship, as another step in
building that relationship and
having an impact on its future.
Reciprocity builds relationships.

A person is a person through other persons. You can't be human in isolation. You are human only in relationships.

—Archbishop Desmond Tutu[1]

Every conversation you have with someone is influenced by the status of your relationship: how long and how closely you have known each other, how often and where you meet, the range of subjects you typically discuss and, most importantly, your last conversation and the basis of your last farewell. Every one of your relationships is thus a work-in-progress. As each conversation has an impact on that relationship, it potentially impacts all future conversations. So, when you're finishing a conversation, as golfer Tommy Armour said, 'Hit the shot that makes the next shot easiest'.

Life-enriching conversations are generally not one-way streets. You are presented with many opportunities to talk with family, friends and colleagues about their opportunities and challenges, and to introduce them to others who may do the same. Anything you can do to help them enhance their Life Capital ultimately enhances your own!

Often, however, you're unable to reciprocate very effectively on the day, especially if you've approached someone else for advice. All you may be able to offer in reply is respect for the other person, their time and their preparedness to help, but that shouldn't dissuade you from accepting their offer. Part of that respect is provided later on when you give them feedback about how you're going. If they're interested enough to spend that time with you and offer ideas, they'll be keen to hear the outcome.

15.1   Knowing who and what you are

Three of Stephen Covey's seven habits of highly effective people relate directly to relationships:

→ thinking win–win
→ seeking first to understand and then to be understood
→ aiming to achieve synergies.

Covey points out that these three habits are only achievable and effective if your 'independent' habits (your personal vision, your personal leadership and your personal management) have strong foundations:

> *Self-mastery and self-discipline are the foundation of good relationships with others ... Independence is an achievement. Interdependence is a choice only independent people can make ... The most important ingredient we put into any relationship is not what we say or what we do, but what we are. And if our words and our actions come from superficial human relations techniques (the Personality Ethic) rather than from our own inner core (the Character Ethic), others will see that duplicity. We simply won't be able to create and sustain the foundation necessary for effective interdependence.*[2]

Therefore investment in your human capital is essential to the growth of your social capital.

Knowing who and what you are is an important basis for what people see in you. Behaviour that's consistent over time, and consistent with who and what you are, establishes your 'brand' and will give others confidence in the level and nature of the relationship they might develop with you. This consistency between the implicit promises you make to others, the distinct personality and emotional attributes you demonstrate and the communications that reflect this is analogous to the authenticity needed in successful product branding.

Former Harley Davidson CEO Rich Teerlink said: 'We don't sell motorcycles. What we sell is the ability for a 43-year-old accountant to drive through a small town dressed in black leather and have people be afraid of him.'[3] People regularly make important decisions the same way as Teerlink's Harley buyer—they first decide emotionally, then try to rationalise that decision.

Emotional factors will influence who you want to talk to and build relationships with. Reciprocally, your 'brand' will influence who wishes to engage with you and the way they do so. If you are known for your punctuality, those meeting you will tend to be more punctual. If you are known for your warmth and your respect for people's confidences, people will engage with you more openly. If your impatience with long meetings is legendary, people will stick to the agenda. If you are respected for your detailed knowledge and insightful questions, people will come prepared.

Charles Handy remarked of his radio programs produced in India: 'If you are carrying a tape recorder with the magic letters BBC on it, it is surprising how ready people are to talk with you'.[4] Bono observed that the people he wanted to meet would do so out of curiosity. If you are a person of perceived importance or influence, you will find it easier to meet people. One of John Whitehead's challenges to those in 'new business' at Goldman Sachs was: 'People like to talk to people who are important. Are you important?'[5]

So, if you don't have Bono's fame, the financial status of an investment banker or a major brand name like Goldman Sachs or BBC to flash, is everything lost? Far from it. It just takes more preparation, guts, resilience, initiative, personality, strategic serendipity ... and with your passion and a big smile, you'll often knock people out more than someone who got in there because of their fame, notoriety or perceived influence.

15.2   First impressions

There's an old saying: you never get a second chance to make a first impression. First impressions are important because they stay with people a long time and are only slowly influenced by fresh observations at subsequent meetings. As demonstrated by the Pygmalion effect or the self-fulfilling prophecy (see 3.4), first impressions can create either a virtuous circle or a vicious circle.

So, if you want an ongoing and positive relationship, impressions from a first meeting are vital. Consciously or subconsciously, the other person will be asking themselves questions about you:

→ Did you make them feel good? Were you refreshing and fun or a bit toxic?

→ Did you waste their time? Were you interesting? Did they take something special away?

→ Were you interested in them or were you focused on someone on the other side of the room? Were you a listener? Did you understand their point of view?

→ Did they feel a sense of trust with you?

→ And the ultimate question: if they have the opportunity to do so, will they invest more of their time in building a relationship with you?

If it sounds a bit like a speed-dating, you're right. Given the short length of 21st-century attention spans, many first meetings in a big city, whether business or personal, are rather like speed-dating. If you're going to invest the energy to build a relationship, positive first impressions each way are vital. Not surprisingly, most relationships have an extremely short life.

Even the committed investor in relationships has to know where to draw the line on those that are destined to go nowhere. Some lessons in making investment decisions translate naturally to relationship lessons:

> If you know why you bought a stock in the first place you automatically have a better idea of when to say goodbye to it.

—Peter Lynch[6]

> Many investors get 'nickled and dimed' into penury by failing to appreciate that the first loss is not only the best, but usually the

smallest. They must learn to avoid defensive rationalisation of their past bad judgements.

—Arthur Zeikel[7]

After 25 years of buying and supervising a great variety of businesses … I have not learned how to solve difficult business problems. What we have learned is to avoid them … Overall, we've done better by avoiding dragons than by slaying them.

—Warren Buffett[8]

For a relationship to grow and survive, let alone flourish, you've both got to invest the necessary effort. And to do this, you've both got to believe it will be a good investment of your energy.

15.3   Building and enhancing a relationship

So you've made a good first impression and you want to invest in building the relationship. There are many forms this investment can take, including the following.

Alertness to opportunity

With any ongoing relationship you have the opportunity and the challenge to take it to a higher level. All you can do, and arguably all you need to do, is to work to retain your seat at the table and be empathically alert for an opportunity to build the relationship. Sometimes it may be a long wait for that opportunity but it could come in many forms: reciprocity of advice, handling a difficult issue with judgement, discretion or empathy, or finding a close common interest.

It is likely to come sooner if you have regular opportunities to talk and to progressively add extra dimensions to your conversations. Imagine the relationships you could build if you had the capacity to identify the interests and potential preferences of others and thereby to help them find new opportunities; it's analogous to the power of amazon.com. Arguably, all it needs is a good understanding of the other person (perhaps just good listening on the day) and a good knowledge of some of the options that are out there—preferably tradeable options as described in 13.7.

In today's complex and time-poor world, people who are capable of identifying such options for others make very welcome and valued partners.

Valuing another person's time

Most people enjoy a chat, exploring new ideas and other disciplines, being helpful and seeming knowledgeable. Hence you can potentially find good opportunities for having further conversations and forging relationships, provided you value the other person's time—and your own.

The more highly you value their time, the better you will prepare and perform, the more of their time you will have access to, and the more you will look to use that access. I call this 'Pollard's Paradox': the more you value someone's time, the more it will be (freely) made available to you—and the more of it that is made available, the more free options will emerge.

Valuing another person's time is a vital dimension of building a relationship, but it should be viewed more as an entry-level requirement. You virtually *have* to do it in order to keep a seat at the table—because a person's time and attention are among the scarcest resources they have.

I was given a wonderful lesson in this some years ago. I had arranged to meet a recently retired senior head-hunter to have a chat about my career. I was somewhat taken aback when he rang and said he was going to charge me for the time on an hourly basis. Although it was unusual in such circumstances, he hoped I didn't mind. He had a policy of charging for his time, so the people he saw put a lot more effort into their preparation and thereby benefited more from his advice. He was right. His charge, although at only half commercial rates, meant I respected his time more, prepared better and got more from the meeting. I have often since envisaged this concept when preparing for important meetings.

By framing a meeting as though you are paying for the other person's time, you prepare appropriately and ensure you deal with the key issues professionally and conclusively. It ensures that the meeting is effective and doesn't drag on longer than is necessary. It's astonishing how often in business you hear of large numbers of senior people meeting on important issues without having a clear agenda or any pre-circulated papers. You wonder whether people who call such meetings ever calculate the costs of the hours invested, or ask whether all the agenda items are necessary or whether the issues can be dealt with effectively on such a basis.

Trust

Trustworthiness lubricates social life. If we don't have to balance every exchange instantly, we can get a lot more accomplished.

—Robert Putnam and Kristin Goss[9]

Trust cannot be commoditised. It is fundamental to building relationships and vice versa. It is developed from respect and concern for the other person, an ability to listen, a respect for confidentiality and privacy, and keeping your word.

Unfortunately, trust is fragile. It is easier to destroy than to create because negative events carry much greater psychological weight than positive events. Bringers of negative news carry much more credibility than bringers of positive news. Further, once an event triggers distrust, the people involved have less contact with each other—providing less opportunity for trust to be restored. One of the great impediments to trust is defensiveness, and the consequent filtering out of critical information or the provision of weak rationalisations or excuses.

Stephen Covey uses the concept of an Emotional Bank Account as a metaphor for the amount of trust in a relationship, and suggests there are six major deposits that build this account: 'understanding the individual, attending to the little things, keeping commitments, clarifying expectations, showing personal integrity and apologising sincerely when you make a withdrawal'. A trust account that's full enables easy and effective communication. For constant relationships, such as marriage or with people you meet often, fresh deposits are needed regularly due to continuing expectations. On the other hand, says Covey, 'when you run into a high school friend you haven't seen for years, you can pick up where you left off because the earlier deposits are still there'.[10]

Mindsets

Some mindsets are fundamental to the building of relationships, others are corrosive.

→ *Seeing others' problems as relationship opportunities, not irritations.* Most problems involving people can be viewed as a significant annoyance, or as an opportunity to build the relationship. Taking the path of opportunity demands an investment of energy with significant potential returns, whereas the path of annoyance leads to just as much emotional investment but less return—whether with family, friends or colleagues.

→ *The ability to empathise with others,* to put yourself emotionally in the other person's situation, is a core emotional competence for leaders. Empathy enables you to read better the emotional signals in any conversation and, by understanding others better, to work towards win–win situations and collaborative relationships. Women are generally more empathic than men.

→ *Be open to be helped:* if we were to satisfy all of our needs by our own independent means, there would be no build up of social capital in our community. Each time someone helps you solve a problem or identify an opportunity (whether you invited them to do so or not), you incur an obligation to that person (whether they intended that or not). Most people like being given an opportunity to help, either because it makes them feel useful, and good about themselves, or because it adds to their social capital. If you try to achieve things totally independently or are too quick to terminate a conversation because you feel you've used enough of the other person's time, you will miss substantial opportunities to build that relationship.

→ *A mindset of equality and autonomy:* the value of a relationship is much diminished if all parties do not feel equally recognised and equally invited to contribute, both to the relationship itself and to any issues or opportunities that result.

→ *A win–win mindset:* Stephen Covey's fourth habit of the highly successful is to think win–win—a mindset aiming for mutually beneficial, mutually satisfying outcomes—instead of such alternative paradigms as win–lose, lose–win, lose–lose or win and let the other guy worry about himself. Covey sees anything less than a win–win as:

> *A poor second best that will have impact in the long-term relationship. The cost of that impact needs to be carefully*

considered. If you can't reach a true Win–win, you're often better off to go for No Deal'.

Covey's fallback paradigm is 'win–win or no deal', citing the example of a family that can't agree on a video that everyone will enjoy, deciding instead to do something else — no deal — rather than having some enjoy a video at the expense of others.[11]

Covey sees three character traits as being essential to a win–win mindset: integrity, maturity and what he calls an 'abundance mentality', the paradigm that there is plenty out there for everybody. People with a 'scarcity mentality', he says, have a very difficult time sharing — even with those who have helped them along the way. The abundance mentality, he says, flows out of a deep inner sense of personal worth and security.

So what do you do when you have a win–win mindset but the person you're dealing with is a win–lose thinker? According to Covey, the relationship is still the key. He suggests focusing on your 'circle of influence', showing respect for the other person's point of view, listening deeply and hanging in there until the other person realises you genuinely want a win–win outcome. Your relationship will benefit from this approach.

15.4 Redefining relationships

The building of relationships depends very much on the mindset of the parties involved. So too does the transformation or redefinition of relationships and the related ability to adapt to new circumstances.

How is it that relationships are transformed or redefined? How is it that the former apprentice achieves credibility as CEO and is not still referred to as 'Young Susan' or 'Young Bill'? How does a business relationship change to become a close personal friendship, a reporting relationship become a peer relationship or an adversarial relationship become more respectful? How does a dissatisfied customer or a sceptic become a positive supporter?

Such transformations don't generally happen by some slow osmotic process, and they certainly won't happen if you don't engage. Whether you're in an adversarial relationship, a dysfunctional upwards-reporting relationship or a difficult personal relationship, the key to any transformation is open-minded engagement with the other party:

→ spotting or making the opportunity for dialogue
→ listening in order to understand their thoughts and position, and frankly communicating your own
→ putting the relevant information and perceptions on the table
→ finding where there is common ground you can build on
→ exploring, clarifying and embarking on paths forward.

It doesn't sound like rocket science but it does take some courage, preparation, empathy and an open mind. My objective here is not to elaborate on the tools, which are thoroughly covered elsewhere, but to highlight the magnitude of the opportunity. That magnitude is well demonstrated where people manage to transform their reporting relationship with their boss—one of the most common opportunities for our clients at Global Coaching Partnership.

Upwards-reporting relationships

Aspects of such relationships have already been explored in Principle 3, in the context of performance reviews, demonstrating how the reporting relationship can become a virtuous circle or a vicious circle, depending upon the mindsets and efforts of the two parties.

When you began your working life, you were probably taught little or nothing about how to report upwards, let alone how to do it effectively. It was just one of the many things you were expected to know how to do using common sense, or to absorb by osmosis from your experiences. Effective upwards reporting is also one of those things people misinterpret as being about institutional politics or even brown-nosing.

The bottom line is that effective upwards reporting is essential for:
→ information
  • ensuring a smooth flow of the information you need to do your job
  • leading your own team more effectively, by providing a more accurate reading of the wider objectives and pressures of your boss and the organisation
→ strategic issues
  • having higher level, more strategic discussions with more options
  • having more support for new initiatives or experiments

- having your voice and your team's voice heard on
  important issues where they have things to contribute to
  the debate (for example, on new products or projects)
→ resourcing issues
  - presenting a strong case for the resourcing of your team
  - being given realistic objectives and timelines
→ influence
  - having a better understanding of how your boss works,
    learns, understands and makes decisions
→ resilience
  - having the opportunity to discuss openly any challenging
    issues and disappointments as they emerge—without
    defensive behaviour
  - a better understanding of the decisions that don't go your
    way, therefore being more resilient in thinking through
    and negotiating alternatives
→ time and energy
  - wasting less time and energy in communications and in
    spinning wheels
  - having a better chance of avoiding micromanagement
→ learning
  - enjoying an accelerated learning curve because your boss
    has increased confidence in delegating to you, discussing
    challenges with you, getting help from you or including
    you in cross-disciplinary discussions
→ networking
  - enjoying more introductions to people of relevance to
    your work, both within the company and externally
→ satisfaction
  - enjoying your work, finding it satisfying and feeling good
    about yourself

In some situations, it's possible to sense or measure the level of
opportunity or opportunity loss inherent in any one of the above
points. One compelling example of the relevance of upwards reporting
and ensuring that your team has context and meaning for its work is

provided by the experience of Richard Feynman (later a Nobel laureate), who worked on the Manhattan Project to develop the first atomic bomb in the 1940s. Then a young but brilliant scientist, he was responsible for a team of talented people working on tedious calculations. For security reasons, Feynman was not allowed to inform his team about the project's purpose or the relevance of their calculations. Concerned by their slow and poor work, he prevailed upon his superiors to talk to his team about the project as whole and the relevance of their contribution. According to Feynman, the transformation in their behaviour once their work had meaning led to it being done more innovatively, with much less supervision and nearly 10 times as fast.[12]

If Feynman had not reported upwards so effectively on this issue, and his team had been left in the dark about the purpose of their work, the opportunity cost may have been a later finish to the Pacific War.

A constructive response to a constructive performance review, as described in 3.2, goes hand-in-hand with an effective upwards-reporting relationship and offers additional levels of benefits. The dimensions and magnitude of the opportunities that arise from a positive upwards-reporting relationship are therefore immense, as is the magnitude of the opportunity loss from a dysfunctional reporting relationship—and therefore also the magnitude of the opportunity, if you can transform a dysfunctional reporting relationship into a positive one.

Other direct benefits of achieving this transformation include:

→ the realisation that you have been able to work at and transform a difficult relationship
→ the lessons you take away from that transformation
→ the template you take away for managing other key relationships, including those with your own team.

15.5   Informed mutual champions

Some years ago a colleague introduced me to the concept of champions—people who will think of you or your business and mention your name positively when they hear of opportunities. In the context of Principle 13, I like to think of champions as the people who will create options for you even when you're not present.

Champions must respect and trust you; just liking you is not sufficient. They will not recommend you and risk their reputations and relationships unless they respect you. The powerful combination of respect and friendship is often built up over a very long period; sometimes respect precedes friendship, at other times friendship precedes respect. Respect, trust and friendship are generally reciprocally felt, so it is not uncommon to find 'mutual champions'.

Having champions is generally a major career asset. However, if your champions are not well aware of your needs and aims, they may introduce to you the wrong 'deal flow'. This will inconvenience you and the person they've introduced you to, and they themselves will feel embarrassed. Hence it is vital for your objectives to be clear to your champions, making them informed champions. This is often most effectively achieved through conversations.

I believe that having informed mutual champions is the pinnacle of a professional or business relationship. Many informed mutual champions have been friends from school, university or sport—warts-and-all envir-onments where they have a shared common history or have fought common foes. Yet nothing precludes such relationships traversing gender, age, culture or technology barriers.

A significant example of informed mutual champions is the relationship between Bill Gates and Warren Buffett. It is of particular interest, given their different ages and backgrounds. The ultimate testimony to their relationship was Buffett's 2006 decision to pledge more than US$30 billion of his Berkshire Hathaway stock to the Gates Foundation, primarily for work to reduce poverty, disease and premature death in the developing world. In Buffett's words:

> The Gateses have set out to try and figure out how they can help the most human lives in the world. So when I can get some people who are ungodly bright, energetic, putting their own money into it...to work for me for nothing, it's not a bad deal.[13]

15.6 Lessons in relationship-building from customer or client service

In *The Ultimate Question*, Fred Reichheld provides an excellent business analogy for the concept of champions. Reichheld, of Bain & Company, carried out two years of research to find out whether a single survey question could be a useful predictor of business growth. He found one:

'How likely is it that you would recommend this company to a friend or colleague?'[14]

Reichheld noted that:

> Two conditions must be satisfied before customers make a personal referral. They must believe that the company offers superior value in terms that an economist would understand: price, features, quality, functionality, ease of use, and all the other practical factors. But they must also feel good about their relationship with the company. They must believe the company knows and understands them, values them, listens to them, and shares their principles. On the first dimension, a company is engaging the customer's head. On the second it is engaging the heart.[15]

These two dimensions seem equally relevant in the context of championing an individual.

Reichheld's approach divides customers into three categories, based on their answers to the Ultimate Question (on a scale of 0 to 10):

→ promoters (9 or 10)—loyal enthusiasts who continue to buy from the company and urge their friends to do the same

→ passives (7 or 8)—satisfied but unenthusiastic

→ detractors (0 to 6)—unhappy customers.

From this data, a Net Promoter Score (NPS) can be calculated, being the percentage of promoters less the percentage of detractors.

Reichheld's observations about businesses and their customers may have some analogy for you as an individual. Try viewing your own relationships in place of company customer relationships in the following statements:[16]

→ Customers that represent a highly profitable relationship and are promoters (profitable promoters) are too often taken for granted and sometimes milked to fund solutions for other less happy or less profitable customers. Systematic underinvestment in these profitable promoters is one way many companies compromise their growth.

→ Bad profits are profits from a customer who then feels misled, mistreated, ignored or coerced, while good profits are those earned with a customer's enthusiastic cooperation.

→ Building high-quality relationships requires investment. It requires reducing a company's dependence on bad profits.

→ Companies materially overrate the experience of their customers: 80 per cent believed they delivered a 'superior experience' to their customers, whereas only 8 per cent of customers thought so.

→ Almost nothing delights customers more than being invited to make meaningful contributions on important decisions.

→ Are customers sticking around out of loyalty, or just out of ignorance and inertia? Are they trapped in long-term contracts they would love to get out of?

And the bottom line according to Reichheld:

→ On average, increasing the NPS by a dozen points versus competitors can double a company's growth rate.

→ High-quality relationships are a necessary but not sufficient condition for growth. A company may build such relationships, but it will squander the potential they create if it cannot then make effective decisions, innovate and do everything else necessary for growth.

→ Companies can grow too rapidly, leading to service problems. Detractors will then begin to choke off the company's growth.

→ Each negative comment by a detractor neutralises from three to 10 positives.

My ultimate question as an executive coach

As I explained at the beginning of Principle 3, in my coaching assignments the client's buy-in has always been the principal determinant of the success or failure of the assignment. Accordingly, I have one overarching measure of the success of each coaching session — the extent to which it increased or decreased the buy-in of my client to their own personal development.

Are there analogous questions you can apply to each engagement in those relationships that are very important to you? For example, in your upwards-reporting relationship, has this engagement enhanced or diminished your boss's buy-in to your reporting relationship? Has it enhanced or diminished your own buy-in? If either has been diminished, why and what can you learn from this for next time?'

Maister's first law of service and the leveraged value of positive surprises

Professional practice guru David Maister's first law of service is: Satisfaction (after) = perception (after) minus expectation (before). This is clearly an 'A = B − C' opportunity, as discussed in Wealth Insert 10A.

By including numbers in the formula to demonstrate the point, consider two outcomes in a service situation:

→ Outcome 1—Perception 110 less Expectation 100 = Satisfaction 10 units

→ Outcome 2—Perception 120 less Expectation 90 = Satisfaction 30 units.

Outcome 2 generates three times the amount of satisfaction for around 10 per cent improvement in perception of the actual service (because you went out of your way to please) and a 10 per cent lower expectation (because you intentionally understated things).

Those emerging differences are basically the positive surprises—the seemingly little surprises which, because of the law of difference of two numbers, have such a leveraged impact on satisfaction or enjoyment and therefore on the relationship:

→ the boyfriend arriving with flowers

→ the parent getting away from work early and arriving at the child's school in place of the nanny

→ you surprising your partner with business-class air tickets rather than economy class

→ the boss giving you a Monday off without having to take leave or giving you a pay rise above your expectations (probably because you exceeded their expectations)

→ being sent an interesting book as a thank you for taking someone out for lunch.

Maister's Law becomes more difficult to apply when you always exceed expectations. Soon the other person begins to expect that there will always be little extra surprises, even if they don't know what they will be. Your challenge is to then keep a lid on their expectations.

15.7   Returns from investment in relationships

Our most important relationships are those that have value way beyond any business or professional benefit—as eloquently described by the 19th-century English novelist George Eliot:

> Oh, the comfort, the inexpressible comfort of feeling safe with a person; having neither to weigh thoughts nor to measure words but to pour them all out, just as it is, chaff and grain together, knowing that a faithful hand will take and sift them, keep what is worth keeping, and then, with the breath of kindness, blow the rest away.[17]

Such relationships are in the innermost of Gene O'Kelly's concentric circles (see 8.6). The relationships in O'Kelly's outer circles are the ones you build up during your professional life, through your investment of time, energy and trust.

As Reichheld demonstrates in *The Ultimate Question* in respect of Dell's consumer business, companies can measure the lifetime value of relationships with their customers. Dell's average consumer's lifetime value was estimated by analysts at $210. According to Reichheld, Dell's promoters were worth on average $328 while its detractors were worth negative $57—because of the detractors' lower retention rates, lower margins, lower annual spend, higher costs to serve and the financial impact of their negative rather than positive word of mouth. Thinking of your professional relationships as customer relationships can lead to some worthwhile analogies.

Alternatively, thinking of your professional relationships as investments in businesses brings one of Charlie Munger's lines to mind: 'The difference between a good business and a bad business is that good businesses throw up one easy decision after another. The bad businesses throw up painful decisions time after time'.[18]

Relationships are very much about investment and the long term. Some of your best investments in relationships are those that start as purely personal relationships at school or university, in a football team or tennis club, and stay that way for a couple of decades. Years later, you find those old friends are captains of industry, leaders in your profession or in the community. They are keen to work with you because they value your friendship, having always appreciated your way of doing things and knowing that they can trust you to deliver what you say you will.

Think of this as my argument in favour of old-boy networks, counterbalancing my thoughts in 10.5, which clearly favour those who reach a position of equality despite coming from a disadvantaged background.

Over to you ...

Reflection

- Do you think of conversations as steps in building relationships and, using Tommy Armour's expression, do you 'hit the shot that makes the next shot easiest'? Which of your conversational habits help or hinder this? First impressions, engagement during the conversation, your farewell, your listening, your use or non-use of people's names?
- What features of your 'brand' most influence the way people engage with you? What opportunities does this engagement lead to?
- Whether personally or professionally, are you investing in relationships destined to go nowhere for either of you? Do you have relationships that regularly throw up painful decisions? If so, what can you do about it?
- Who are your champions? Do you keep your champions informed about your plans or priorities? Who do you champion? Do they keep you informed?
- Do people trust you because of your ability to listen, respect confidentiality and do what you say you will do? Do you naturally respect others' time and reflect that in your behaviour?
- Do you typically take a win–win mindset into a conversation?
- In a work environment, do you report upwards effectively and are you gaining the most out of your relationship with your boss?

Action

- Select one of your relationships that you suspect would benefit materially from redefinition. Determine how it would benefit and how significant those benefits are (appendix B1 may prompt further thoughts). Plan to redefine that relationship and implement the plan.
- Following several engagements, whether personal or professional, ask yourself whether each engagement has enhanced your

commitment to the relationship or diminished it, and why, and/or enhanced the other person's commitment to the relationship or diminished it, and why.

- Find an opportunity, personal or professional, to test the leverage in Maister's Law by both under-promising and over-delivering.
- Be conscious of the significance of first impressions by ensuring you bring genuine warmth and enthusiasm to your engagement with people.

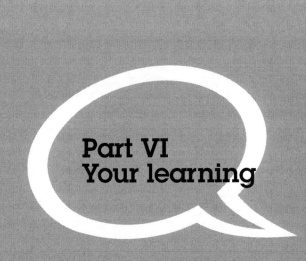

**Part VI
Your learning**

Learning is the process of enriching your human capital. The richer your human capital, the better placed you are to spot opportunities, converse effectively and make sound decisions—all fundamental to the growth of your Life Capital.

Charles Handy understands the importance of learning experiences, and believes that having a passion is the ultimate secret to learning:

> *The lesson I learned from the study of people who create something in their lives out of nothing... alchemists... [is] that you can learn anything if you really want to. Passion was what drove these people... If you care enough you will find out what you need to know and chase the source of the knowledge or the skill. The alchemists never spoke of failures or mistakes but only of learning experiences. Passion as the secret of learning is an odd solution to propose but I believe that it works at all levels and all ages.*

—Charles Handy[1]

Part VI presents the following three principles about learning:

→ *Principle 16:* The enrichment of your human capital will be most effective if, after due experimentation, you understand your preferred learning methods and your strategy capitalises on them.

→ *Principle 17:* A comparison between your vision and your current reality provides both the insights and the energy for growth.

→ *Principle 18:* If you collaborate effectively, the growth in your Life Capital will be accelerated.

Principle 16
Learning methods and strategy

The enrichment of your human capital will be most effective if, after due experimentation, you understand your preferred learning methods and your strategy capitalises on them.

The best thing for being sad is to learn something... That is the only thing that never fails... the only thing which the mind can never exhaust, never alienate, never be tormented by, never fear or distrust or never dream of regretting.

—Merlin[1]

Learning is defined as any increase in your human capital. Naturally, it includes any enhancement of your emotional, intellectual, physical, sensory or spiritual capital.

The importance of having a learning strategy as part of the framework to build your Life Capital was discussed in 5.8. You are the person best placed to devise and modify that learning strategy. This ensures your buy-in, that it works for you and that you enjoy it.

This principle explores my views about learning processes. I have formed these views without any formal training in the field, but with decades of interest in it. My aim is to increase your interest in learning strategies, especially your own.

16.1   Learning journeys

Whatever the context, learning is a journey, and often a long one. The milestones you reach might include:

1   *interest*
2   *base knowledge*: some facts, some jargon and a
    basic understanding
3   *interpretation*: the ability to express what you have learned in
    your own words
4   *own ideas*: incorporating your experience from other fields
5   *engagement with others*: the confidence and ability to start
    discussing what you have learned
6   *deep understanding*: as a result of much engagement with others
7   *mastery*: you have the ability to engage with anyone on what you
    have learned, in any situation, and the ability to solve problems
    and take tough decisions.

Circumstances don't always give you the luxury of having a great deal of time in which to make the journey, requiring you to reach that final milestone quickly and perhaps jumping a couple of stages along the way. An inspiring story of urgent learning and self-teaching was told by multiple Tour de France winner Lance Armstrong in his autobiography, *It's Not About the Bike*.

Armstrong, a high-school graduate but not a big reader, immediately became a student of cancer when he was diagnosed with testicular cancer. He read every book or internet download he could find on the subject. In the first week after his initial diagnosis, Armstrong had to deal with immediate surgery, a press conference, banking sperm, starting chemotherapy, learning that the cancer had spread not only to his lungs but also to his brain, and realising that he had no health insurance. Despite all this, he rapidly developed an in-depth knowledge of cancer, including the language of the disease, which he found had much in common with the language of cycling, both being about blood.

Consequently, Armstrong was empowered for what lay ahead. He understood the need to seek multiple opinions regarding alternative treatments: one treatment could be tailored so he could cycle again; another held no such promise. His research also prepared him to make his choice of doctors, a decision he was able to make because he had asked the tough questions and understood the doctors' answers. He found knowledge more reassuring than ignorance, and the more research he did, the better he felt his chances of recovery would be. It also enabled him to view his treatment program as a collaboration in which he shared responsibility with his doctors.

Armstrong didn't restrict his focus to the technical and treatment aspects of his situation. He read books about anything whatsoever that might give him an advantage over the disease—including diet, coping emotionally and meditation. He also found it a relief to talk with others with the same illness and compare experiences.

Armstrong won his battle with cancer, and his story underscores two major points. Firstly, that genuine interest and a sense of urgency are key drivers of learning. Secondly, that a thirst for knowledge can override a lack of formal training. You need not be afraid of embarking on a learning journey because of your lack of knowledge or background. If you're passionate enough, give it a shot.

16.2　The engagement gap

In a learning journey like Armstrong's, the tipping point is most often when you reach the fifth milestone—engagement with others. Everything accelerates from there, often in unanticipated directions.

Two valuable learning concepts, both potentially measurable, are:

→ the 'engagement gap'—the difference between your current capability in the subject and what you think you need in order to start engaging with others
→ the amount of time you need to bridge that gap.

That time period can be significantly reduced if you have a clear learning strategy, a sense of urgency and the right tools—books, videos, audio tapes, internet, software and so on. It also helps if:

→ you are a good self-teacher
→ you have good judgement of what you do and don't know

→ you practise deliberately (see 16.4), focusing on the genuinely challenging steps that will advance your progress

→ your general self-confidence enables you to engage with others without having to be perfect first.

A classic example of an engagement gap is a person who is aiming to learn a foreign language, a new technical language or to adapt to a new culture, even one that uses their own language. Their learning curve will accelerate markedly as soon as they have the competence and courage to converse with others. Initially, there will be obstacles that discourage or prevent them from reaching that stage, collectively constituting the engagement gap.

Imagine you are an aspiring French speaker but you lack the confidence to enter into conversations. You identify that this engagement gap is not due to your vocabulary, grammar or accent, but your inability to understand what the average French person is saying. If that's the case, you have to find a way through this engagement gap; for example, by:

→ improving your ear for the language by listening to French tapes or the French news on television or radio, then progressing from clearer speakers such as politicians and reporters to members of the general public being interviewed

→ improving your fluency at identifying idiomatic expressions, numbers and times of day—or other topics that typically cause you to stop and think, and thereby miss the next sentence

→ selecting the contexts in which you first try to engage in conversation, such as quieter environments or with people in a shop where you might buy something

→ at all stages aiming to build not only your ability at understanding but also your confidence.

The same concepts—identifying the gap and its causes, and implementing a clear strategy to overcome it—are just as applicable when you're taking on a new role, especially if you're joining a new organisation. Induction programs are targeted at rapidly reducing the engagement gap, and thereby accelerating the effectiveness of new recruits.

Change and the engagement gap

If you don't like change, you'll like irrelevance even less.

—Peter Drucker

The ability to bridge engagement gaps through learning helps take some of the stress out of unfamiliar situations. These unfamiliar situations don't tend to be the result of your own decisions but because of a change in your environment—new technology, new processes, a new boss or new owner with new expectations, new tax rules, new economic conditions or general cultural change. The more rapidly the world changes, the less critical what you already know becomes, and the more critical your ability to learn new things. These days, the saying 'You can't teach an old dog new tricks' has to be a thing of the past.

Being able to bridge engagement gaps quickly will help you to become more comfortable with change.

16.3 Personal mastery and accessing the subconscious

In *The Fifth Discipline*, Peter Senge talks about the concept of 'learning organisations' and the relevance of five disciplines to organisational learning. One of the five disciplines is personal mastery, an ongoing process of:

→ clarifying what matters to you
→ learning to see current reality more clearly
→ using the difference between what you want and where you currently are at to build and sustain creative tension in your life.[2]

According to Senge, if you have a high level of personal mastery, you not only have a clear picture of your desired future but you are also acutely aware of where you need to grow to reach that future. You are continually learning—expanding your ability to produce what you want in life. You therefore tend to lead a creative rather than a reactive life.

Senge asks you to imagine that one of your goals is fully realised, and to then ask yourself where this would actually get you. On reflection, you may discover that the goal is just an interim step towards a more important result or deeper desire.

Senge considers that the ability to access the vast capacity of your subconscious is essential to dealing with complexity and achieving personal mastery. For example, such tasks as developing a particular stroke in a sport, learning to play a musical instrument or driving a car all initially require significant conscious attention. Ultimately, however, the mechanics of these achievements become automatic and subconscious, so you can then focus your conscious attention on your sporting opponent, your musical performance or the other cars on the road.

According to Senge, most of us take our subconscious for granted. Through meditation to quieten the conscious mind, we can learn to work more productively with our subconscious. When you have made conscious choices about what matters to you, your conscious mind has performed a major part of its job and passes on a clear vision to the subconscious, which can then be less distracted by contradictory thoughts and thereby more effective as you work towards your goals.

16.4   The 10-year rule and deliberate practice

According to academic studies, it takes around 10 years for a person to become world class—almost regardless of their field and their innate ability. Importantly, it's not just any 10 years. For the years to count here, they must be years of deliberate practice, devoted to activities explicitly dedicated to improving performance, reaching for objectives just beyond current competence, providing feedback on results and involving high levels of repetition. Hitting tennis balls or golf balls is not deliberate practice unless it is done with a clear 'stretch' purpose; performance is assessed, adjustments are made to the stroke or swing and the experiment is repeated—over and over.[3]

An important part of deliberate practice is to review your performance: analysing what you felt, learned, experienced or observed; how you performed against your objectives; and the quality of your strategy, judgements and decisions. It also relates to the wider context of your performance, the situations or opportunities that you would like to recognise and capitalise on if they recur. A performance review therefore builds both self-awareness and awareness of the full context of your performance.

Deliberate practice is also enhanced by keeping a diary of your practice and your progress against your objectives. This valuable discipline sharpens your analytical skills, ensures you are focused and thinking during practice, and enhances your objectivity by helping you avoid hindsight bias. Reviewing the diary from time to time can remind you of the significant progress you have made or any shortfall against your original objectives.

Research suggests that the ability to practice deliberately is more fundamental to success than any innate ability in the specific field.

16.5   Learning methods

There is a wide range of learning methods to choose from. For example, you will know whether you prefer information to be presented in writing or during discussions, lectures or video presentations; whether you prefer figures over graphs or logic versus a diagram or picture. You might find it hard to learn from others' mistakes, but be good at learning from your own. You might be a keen experimenter, or maybe not. You might prefer live projects and tangible outcomes, whereas others might prefer theory and models.

As explained in 4.2, finding the right environment, method or tools to suit you and what you are trying to learn can double or treble your learning speed, along with other important impacts. You will find the learning process less draining, more satisfying and more likely to build your self-esteem. In addition, you will have a much higher probability of persisting and taking something away from your efforts.

The combined effect of these factors could be a five- or 10-fold increase in your learning for the effort required. In addition, the length of your engagement gap will be reduced so your learning will be adding value sooner.

Education and learning experts have developed many alternative theories of learning styles. You may find it instructive to examine at least one model and apply it to better understand your own learning preferences. Fortunately, on most subjects your choice of learning methods, environment or tools is vast, so you can choose those that suit your learning style and thereby accelerate your learning curve. Here are a few observations on some of them.

One-on-one tutor, mentor or coach

Teaching in a large class will always have casualties as instruction can't be pitched at each person's diverse needs. An opportunity for a one-on-one tutor or mentor is therefore a privilege to be capitalised on. Ideally, all the tutor's energy will be focused on your mind, thoughts, needs and progress. The most effective teachers will ask for your thoughts before offering their own. We all experience these one-on-one relationships — at home, in sport or the arts, academically or at work.

The privilege of one-on-one teaching brings responsibilities for both you and your tutor — preparation. If you're prepared, with your homework or practice done, a supply of challenging questions to ask and some reflections on failed experiments, your tutor or coach will be fired up and ready to stretch you further.

Teaching others

Charles Handy, a graduate in Latin and Greek and fairly new to Shell in Singapore, was asked to give a lecture on the Future of Oil. It was then that Handy discovered that 'a degree was not a qualification but a licence to learn' and that 'the best way to learn something is to try to teach it to someone else. It's bad luck on the students, I often think, but I have found it an excellent way to develop my thinking ever since'.[4]

Teaching someone else is not just an important learning tool intellectually or physically. It can also be a significant emotional challenge, and therefore a source of personal growth. Your learning will vary depending on whether you are teaching mainly didactically (by giving a lecture), socratically (by involving discussion, questions and answers) or by coaching.

Conversation and discussion

As explained in 16.2, the 'tipping point' in a learning process often occurs when a standard of competence and the confidence to engage with others is reached. You then learn from their ideas, their exposure of weaknesses in your logic or performance and your inevitable preparation to ensure you do better next time.

Writing

The discipline of writing your thoughts down applies further scrutiny to your logic. For this reason, if you ever need to get some important professional advice from someone, always get it on paper—not so you have written evidence of the advice, but so you can have confidence that your adviser has thought the matter through and reviewed their logic to the best of their ability. Importantly, it also gives you the opportunity to thoroughly review and understand their logic.

Visualisation

The visualisation and mental rehearsal of processes can train your natural reactions under pressure. A variation of this theme is to reproduce in your mind the logic of a subject—to check or embed your understanding of it. It's an important test of your fluency or understanding of a subject, requiring the same level of comprehension as would be required to deliver a speech without notes.

Self teaching

This is well demonstrated by Lance Armstrong's study of cancer in 16.1, and is often the most efficient way to bridge the engagement gap.

Experience curves

> Any experience that does not violate expectation is not worthy of the name experience.
>
> —Georg Hegel

The principle behind experience curves is that the more you have performed or tried to perform a particular task, the more efficiently or effectively you will be able to do it and variations of it. That's great news up to a point, and is fundamental to the concept of deliberate practice (see 16.4). However, it is important in terms of learning to be aware of the distinction between three years' experience and one year's experience repeated three times (see 10.4). That's why one of the premises behind deliberate practice is that the objectives must be just beyond your current competence.

Action learning

Action learning is a form of team experiential learning based on solving complex practical problems of importance to an organisation. It was first developed in the 1940s by Reg Revans when he was director of education at the National Coal Board in Britain. The basic principle is an ongoing cycle of understanding, action and reflection, conducted in the company of a group of others who are doing likewise to work on their own problems. The group is known as an 'action learning set'. The set's meetings, ideally of short duration, not only provide new ideas but are also vehicles for significant learning. Thus action learning is active rather than passive, focused on the future rather than the past, and taking place in a real-life rather than simulated environment.

Revans' experience was that action learning is most effective if the level of familiarity of the problems selected is related to the capacity and experience of the individual. For example, CEOs would work on problems related to unfamiliar tasks in unfamiliar situations, whereas a foreman's problem would be better related to a familiar task in a familiar situation.[5]

16.6   Learning accelerators and inhibitors

Research supports the view that EQ actually improves with age...the older you get the more emotionally intelligent you become, at least up until your late 40s or early 50s...IQ has been found to peak in the late teens, level out until the late 50s and even mildly decline later in life. So the real question is not so much about whether EQ can be improved—but rather, how can we take the necessary steps to accelerate the development of our EQ.

—Martyn Newman[6]

Whether we are seeking to develop our emotional intelligence quotient (EQ) or any other part of our human capital, one of the most valuable skills is to be able to identify accelerators and inhibitors of development.

Accelerators

→ *Trying something new*: any new challenge builds your thinking and feelings in ways that make you more effective in other contexts

→ *A safe environment for unlearning and learning*

→ *The right mentor, coach or teacher*

→ *An open mind*

→ *Peer pressure*

→ *Taking on more responsibility and pushing your boundaries*

→ *A major short-term goal or challenge*

→ *Understanding the full context of your work*

→ *An outsider's fresh view*: according to a Polish proverb, 'The guest can see more in an hour than the host can in a year', so it is always worth asking to hear the observations of someone new on the scene (a new employee or a coach who has never seen you play before)

→ *Reflection and a diary of progress*: this is as important to learning as the experience itself

→ *Discipline*

→ *Pressure and stress:* if something puts you under pressure, the experience will generally build your emotional capacity. The challenge is to maintain a healthy balance between stress and invigoration. Your ability to maintain that balance will depend on you being able to stand back from time to time and achieve some emotional distance from the issues at hand, along with some emotional renewal.

Inhibitors

→ *Doing the same thing all the time*

→ *Being afraid to try something new:* you may fear failure or not want to look stupid, give up old successful habits or lose your standing in your bonding network

→ *A closed mind*: for example, the biggest reason for medical misdiagnosis is 'premature closure', where doctors, in the belief that they have the correct diagnosis, close their minds to other possibilities[7]

→ *If your previous success causes risk aversion*
→ *Absence of a linking of the learning to immediate priorities*

If much of your life is spent working in a single organisation, the learning disabilities in that organisation can also inhibit your own learning. Peter Senge cites seven learning disabilities:[8]

→ focusing only on your own job, confusing your job with your identity and not seeing your role in a whole enterprise context
→ finding someone or something else to blame if things go wrong
→ acting before you understand how you have contributed to the problem
→ focusing on short-term events (like last month's sales or a product delay)
→ being unable to see gradual change
→ not directly experiencing the consequences of many of your important decisions because the primary consequences will occur well into the future or in other parts of the organisation
→ inability to work as an effective team member when things get complex, embarrassing or threatening. In this instance, long training in hiding ignorance blocks out any new understandings that might be a threat.

Other issues in team and organisational learning are covered in Principle 18

16.7   Learning to manage your health

If your health fails, everything else stops in its tracks. Your physical and mental health are your most important life assets, and you should treat them as such. It's your job to manage them and it's not something that can be delegated. Just like Lance Armstrong in 16.1, you're the person who chooses your doctors and treatment, including having to give *informed* consent to any operation.

You can't manage something you don't understand, so you need to be alert to your own body and mind, and deal with changes or concerns with an appropriate sense of urgency. Unfortunately, some changes, such as poorer physical capacity because of the progressive blocking of arteries, are sufficiently gradual that you might not realise anything has changed until you have a heart attack—hence the importance of having regular medical check-ups.

Other, more sudden changes are obvious. A couple of years ago, my wife suffered progressive loss of vision in her left eye. When Tori realised her condition was becoming worse, it was 11 pm. She googled 'sudden loss of vision' and in a couple of minutes ascertained that she had probably suffered a retinal detachment—which required surgery within 24 hours to avoid blindness in that eye. She then understood the possible urgency of receiving prompt medical diagnosis and treatment.

The internet can help you take greater control in managing your health. In *Super Crunchers*, Ian Ayres writes that the Medline website, originally compiled by the US National Library of Medicine for physicians and researchers, receives more than a third of visitors from the general public. Consequently, MedlinePlus was added as a sister site specifically for patients, along with 12 consumer health journals. Ayres believes the internet is transforming the culture of medicine and changing the way patients interact with doctors.

As an alternative to MedlinePlus, you could try <www.mayoclinic. com>. Apparently, more than half of the women and more than three-quarters of the men who suffer from the potentially embarrassing, sleep-depriving and socially limiting problem of having an overactive bladder never talk to their doctor about the issue. If they looked up their condition on the Mayo website, they would find many pages of easily readable information on the condition's definition, symptoms, causes, risk factors and complications, along with advice on preparing for their appointment, tests and diagnosis, treatment and drugs, coping, support and prevention. They would then be fully empowered to manage their dialogue with the medical profession and tackle the issue rather than hide from it.

Discussing health issues with friends or family can also put you in a better position to manage your health. Friends in your age group can be valuable confidants or sources of shared experience—even if they're just having the same regular tests as you. Obviously, such discussion is no substitute for seeing a doctor, but your friends may be able to point you in the direction of a doctor who impressed them in circumstances similar to your own.

According to Dr Hilary Jones on <www.netdoctor.co.uk>, men who experience medical problems are much less likely than women to consult a doctor, and much more likely to require an emergency hospital admission with a serious or life-threatening condition. She attributes men avoiding seeing their doctors to embarrassment about their bodies, an aversion to doctors, avoidance of intimate examinations, male machismo, male reluctance to talk to one another about their medical problems (unlike women) and an overriding failure to take responsibility for their health.

If mental health is the issue, the effects can be progressive. A sense of despair or anxiety can be readily attributed to workplace or family stress. Prolonged feelings of despondency, lack of life control, inability to sleep or indeed sleeping too much are all signs that the body and mind are out of sync with one another. In many cases, however, mental illness can be managed and resolved in the same way as physical illness. Friends, family and work colleagues are generally the first to recognise that all is not well, and a visit to the general practitioner can be the first step in resolving what would otherwise seem to be overbearing, life-threatening problems. Mental health information is included on most health websites, and there are numerous specific websites dealing with the subject.

Medicine *is* rocket science; managing your own health and health care is not — provided you:

→ recognise that your health is important and consequently take it seriously

→ recognise that your health is your responsibility, not your doctor's

→ organise yourself and your health records

→ build a relationship with medical professionals

→ visit your medical professional when you have health issues

→ keep asking questions until you clearly understand the issue, and if decisions are necessary, keep asking questions until you can make those decisions on an informed basis.

It's important to note that these are the same principles as would apply to managing your financial capital.

Over to you ...

Reflection

- Have you assessed what learning methods work for you? Do you have a learning strategy in life? In the broadest sense, are you regularly adding knowledge to your life?
- Is there a context in which you are lacking the confidence to engage? What is the nature of your engagement gap? What steps are needed to traverse it? Are you able to take a leap of faith and ignore the gap between what you know and what you think you need to know in order to engage with others with confidence?
- Are you comfortable with change? Can you identify any engagement gaps influencing your reaction to change? What can you do about them?
- Can you access your subconscious more and allow it to work for you more effectively?
- For your most important learning goals, are you deliberate in your practice, with a clear purpose and constant reviews of performance?
- Do you have current first-aid training? It's a valuable source of learning about the body, as well as an important part of your family and workmates' social capital. Do you contribute to your community's social capital by giving blood?

Action

- Analyse the benefits of using your optimum learning methods and how significant those benefits are (appendix B8 may prompt further thoughts).
- Make it a habit to ignore the 'engagement gap' and start conversing.
- From time to time, review your learning against your objectives and strategy. Keep a diary of your progress, identifying what's working and what's not.
- From each important conversation, identify what you learned from it and where that knowledge takes you.

- Analyse the negative impacts of failure to deal with a significant medical discomfort; for example, persistent neck problems or headaches (appendix B14 may prompt further thoughts).
- Be proactive in managing your health and practise preventative medicine.

Principle 17
Learning from
success and failure

A comparison between your vision and your current reality provides both the insights and the energy for growth.

Experience is not what happens to a man; it is what a man does with what happens to him.

—Aldous Huxley

Superficially, successes are career assets, highlighted on your CV; failures are career liabilities, omitted from your CV. You would think that distinction is pretty clear, especially in sport, where you either win or you lose.

Equally superficially, success and failure are often perceived as being opposites and mutually exclusive—if you didn't succeed, you failed. However, is it success or failure when:

→ You swim a PB, but do not win the race?
→ You work on a new grip or stroke and feel increasing confidence in it, but do not win (as Tiger Woods did for 18 months—see 4.2)?

→ You complete your comeback game injury-free, but your team does not win?

→ You don't win, but you identify how you can win next time?

On closer inspection, it appears that success and failure are neither mutually exclusive, nor opposites. They are both major sources of learning—experiential learning.

17.1 An empowering perspective on success and failure

For me, the most empowering perspective on success and failure is provided by Peter Senge in his book *The Fifth Discipline*. In his chapter on 'Personal Mastery', Senge defines failure as 'simply, a shortfall, evidence of the gap between vision and current reality'.[1]

Senge's definition appeals to me because:

→ it is simple and unemotive

→ it identifies the opportunity to learn about 'your picture of current reality, about strategies that didn't work as expected, about the clarity of the vision'

→ it is empowering to recognise the gap between vision and current reality as a source of 'energy for change'—your choice is whether you work to improve your current reality or take the easy way out and rein in your vision

→ it recognises that success—reaching the vision—leaves limited opportunity for further learning or growth unless the vision is extended.

Senge cites the wonderful example of Bill Russell of the Boston Celtics. Russell's personal scorecard shows he never gave himself more than 65 out of 100—not once in over 1200 games, including 11 pro basketball championships in 13 years. Senge says: 'given the way we are taught to think about goals, we would regard Russell as an abject failure. The poor soul played in over 1200 basketball games and never achieved his standard! Yet it was the striving for that standard that made him arguably the best basketball player ever'.

Objectivity in assessing your current reality is vital. Any significant difference between 'current reality' and 'your perception of current reality' will affect the amount of energy you have for change.

17.2   Long-term success and failure

Success is said to have many fathers, while failure is an orphan. One of the most important fathers of success is failure. This is axiomatic, whether success is as defined by Senge or as defined by Churchill: 'Success is going from failure to failure with no loss of enthusiasm'.[2] Thomas Edison exemplified this view. He failed in his first 6000 attempts to develop a light bulb, but when asked if he was discouraged, he replied: 'No. I am now well informed on 6000 ways you cannot do it'.

Churchill thus suggests that resilience, like Edison's, is another of the fathers of success. Also high on the list must be learning, which has, in turn, a number of fathers—curiosity and an open mind, questioning, listening, experimentation, courage...

The DNA of long-term success is complicated indeed, but the DNA of long-term failure is often much simpler. Having a closed mind or not listening is almost sufficient in itself to ensure long-term failure, as is a lack of resilience, lack of courage or a reluctance to give new things a go.

17.3   Disciplines for learning from success and failure

Questioning yourself must become a habit, one strong enough to surmount obstacles of overconfidence and dejection. It is a muscle that can be developed only with practice.

—Garry Kasparov[3]

A major source of enrichment for your Life Capital is a willingness to learn from both successes and failures. The keener you are to learn, the more you will find tools or approaches that can make this learning more effective for you.

The following tools will be valuable if you have an open mind, but they're of little value if you have an unqualified commitment to preconceived ideas or constantly find external forces and events to blame.

Clarity

→ *Clear visions and objectives* are essential if you are to learn effectively from failure, as defined by Senge. A professionally coached athlete will have a clear vision and, for most training sessions, defined objectives. If it's good enough for them, why not for you? Don't worry about the luxury of having a coach. Before you embark on an assignment, a training session, a meeting or any experiment, if your vision is clear you'll soon be able to define your principal objectives. And if your vision isn't clear, the extra time spent on your objectives will lead to healthy reflection on your vision.

→ *Experimentation* is a major tool for achieving low-risk progress — testing boundaries, theories, new business propositions, alternative approaches to relationships or tactics in sport. It's also of great value in testing what works for you. One key is to recognise that you have many opportunities to conduct experiments — and the more you experiment, the more successful they will be. Gaining the maximum benefit from any experiment involves *clarifying what you are trying to test* (your theory); structuring and performing the experiment; collecting, analysing and interpreting the data; then drawing some conclusions — and then perhaps retesting the experiment. These steps need not be applied with the rigour and documentation of a scientist, but with sufficient forethought that the key learnings from the experiment can be identified.

Due scepticism

As Einstein said: 'No amount of experimentation can ever prove me right; a single experiment can prove me wrong'. This view is reflected in the ideas of Karl Popper on scientific discovery. Popper argued that all progress in knowledge results from efforts to disprove our theories, not efforts to confirm them.

The compound benefits of dealing constructively with failure or disappointment

If your environment and your psychology allow you to deal with failure and disappointment constructively, and to learn from them, you will more actively experiment or seek out new experiences from which to learn. These strengths have a multiplier effect. Simply put, if you have twice as many new experiences as others who are less comfortable with failure or disappointment, and you learn twice as much as them from each experience, your learning from experience will be four times faster than theirs.

Discipline

→ *Post-decision reviews, documentation and good record keeping* are important tools, whether for individuals or for companies. Because humans have a tendency known as 'hindsight bias',[4] we are generally poor at recalling the way an uncertain situation appeared before we learn the results. Hence the value of post-decision reviews. However, the value of a company carrying out a post-decision review is limited by the quality of the original board minutes and detailed investment proposals. The personal equivalent of corporate records is a diary of major events, decisions, outcomes, progress and learning. While it takes effort to maintain a diary, it is an investment in making better decisions and more valuable post-decision reviews.

→ *Measurement* is also important, as the old adage 'Whatever isn't measured doesn't happen' affirms. One of the key areas where you may elect to measure things is how you spend your time or energy. For example, if your key responsibility and objective at work is sales yet you're spending 50 to 70 per cent of your week on administration, there is clearly something wrong in your resourcing or your personal discipline.

→ *Objectivity and openness in reflection.* Much of the learning benefit from experiences or experiments can be lost if they are not followed by objective, open-minded reflection. This can take the form of Bill Russell's post-game performance assessment (see 17.1), a coach's post-game analysis or an employee's performance assessment by their boss (or vice versa).

→ *Reflection on the opportunities you didn't take up.* Many of the decisions you take in life involve *not* proceeding with an opportunity. Sometimes the difference between your expectations and the results someone else achieves by taking that opportunity can be so great that, much as it might hurt, it begs further reflection. Such circumstances may well recur and maybe you will be better placed to identify the opportunity next time — and thereby avoid a major opportunity loss. As ice hockey great Wayne Gretzky said: 'You miss 100 per cent of the shots you don't take'.[5]

The discipline of performance analysis is fundamental in investment management — for learning by both investment managers and their clients. The first step in performance analysis is the identification of suitable benchmarks.

Wealth Insert 17A: benchmarking

In professional money management relationships, client and manager usually agree a benchmark with which performance will be compared. Typical return benchmarks would be the performance of the stock exchange or bond indexes that are best aligned with the strategy of the fund.

For example, a manager of international equities may adopt the MSCI World Index as the benchmark for a fund. An alternative benchmark could be the median or mean performance of all the funds of other managers with similar investment strategies. The measurement of the fund's performance against that benchmark is the first step in shining a light both on the fund's adherence to its strategy and on its performance in that strategy.

The next step in performance analysis is the attribution of the performance to specific factors.

Wealth Insert 17B: performance attribution

> Decisions shouldn't be evaluated only on the basis of results ... Anyone who is honest about having done well will acknowledge the enormous role played by chance.
>
> —Robert Rubin[6]

Typically, an investment manager and his client agree on investment policies that link the work of the investment manager with the objectives of the client.

The performance of the investment manager should be assessed only in comparison with the agreed policies and benchmarks or indices that are matched to the policies. For example, the performance of a portfolio of value stocks should not be compared with the total stock market because this comparison confuses two issues: an underperformance could occur because value stocks were a rotten place to be during that period (a policy issue) or because the manager's selection of individual value stocks was poor (a manager performance issue).

When an investor or investment manager has compared the performance against appropriate benchmarks, the next step is the key to learning. When any under- or overperformance against benchmarks is attributed to a specific source, this plays a vital role in enabling the investor to identify results which, while they may look good, are not sustainable or are not in accord with the agreed business or investment model.

This essentially quantitative analysis has one principal purpose: to throw up the core questions that need to be asked of the investment manager. Charles Ellis points out that only after many years of measurement could you determine whether an investment manager with superior results is skilful or lucky, so you have to ask core questions.[7] Do the manager's explanations of decisions make good sense? Are they consistent with previous statements? Do you find your confidence in the manager's abilities, knowledge and judgement rising or falling?

The same quantitative and then qualitative principles of performance attribution are applied in most areas of business:

- company management or boards compare revenues, expenses and profits against budgets
- financial analysts compare company results against their forecasts — some seemingly excellent results are shown, under scrutiny, to have been substantially attributable to activities such as currency or commodity trading, which the company should not even be conducting
- actuaries compare the performance of financial institutions against the expectations per their actuarial models.

My profession has a simple problem-solving algorithm — 'the actuarial control cycle'.[8] It involves a cycle of four basic steps, as shown below in figure 17.1.

Figure 17.1: the actuarial control cycle

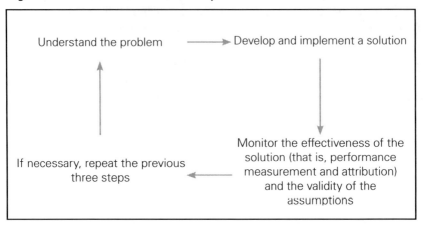

As there is nothing uniquely actuarial about this common-sense approach, you can apply it to problems in most fields. What is important is the discipline it brings and the consequently increased chance of receiving an early-warning sign that something is not going as you expected. It is targeted at overcoming the assumption, generally invalid (as will be discussed in 21.1), that things will work out as you forecast.

These simple and powerful disciplines are nothing more than common sense and you can master them, even if you can't solve every problem. But, believe it or not, that's not what most people do. According to Peter Senge, we are most likely to respond to unexpected outcomes by reverting to problem-solving mode or by just trying harder — rather than searching for new learnings that may challenge or modify our underlying assumptions.[9]

One area where you might apply your own versions of the above cycle is in reviewing and improving how you invest your time. As evidenced by the example of the aspiring musician in 10.1, you don't have to make your version as complicated or technical as investment managers or actuaries tend to do. To be effective, however, it does demand a few basic steps and a reasonable level of detail.

1 Be clear how many hours a week you expect or are expected to be working.

2 Be clear on your objectives or key performance indicators (KPIs) at work. Estimate how it would make sense to allocate your time, and break your hours down into one of the following ways:
   → by type of activity (administration, meetings, reporting, people management, selling, training, reflection)
   → by linking it to your objectives or KPIs
   → in a matrix ranking urgency and importance.

3 Record how your time is actually spent in the chosen categories.

4 Compare the actual versus the expected to see what differences emerge. If your office hours roughly equate to those of your model lifestyle, and the way you spend your office hours is well aligned with your objectives, you'll be the great exception—proceed to Step 8, or go back to Step 2 and choose a different breakdown.

5 Study those differences to understand the problem/opportunity.

6 Develop strategies to fix the situation.

7 Try to implement those strategies, continue recording your time and return to Step 4.

8 Life is great and you're getting good results. If you haven't already done so, stick a brightly coloured pie chart on your wall with your expected time allocation as a healthy reminder and make a diary note to review how you're going in six months.

An important outcome of such a process should be a clear distinction between apparent and real success. For example, you may have succeeded in reducing your work hours to your targeted 40 hours per week but find that you are only achieving this target by spending no time at all on important but non-urgent matters—deferring them at the long-term expense of your career.

Over to you ...

Reflection

- How do you view failure? Do you choose to view failure as a learning opportunity—to understand what does not work and to create energy for change?

- Where your performance doesn't match your vision, do you typically reduce your vision or energise yourself for improved performance?
- Do you typically record your performance and reflect on it with an open mind?
- If your performance is regularly meeting your vision, are you setting your vision too low and hence not extending yourself?
- By not risking failure, are you setting yourself up for opportunity loss?

Action

- Analyse the potential benefits from benchmarking and how significant these benefits are (appendix B13 may prompt further thoughts).
- Examine any failures and, with an open mind and with energy for change, analyse what you can learn from this failure.
- Analyse an example where you chose not to risk failure by not participating, and assess whether it was an opportunity loss and what, if anything, you would do differently the next time.

Principle 18
Collaboration

**If you collaborate effectively,
the growth in your Life Capital
will be accelerated.**

*When teams operate at their best, the results can be more than
additive—they can be multiplicative, with the best talents of
one person catalysing the best of another and another, to produce
results far beyond what any one person might have done. The
explanation of this aspect of team performance lies in the members'
relationships—in the chemistry between members.*

—Daniel Goleman[1]

If a person has been working on an idea and then bounces it off
another person, the two minds working together are likely to improve
it. The improvement is likely to be greater if the second person comes
from a different background from the first, whether in gender, age,
profession or culture … and better still if a third person brings other
attributes—provided they can all work together! This is a simple
example of collaboration and cross-fertilisation.

18.1   The characteristics of great groups

While the cult of the individual is still alive and well in Western society, success in our increasingly complex world is becoming progressively dependent on the ability of teams to collaborate.

In *Organising Genius: The Secrets of Creative Collaboration*, authors Warren Bennis and Patricia Ward Biederman share the stories of diverse 'great groups', which accomplished so much more than talented people working alone and in some cases reshaped the world. These groups had missions as diverse as the artists working on Disney's 1937 animated feature film *Snow White and the Seven Dwarfs*, the team behind the 1992 Clinton presidential campaign, the engineers building radically new planes for Lockheed and the scientists working on the Manhattan atomic bomb project in World War II.

Bennis and Biederman identified the common characteristics of these great groups, including the following:

→ through their networks, they knew where to find talent and diversity and were unafraid of hiring people better than themselves, focusing on excellence and the ability to work with others

→ they tended to encourage dissent to enhance the spirit of discovery

→ their collaborations tended to be collegial, with a strong leader who was also perceived as one among equals

→ group members were often so attuned to each other and to the nature of the task that they rarely needed to speak to each other

→ they solved complex problems relatively quickly because, being a group, they had more options to discuss, discarded the dead-end options more quickly, improved each others' ideas and no-one bore sole responsibility for the result

→ they saw themselves as being on a mission from God, as winning underdogs with an enemy to beat

→ they were focused and optimistic, with the right people acting in the right jobs.

The challenge for someone organising a collaborative session is to set up the best conditions for success. A climate of trust is essential to encourage the raising of alternative views or the sharing of information. To achieve this, some forums run their discussions subject to Chatham House rules, devised in 1927 by the Royal Institute of International Affairs (Europe's leading foreign policy think tank, better known as Chatham House) to encourage free discussion and openness. They operate on the basis that 'participants are free to use the information received, but neither the identity nor the affiliation of the speakers, nor that of any other participant may be revealed'. Thus people can speak as individuals and express views that may not be those of their organisations, without fear of being publicly quoted.

An important aspect in collaborative, brainstorming discussions is the role played by the team leader. By bringing in an external facilitator, the leader has the option to act as one of the team or to absent themselves for part of the discussion so that others can throw in their ideas without being intimated by the team leader's presence.

While diversity within groups increases group knowledge, it may also disrupt the group's social integration, thereby impairing performance. Research by Fabrice Cavarretta and other organisational theorists suggests that:

→ diverse teams will on average perform worse than more homogeneous ones, as improved knowledge is outweighed by poorer social integration

→ the variability of performance is higher for highly diverse teams than for more homogeneous ones.

Thus highly diverse teams can produce both very low and very high performances, whereas the performance of homogeneous teams will be within a narrower band. Accordingly, the level of diversity you seek for a team should be influenced by your objectives and the risk profile associated with it.

If you have low hurdles and your priority is to avoid disasters, for example, a more homogeneous team would be favoured. If you have high hurdles to reach (for example, to be in the top 10 per cent of the population to survive), it may be that you have to take the high diversity approach as being the only one that can get you over that high hurdle.[2]

18.2 Team learning — dialogue and discussion

*Until we have some theory of what happens when teams learn
(as opposed to individuals in teams learning), we will be unable
to distinguish group intelligence from 'groupthink'.*

—Peter Senge[3]

When writing on team learning, Peter Senge emphasises the distinction between:

→ *Dialogue:* where you explore subjects collegiately, freely and creatively; expressing your views clearly, along with your underlying assumptions; listening deeply to one another; and not trying to win individually but collectively. You thereby come to a deeper collective understanding of the subject and also learn individually about your logic and assumptions.

→ *Discussion:* where you present your individual views and defend them in a search for the best view to support the decisions you have to take.

The power of both dialogue and discussion lies in their synergy, but this is unlikely to occur without an understanding of the distinctions between them. 'Discussion' is targeted at the making of a decision, whereas 'dialogue' aims for a deeper exploration and understanding of the issues.

Senge considers that most teams lack the ability to distinguish between dialogue and discussion, and to move constructively between them. Hence an important role of a chairman or facilitator is to encourage and maintain dialogue long enough before the inevitable focus on the decision at hand.

According to Senge, regular dialogue develops your skills of enquiry and reflection, your understanding of the uniqueness of others' points of view and your awareness that you will learn more by holding your point of view 'gently'. Also, through dialogue your team will develop a deeper trust, which it can carry over to its discussions. It will also learn to distinguish between a discussion's 'focusing down' consensus based on seeking the common denominator in multiple individual views and a dialogue's 'opening up' consensus, which seeks a picture larger than any one person's point of view.

Senge quotes the work of organisational learning expert Chris Argyris and his colleagues, who for decades have studied why capable managers often fail to learn effectively in management teams. They believe that the key difference between great teams and mediocre teams is how they deal with conflict and the defensiveness that invariably surrounds it—a fear of exposing the thinking that lies behind their views. That defensiveness then inhibits learning about the validity of their reasoning.

18.3 Team learning—individual and organisational defensiveness

Deep within the mental models of managers in many organisations is the belief that managers must know what's going on. It is simply unacceptable for managers to act as though they don't know what is causing a problem. Those that reach senior positions are masters at appearing to know what is going on, and those intent on reaching such positions learn early to develop an air of confident knowledge. Managers who take on the burden of having to know the answers become highly skilful in defensive routines that preserve their aura as capable decision makers by not revealing the thinking behind their decisions.

—Peter Senge[4]

According to Senge, the more seemingly effective defensiveness becomes, the more it covers up problems and the worse they then become. In contrast, enquiring into problems in a way that reveals your own assumptions and reasoning, and encouraging others to do likewise, makes defensive routines less likely to occur. Fundamental to overcoming defensiveness in an organisation is the recognition that it is not just an individual's problem but a jointly created systemic one, and that you have had a role in encouraging others' defensiveness.

Organisational learning expert Chris Argyris believes that most people don't know how to learn because they misunderstand what learning is all about and how to achieve it. In particular, most people focus on identifying and correcting specific business problems (in Argyris's language, 'single-loop learning'), rather than also critically reflecting on how their own behaviour has contributed to the problem or to the failure to deal with it earlier ('double-loop learning').

According to Argyris, this double-loop learning and its essential ingredient of reflection is discouraged by both individual and organisational defensive routines.

Individual defensive routines

All over the world, in every kind of business and organisation, in every kind of crisis and dilemma, the principles of defensive reasoning encourage people to leave their own behaviour unexamined and to avoid any objective test of their premises and conclusions.

—Chris Argyris[5]

Chris Argyris has noted that when we face embarrassment or a threat, we resort to different programs of behaviour from the ones we think we use, which fit our intellectual and philosophical backgrounds—and we are not aware of the contradiction.

Most of us resort to behaviour designed to keep us in unilateral control (for example, by advocating our views but not encouraging enquiry), to maximise winning and minimise losing (by changing targets to suit emerging performance, the selective presentation of data or not engaging with people who we think have a contrary view) and to suppress collective embarrassment (by not being frank about others' accountabilities, performances or views, or by changing the subject entirely). All these responses are aimed at avoiding risk, embarrassment and any appearance of incompetence. These deeply defensive strategies, says Argyris, are a recipe for ineffective learning. He has found them to be universal, regardless of country, age, gender, ethnicity, education, wealth, power or experience.

Chris Argyris conducted 15 years of research into the behaviour of management consultants, mainly MBAs from the top US business schools. He found such professionals are very good at solving real-world problems (single-loop learning) but, because of their inexperience at failure, they have never learned from failure. Hence, if their real-world solution fails, they become defensive, screening out criticism and blaming others—shutting down their ability to learn just when they need it most.[6]

Organisational defensive routines

Organisations have policies and practices in place to protect employees from embarrassment or threat by effectively censoring negative messages; for example, by sending out persistent but inappropriately positive messages or by stressing the problem rather than any people issues that may have caused or exacerbated it.

Argyris believes an emphasis on being positive can be counter-productive as it avoids the important roles that 'negative attitudes can play — often *should* play — in giving an accurate picture of organisational reality, especially with regard to threatening or sensitive issues'.

18.4   Team communication and learning

Systems archetypes are used to describe common patterns of behaviour in organisations, and can be used to deal with complexity and enhance objectivity. They can serve as diagnostic tools or as prospective tools to alert you to future unintended consequences, and are well explained in William Braun's *The System Archetypes*. Examples include:

→ *Limits to growth*: in any system, growth cannot continue on an unrestricted basis. Ultimately, something will push back and limit growth.

→ *Eroding goals*: where people faced with underperformance against a stated vision seek a rationale for changing the goal to something more attainable, rather than rigorously considering what is preventing the original goal from being realised.

→ *Shifting the burden*: where a symptomatic solution rather than a fundamental solution is applied to a problem, alleviating the symptoms and reducing the pressure to implement a fundamental long-term solution. There is an obvious tension between the relative ease and lower cost of the symptomatic solution and the more permanent benefit of a fundamental solution.

→ *Escalation*: when one party's actions are perceived by another to be a threat, and the second party responds similarly and thereby increases the threat — resulting in exponentially bigger threats over time.

Peter Senge believes that problems can become compounded in diverse teams, as each team member carries simple models focusing on different parts of the problem. This makes it virtually impossible for a shared picture of the system as a whole to emerge in normal conversation, unless there is a shared language for describing complexity. He also notes that although there are some widely used languages of business, only one is universal—financial accounting—and none of the languages deal well with dynamic complexity. Senge proposes systems archetypes as a powerful basis for developing a language to deal with complexity, leading to more conversations about underlying structures and leverage, and fewer conversations about crises and short-term 'fixes'.[7]

Advocates of systems archetypes see them as having two benefits in conversations about complex and potentially conflictual issues:

→ the common language makes communication easier
→ systems archetypes can help make the conversation more objective as they focus the discussion on 'the structure', the systemic forces at play, rather than on personalities or leadership styles.

Difficult questions can therefore be raised in a way that carries less or no innuendo or implied criticism.

18.5 Collaboration and cross-fertilisation in research, innovation and problem solving

The increasing complexity of knowledge makes collaboration vital, especially the inter-disciplinary collaboration that results in cross-fertilisation. Such cross-fertilisation may occur across academic disciplines, across sports or arts, between left- and right-brain thinkers, engineers and marketers, public and private sector, or commercial and not-for-profit sectors.

Today, major companies are building their capital through the global collaboration made possible by the internet. Some of the principles applied by companies as they collaborate globally on research, innovation and problem-solving can be used by the individual to innovate and solve problems.

Collaboration Principle 1: Trust makes collaboration cost-effective

Philip Evans and Bob Wolf of the Boston Consulting Group have noted that transaction costs, typically related to the negotiation and enforcement of transactions, cause a high proportion of potential value-generating ideas to be ignored. Alarmingly, they have estimated that 'in the year 2000, cash transaction costs alone accounted for over half the non-governmental US GDP!'—suggesting that people and businesses in the US spend more money on negotiating and enforcing transactions than they spend on fulfilling them.[8]

Evans and Wolf cite Toyota as a wonderful precedent where agreements are enforced by mutual trust, thereby lowering transaction costs. Toyota's component suppliers share process knowledge daily, trusting the company not to use it to push prices down. Information about problems and solutions is also shared widely, frequently and in small increments, consistent with the Toyota philosophy of continuous improvement comprising a thousand small collaborations. Evans and Wolf note the estimate by Brigham Young University's Professor Jeffrey Dyer that transaction costs between Toyota and its tier one suppliers are one-eighth those at General Motors—a disparity he attributes to different levels of trust.

Evans and Wolf argue that organisations that can work more on trust rather than legal contract can reduce transaction costs and thereby afford to embrace more of the potentially value-generating ideas that are otherwise rejected. This enables them to place 'a hundred small bets instead of a few big ones'.

Collaboration Principle 2: Transparency leads to a virtuous circle

The benefits of collaboration have best been demonstrated over the centuries in the sciences, where the tradition of open publication enables new work to be challenged, rejected or confirmed, used and enhanced. This leads to the identification of new, often inter-disciplinary problems and solutions, followed by further open publication and the creation of an ongoing virtuous circle.

A classic example of this collaboration is the successful development of the Linux open-source operating system. Linux calls to mind that open scientific heritage, being free for use or modification, provided users in turn make their changes freely available to others. The Linux operating system has been built up by the collaboration of thousands of people since the release of the first simple version by Linus Torvalds in 1991. Some of those people operate as independent agents, many anonymously; others work with affiliations with major organisations such as BMW, IBM or Intel. According to Evans and Wolf, more servers run on Linux than on any other operating system.

Collaboration Principle 3: Easy, low-cost communications

The success of Linux demonstrates the power of transparency combining with low-cost modern communications. This phenomenon is described in Don Tapscott and Anthony Williams's *Wikinomics: How Mass Collaboration Changes Everything*, published in 2006. Their stories range from Wikipedia, MySpace and Skype to that of Canada's Goldcorp Inc. The key to Goldcorp's growth from a $100 million company to a $9 billion company was an astute decision to disclose on the internet all the company's proprietary data about its exploration leases and to offer substantial prize money for on-line prospectors who came up with the best methods and estimates of recoverable gold.

You may think a direct analogy between you as a collaborator and Linux or Toyota is a little far-fetched. Not necessarily so. If you are to collaborate successfully you need to be clear, not only about what you can contribute or benefit from, but that your guiding principles make you an effective and low transaction-cost collaborator. If you are trusted, easy to work with and generous in sharing your thoughts, you are likely to be a sought-after collaborator and enjoy a range of collaboration opportunities.

18.6   Building bridges between people

In some conversations, a person or a group of people can play an important role as bridges between other parties, helping to achieve things that would be impossible or unlikely in their absence. They can act as:
→ mediators
→ marriage guidance counsellors

→ interpreters, whether between languages or between technical
jargon and plain language

→ complete outsiders who know nothing about a married couple
and, by chance, introduce subjects or issues that would never
arise in the couple's normal conversation

→ an outside presenter invited to raise issues that will challenge
the thinking of a normally closed group such as a board or
management team

→ clients who are promoters (per Reichheld's concept in 15.6),
being invited by a business to rub shoulders with target
clients and thereby provide social proof of the quality of the
company's services

→ connectors in a business between the male and female internal
networks that might otherwise be somewhat segregated. These
people could have a particularly important impact in changing
attitudes to gender diversity.

Because of their position, objectivity or independence, some people or
organisations are uniquely able to engage with all parties in a dispute. They
are then well placed not only to contribute some thought leadership, but
also to get others talking more constructively. This role is often played by
think tanks or NGOs. The role of NGOs was highlighted by the founder
of Body Shop, the late Dame Anita Roddick, when discussing the World
Trade Organization talks held in Seattle in 1999. Amidst the riots and
protests, NGOs were the only party who could build bridges to talk to
politicians, corporations, campaigners and protesters.[9]

Organisations with which I am associated have regularly played
similar roles in two contentious areas in Australia where it is vital
to get academia, the government and public service and business
talking—environmental issues such as water, timber and climate
change, and industry policy issues such as innovation and free trade.

The significant opportunity is to be aware when your group would
benefit from having someone else present to act as a bridge:

→ to create opportunities for enhanced communications or
changed attitudes

→ to assist in presenting or endorsing your case

→ as an additional source of ideas options

→ to build dialogue in order to find a bigger picture than the
solutions proffered by individual vested interests (or, as a
fallback, solutions that all parties can live with).

Over to you…

Reflection

- In general, do you value collaboration and cross-fertilisation?
- When seeking others' input, do you actively seek independence and diversity of background or do you seek out a single expert? Do you seek out people smarter or better than yourself? Or experts from a single field?
- Was the last collaborative session you attended effective? How could it have been improved?
- When and why do you find yourself or others becoming defensive in a team environment? What can you do to change that?
- Do you and your team understand what learning is about, and how you intend to achieve it? Does your team have a shared picture of the whole, so communication is clear? If not, how do you achieve that?

Action

- Analyse the negative impacts of thinking that you have to be seen to know everything and how significant these impacts are (appendix B9 may prompt further thoughts).
- Analyse the benefits of being an effective collaborator and how significant these benefits are (appendix B11 may prompt further thoughts).
- Identify what additional diverse sources of information or ideas could be of value to you or your team. Plan to access the most significant.
- Identify ways in which your cost-effectiveness as a collaborator can be enhanced.
- Identify a situation in which a bridge would be of value to you in resolving differences or progressing an opportunity.
- Next time you identify a prevailing mood, push against it by playing devil's advocate to some of the core assumptions others are making.
- Next time you're involved in a discussion leading towards a decision, ask yourself whether the discussion should be preceded by dialogue to ensure the issues are deeply and objectively explored, whether additional sources of information or ideas should be sought, and whether any external input has been independent or diverse.

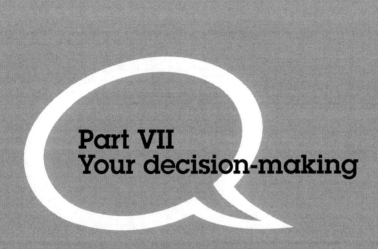

Part VII
Your decision-making

In 6.3 I noted that there are few more important life assets than the ability to make good decisions. This maxim is emphasised by Kamal Sarma in his book *Mental Resilience:*

> It is in our moments of decision where we add or destroy value to ourselves and people around us ... The most important factor in effective and sound decision-making is clarity of mind.[1]

Yet, as is the case with conversation and relationship-building, we are formally taught little or nothing about decision-making, but are expected to be able to make good decisions naturally and competently.

My five final principles are devoted to decision-making:

→ *Principle 19:* You can identify many of the big points in life and thereby set yourself up to make better decisions.

→ *Principle 20:* Achieving your goals will be easier and more likely to happen if your decisions help to maximise the impact of your successes.

➡ *Principle 21:* Achieving your goals will be easier and more likely to happen if your decisions help to minimise the impact of your failures.

➡ *Principle 22:* You can get better at making decisions and thereby make both the uncertainty and serendipity of the world work better for you.

➡ *Principle 23:* The more capable you are at accessing, objectively assessing, and reframing relevant information, the more soundly based your decisions will be.

In writing about decision-making, I have focused on those areas where the lessons from the great investors have significant relevance. The many other dimensions surrounding decision-making, such as how to set yourself up to make sound decisions or how to avoid making unsound ones, are covered by many other authors elsewhere.

Principle 19
Big points

You can identify many of the big points in life and thereby set yourself up to make better decisions.

As you go through life, there are thousands of little forks in the road, and a few really big forks—those moments of reckoning, moments of truth.

—Lee Iacocca[1]

It's the big points that separate the sporting greats from the journeymen. How the sporting elite play those big points is obviously important, but more subtly yet equally important is how they create or spot those big points, and how they respond after attaining them.

Some big points in sport are obvious in advance—tennis tie-breaks, soccer penalty shootouts, sailing starts, and the third and final jumps by pole-vaulters. At other times, a big point might occur without warning, the result of the unrelenting pressure applied by one of the contestants. Some big points might pass unnoticed by everyone but one of the contestants or the most experienced commentator.

Unlike most of life's big points, your sporting opponent aims to make it as hard as possible for you to win that point—like Rafael Nadal's remarkable performance in allowing Roger Federer to win only one of 17 break points in their 2007 French Open final, and only one of 12 in their 2008 Wimbledon final. Nadal won both matches.

For many of your big points in life, you have no opponent but yourself. Certainly, you don't have an opponent as mentally and physically tough as Rafael Nadal. In fact, you probably have many people willing, even keen, to help you, if you're prepared to ask.

19.1   Identifying the big points in life

So what are the big points in life—those moments of truth, of opportunity, of crisis, of disaster, of transformation? Some of life's big points play through in seconds or minutes; others can play out over weeks or months. Being able to identify these big points in advance is a major asset, as is being able to lift your game to play them well. Some big points have their subtleties, and you may only be able to recognise them after the event. In fact, their full significance can sometimes take years to unravel, by which stage their impact can be enormous.

Some generic big points in life include the following:

The morally tough points

→ When you've really screwed up, as we all do from time to time: the decision to acknowledge it, deal with it, learn from it and move on—or risk digging a bigger hole.

→ When you're aware of something significantly unacceptable that someone else has done: the decision to report it, deal with it and move on ('to whistleblow'), or the decision to sweep it under the carpet. Such damaging, potentially long-term situations could involve domestic violence, sexual abuse in religious institutions, corporate malfeasance, professional misconduct, manipulation of research results or failures in health institutions.

When we are faced with these morally tough points in life, doing nothing and hoping that no-one finds out may appeal. The whistleblowing dilemma is particularly challenging. If you read stories about whistleblowers around the world, as I once did in a study I carried out on behalf of the actuarial profession, you could be very tempted to take the easy way out. To quote Professor Fred Alford, author of *Whistleblowers: Broken Lives and Organisational Power*: 'The average whistleblower of my experience is a 55-year-old nuclear engineer working behind the counter at Radio Shack. Divorced and in debt to his lawyers, he lives in a two-room rented apartment'.[2]

The strategically tough points

→ *Where a changing world means the past is not a sound guide to the future,* and those who view the world historically are at odds with those who see signals of change. For example, you're convinced that the early signs of a downturn are evident, but your business partner is convinced that you should be borrowing more and investing more into your business to buy out a competitor or take on more people.

→ *The big decisions that can't easily be reversed if they turn out wrong:* you could choose an approach that keeps your options open and delays making a decision, but this will require you to overcome the desire to release the tension by just getting the decision made. For example, making the decision to marry if your partner is putting pressure on you to tie the knot, or making the decision to have children if your partner wants kids but you're not sure.

The opportunity to change a vicious circle into a virtuous circle

In 3.2 I contrasted virtuous and vicious circles in the context of work reporting relationships and performance reviews. Any opportunity to convert a vicious circle into a virtuous one is a big point in life, as is any decision that risks doing the reverse.

An example of a vicious circle in personal development is when someone experiences reading difficulties, causing poor understanding, slow learning and behavioural problems. Like many boys, my son Stuart had no interest in reading when he was young. He did, however, have a vast interest in sailing. When Stuart was about seven, Tori and I bought him a sailing magazine, which he read cover to cover. He's since read every monthly edition of that magazine and still has them all. That one decision to buy a sailing magazine led to Stuart seeing the rewards of reading, reversing a vicious circle.

In an example from the big league of vicious circles, we now know that Ken Lay and the Enron Audit Committee confronted accounting irregularities as far back as 1986–87 and didn't deal with them.[3] That decision probably set the tone for the next 15 years and was arguably the seed of the world's then largest corporate collapse. Lay and his board never managed to reverse that vicious circle.

On a more modest but far more impressive scale, microfinance is offering tens of millions of women in developing countries the opportunity to change a vicious circle of indebtedness to moneylenders into a virtuous circle of entrepreneurship. Microfinance offers loans as small as US$50 or US$100, sufficient to repay the moneylender. The failure rates on these loans to former 'banking untouchables' are lower than for the more traditional customers of the major banks, due to a range of factors including peer support and peer pressure.

For these women, an approach from a microfinancier is one of the biggest points in their lives. However, the family, social and religious pressures and related self-worth issues have made these decisions very difficult for many. Microfinance inventor Muhammad Yunus, winner of the 2006 Nobel Peace Prize, tells the story of Hajeera, who told him:

> All my life I was told I was no good, that I brought only misery on my parents because I was a woman and my family could not pay for my dowry. Many times I heard my mother say she should have killed me at birth. I did not feel I was worthy of a loan, or that I could ever repay it.[4]

Supported by her peer group, Hajeera took on a loan of US$50, which she used to buy a calf and a rice paddy. She paid off the loan in under a year, and took on a second to rent some land and grow bananas. Today she owns a rice field, goats, ducks and chickens, and her husband no longer speaks of divorcing her.

Hajeera's brave decision in the face of major cultural and family tensions, transformed a vicious circle into a virtuous one. While her home and circumstances may be very different from yours, her story is a healthy reminder that the pressures and opportunities surrounding your major financial decisions can also build your human and social capital.

The big deal

Because of its implications for your financial capital, any big dollar transaction is a big point for you, whether it be Hajeera's US$50 loan, your first home loan or the US$20 billion-plus buyout of RJR Nabisco, described in Bryan Burrough and John Helyar's 1990 book *Barbarians at the Gate*. The same applies to negotiations with a major customer or with your first landlord.

The missing link

With this last link in the chain in place, your project or ambition flies; without this final link, it falls over. The leverage inherent in the following examples is enormous:

- → the final piece of funding for your new business
- → attracting that key employee, champion or partner who brings the remaining missing skills to your business
- → the bridge to your new career; for example, the foundation client for your new business or your first role as a non-executive director after leaving a full-time career.

The first meeting

It can take a lot of work to reverse first impressions. Hence, that first meeting with anyone of significance in your life or career is a big point.

Periods of change and uncertainty, stress and invigoration

Life brings many periods of change and uncertainty—your first child, added work responsibilities or a new boss, a new overseas posting (though surprisingly, the return from an overseas posting is generally more stressful than the cultural challenges of the posting itself), retrenchment, injury or retirement, whether from companies, professions or sports.

These big points in life are not over in a day or two. They merit clear strategies to maximise your invigoration and minimise your stress. You may be able to use the adrenaline of the situation to lift your effectiveness all round, but you can be sure that:

- → these periods of change and uncertainty will be episodes of significant personal growth

→ you will come through them more strongly if you have confidants or mentors to share them with, especially if they have been there before.

Having spent four years successfully defending a $760 million shareholder class action against me and my fellow directors of insurer GIO Australia, I have some personal experience in the subject of change and uncertainty. The board recommended to shareholders that they reject a hostile takeover bid from AMP; at that time it was Australia's largest financial services takeover. AMP initially acquired control of 57 per cent of the capital, and the 43 per cent who stayed in as minorities were later bought out by AMP for a lower share price, allegedly as a result of significant losses in GIO's reinsurance business.

More than 30 years earlier, my father had defended something remarkably similar and equally high profile. I had clear memories from my youth of my father's resilience through those personally, professionally and financially difficult times. I was thus in the fortunate position of having someone to call on who had been there before, and who was also an expert in the technicalities of the issues on which our case would be decided. Having the opportunity to talk through all the steps that led to our recommendation to shareholders increased my confidence in the appropriateness of that advice, given the information then available to us.

Fortunately, I had a number of other business interests in my life at the time and it was very significant for me that my colleagues on other boards gave me strong support and encouraged my continued association with their companies. Nevertheless, the outcome for me was four years during which my career was somewhat on hold—leaving considerable time for reflection.

Of the many valuable lessons I learned during that time, the most memorable story related to one of the key themes of this book: the importance of keeping an open mind about whose input will be valuable.

In early 2000 I helped raise capital for an internet software company. The youngest principal, Adam Ginsburg, had a ponytail and regularly wore a T-shirt and jeans to work, and occasionally no shoes—often he came into the office straight from the surf. In the internet software world, this came as no surprise. What did surprise me, however, was when Adam arrived for a vital meeting accompanied by his German shepherd, Billy. This magnificent animal, wearing a studded collar and leash, sat under the table at my feet for over two hours as we pored over the documentation with our lawyers.

Later, with the capital raising completed, an independent chairperson was required. One of the founders suggested me, and the private equity backers were happy to take me on. The devil's advocacy was posed by Adam, who had the good judgement to ask: 'What if this GIO thing goes the wrong way for Ian? What might be the implications for our company — especially as AMP is our largest client?' After some discussion, I did become the chairperson of that company. Throughout my time as chairperson, until IBM bought the company, Adam was an inspiration to me in his work ethic, his thinking and his judgement. Working with him was a great lesson about keeping an open mind about people, especially other generations in this ever-changing world.

Realising it's okay to be yourself and to strive for what you want

Young adults often wonder who they are trying to please — their parents or themselves? In due course, they realise that it's okay to be themselves and to strive for what *they* want in life — and not what anyone else wants. There can be few bigger points in life, and for some people it can be a long time coming.

The realisation that it's okay to strive for what you want can be quite emotional, and like all big points in your personal growth, it deserves significant reflection after the event. Why didn't I see it coming? What led to it? How long have I really felt like this? Why did it take so long to realise? What changes as a result? Who should I talk to about it?

19.2 Decisions where all your eggs will be in one basket

Investors can spread their risk by holding 10 or 50 stocks; or 20 stocks, two properties, a bond portfolio and some cash for good measure. When it comes to selecting your life partner, home, profession, employer or business, however, you don't have this luxury. Selecting one option will preclude all others for a significant period. There are two critical implications for the risk involved in making such decisions:

→ *Risk of failure*: because you can't hedge your bets, there is a significant risk of failure in the single option you choose, as shown in the failure rates of new businesses and marriages.

→ *Opportunity cost*: by taking one option, you are cut off from other options that may have had significantly brighter outcomes.

Such life-building choices are further complicated by the potentially substantial transaction costs required to reverse or change such decisions.

Only change baskets if the new one is materially better than the current one

When I was looking for my first job, I met with an actuary friend John Corbett. He was unusual among actuaries of his generation in that he had very successfully changed jobs a number of times. When I asked him if there was any secret behind this, John replied with a story that is potentially valuable for anyone considering a job or career change:

> *I never left job A for job B unless I felt that job A was going about as well as it could, and therefore provided an excellent benchmark against which to assess the prospects of job B, and I also felt B still exceeded A by a healthy margin.*

John's story incorporated two fundamental principles of investment management, which are also great tools in life: benchmarking (see Wealth Insert 17A) and having a margin of safety (Wealth Insert 19A).

Wealth Insert 19A: Benjamin Graham's 'margin of safety' concept

Many of the great lessons of investment come from the father of 'value investment', Benjamin Graham. The first edition of Graham's investment tome *Security Analysis* was published in 1934. As a professor at Columbia University, he was the teacher or mentor of many of America's most successful investors, including Warren Buffett. For over 50 years, Buffett has followed a number of Graham's core principles, including the 'margin of safety' concept.

Only a few paragraphs of the 700 pages contained in *Security Analysis* are explicitly devoted to this principle, yet Benjamin Graham describes the presence of a measurable margin of safety as 'the touchstone or distinguishing feature' of true investment — 'the underlying element in every investment operation and … the most fundamental quantitative concept in security analysis'.[5]

In the case of a common stock, the margin of safety would be the excess of the intrinsic value of the stock (as calculated by the analyst) over its market price — sufficient to absorb any unfavourable future developments yet still permit a satisfactory outcome for the investor.

Optimise the current basket so it is a valid benchmark

In addition to its emphasis on having a 'margin of safety' in such decisions, John Corbett's story implicitly poses the question: what can I do to make my current job go as well as it can? The same question can also apply to your home, business or life partner, so it really is a valid benchmark. So, when you are putting all your eggs into one relationship, career or job basket, keep asking yourself, 'What can I do or influence to make the current basket stronger?' Relevant to this is Marcus Buckingham's 'strengths movement' concept:

> Before you make this final decision [to change jobs], give your current role a chance. It may be that the perfect role for you is hiding in plain sight, beneath layer upon layer of the wrong activities. With a little discipline, you may be able to peel away these activities, and, week by week, reveal a role that plays to your strengths.[6]

This characteristic of adding value distinguishes strategic investors from portfolio investors. The strategic investor, such as a private equity fund, will forever be looking for opportunities to add value by applying any distinctive competence they bring.

This can also apply to career opportunities, as a job vacancy may present different opportunities for different individuals. This is most obviously the case for CEO positions, as the successful candidate has the opportunity to mould or totally rewrite the organisation's strategic direction. For those with initiative, however, the opportunity and challenge to identify how value can be added, and then influence the organisation to do so, can apply at many levels in a company.

Minimising opportunity loss in all-eggs-in-one-basket decisions

There is another concept widely applied by private equity investors that is highly transferable to all-eggs-in-one-basket decisions.

Imagine you are looking to buy your first home. Once you commit to purchasing a particular house, you will be unable to buy the better and cheaper house that you see the following day. Hence, opportunity cost is a major potential issue in making such a decision. Why hadn't you seen the other house before? Perhaps because you hadn't thought through how best to maximise your 'qualified deal flow' in advance of your decision time.

Wealth Insert 19B: qualified deal flow

An investor's lifeblood is their access to investment opportunities ('deal flow'), in particular the types of deals that potentially meet their investment criteria ('qualified deal flow').

The private equity funds that have been major participants in the takeovers of recent years raise their funds from big financial institutions and pension funds. When doing so, a significant part of their pitch is the demonstration of their past performance, the source of that performance and thus their qualified deal flow. In anticipation of their next fund-raising roadshow, and as a healthy business practice, they measure and analyse their deal flow—the deals looked at, the deals worked on in detail, the deals bid on and the deals closed.

The nightmare for such private equity funds is too much money chasing too few deals; their heaven is plenty of well-qualified deals and little competition for them. Most valuable are the well-qualified deals that have not been widely shopped.

So, if you're looking for a new profession, job, business, home or partner, the higher your rate of qualified deal flow shortly before your decision time, the greater your choice and the more you will learn from examining the alternative options. Hopefully, as a result, the greater your chance of making the right selection and the lower your risk of opportunity loss. Also, if negotiation is involved, the more options you will have and hence the stronger your negotiating position will be.

Taking an objective view after your decision

So you've made the big decision and changed jobs. Will you have an objective view of your new employer, work environment, boss and job from the start—or will you fall prey to confirmation bias?

Wealth Insert 19C: confirmation bias

Confirmation bias refers to the human tendency to remember, notice or seek things that confirm our decisions or theories, and to forget, not notice or avoid things that contradict them. This is demonstrated in many dimensions of life, including having higher confidence in bets after they are placed rather than immediately before,[7] or hoping to confirm that we've bought a bargain by looking for the same product in a more expensive store.

As Michael J Mauboussin notes:

> After making a decision, we feel both internal and external pressure to remain consistent to that view, even if subsequent evidence questions the validity of the initial decision ... So an investor who has taken a position in a particular stock, recommended it publicly, or encouraged colleagues to participate, will feel the need to stick with the call. Related to this tendency is the confirmation trap: post-decision openness to confirming data coupled with disavowal or denial of disconfirming data.[8]

A study of employee engagement data in companies revealed a high level of engagement in the first six months or so of employment, followed by declining engagement and significant turnover in the six- to 12-month period. Is this a reflection of employees falling into the confirmation trap—initially ignoring issues that might suggest they have made a bad decision and thereby deferring the discussion of issues that should be dealt with? This can be a disappointing lost opportunity:

→ for the employee—delaying making improvements in their own position or engagement

→ for the company—after all, who better than someone with fresh eyes to question the status quo and identify opportunities for improvement?

Mauboussin suggests a useful technique to mitigate confirmation bias: acknowledge upfront the multiple scenarios that are possible. You are thereby psychologically prepared for the scenario that ultimately emerges, and well placed to adjust your views accordingly rather than remaining blindly committed to your initial decision.

This approach can be applied when making a choice between two candidates. Mauboussin suggests that such yes/no decisions aren't black and white. If we identify the candidates' shades of grey (their relative strengths and weaknesses) at the time of decision-making, and retain them for ongoing reference, we are then better placed to view future performance on an informed and more objective basis. For example, having chosen Fred, knowing that he is strong in marketing but not in budgeting, you need to keep this information in the front of your mind as you invest in his development and assess his performance. With this perspective, you will be more objective and less prone to confirmation bias.

Choosing where you live

Fundamental to your life is the country in which you live. As Warren Buffett said: 'If you stick me down in the middle of Bangladesh or Peru, you'll find out how much this talent is going to produce in the wrong kind of soil'.[9]

According to a 2007 World Bank study, *Where is the Wealth of Nations?*, the bottom line is that 'rich countries are largely rich because of the skills of their populations and the quality of the institutions supporting economic activity'—important components of human capital and social capital respectively. According to the World Bank's analysis, 57 per cent of a country's intangible economic capital is determined by the efficiency of its judicial system and governance, and 36 per cent by its education system.[10] Thus your country of domicile is a major life asset or liability. You can't choose your birthplace but you can, within the constraints of immigration laws, elect to change it once you are an adult.

Over to you ...

Reflection

- Are you alert to identifying the big points in your life? Do you typically have a strategy for dealing with them or are you normally caught on the hop?
- Do you typically find that periods of uncertainty or crisis bring learning and personal growth?
- How did you approach the last big point where your decision meant putting all your eggs in one basket?
- After any of your recent big decisions, have you demonstrated some confirmation bias? If so, how? What impact did your confirmation bias have?

Action

- Look for the big points in life.
- Think of a moral or strategic decision you are familiar with and analyse how you would have dealt with it if the decision had been yours. Review what that tells you about yourself.
- When you next meet someone new, aim to create a positive first impression—whether by the clothes you wear, your punctuality or your warmth and enthusiasm.
- When you have to make a decision that will close off other opportunities, be sure there are as many choices available as possible.
- Keep on the lookout for an opportunity to convert a vicious circle into a virtuous one, or an adversity into an advantage.

Principle 20
Success
maximisation

**Achieving your goals will be easier
and more likely to happen if your
decisions help to maximise the
impact of your successes.**

Too much of a good thing can be wonderful.

—Mae West

In 7.4 I demonstrated that very high growth rates in human and social capital are achievable and, if sustained, will lead to a vast increase in Life Capital.

So, what are the steps that lead to this vast increase in Life Capital? Such an increase must be the result of many positive steps—perhaps the majority of them small steps, compounding with the occasional big ones!

20.1   One life-enriching conversation per month

The island of Manhattan's increase in land value from US$24 to US$200 billion over 380 years is an inspiring example of the power of compounding benefits (see Wealth Insert 3A). The land value compounded 380 times, increasing by an average 6.2 per cent on each occasion.

We don't have 380 years to play with in our lifetime, but most of us do have 380 months in our career. Imagine if we could achieve the compounding benefits of one seriously life-enriching conversation per month for 380 months! The combined impact would be enormous.

I believe that one life-enriching conversation per month is a realistic challenge, and many of the resulting increments could be much greater than 6.2 per cent. For example, meeting your life partner, receiving an introduction to a major network of people, discovering an innovative business model, reading a life-changing book, taking a significant step in self-awareness arising from feedback, meeting a new mentor or having a new life vision.

As I explained when describing John's search for a new job in 12.2, 'if you can have five jobs to choose from rather than just one, the fit of the ultimate job is likely to be 10 to 50 per cent better—perhaps more'. This falls into the category of life's big points, and at such a time you may need to have several potentially life-enriching conversations in one month to maximise your choice, your information and, thereby, the upside of the particular opportunity you decide to pursue.

A classic example is the choice of which school, college or university to attend if you have gained the right to admission to a number of institutions that appear to meet your most basic criteria. You will be better informed to make this challenging decision if you seek a number of conversations with friends, teachers, counsellors and students who have attended those institutions, as well as visiting the institutions in question.

20.2   Maximising the big increments

The frequency and potential impact of special situations or insights will vary widely from person to person, and their benefit will depend on the extent to which you back the opportunity. You will:

→ achieve the greatest positive impact if you have the skills and judgement to pick those winners, and the courage, discipline, time and energy to back them seriously over a long period of time

→ suffer the greatest potential negative impact if you lack the skills or judgement but still bet heavily

→ be like the majority of people and probably generate an average result if you back many different opportunities but without making a substantial commitment to any of them.

Three investment lessons provide valuable inspiration for building your Life Capital:

→ be very selective (see Wealth Insert 20A)

→ when the right opportunity arises, really commit (Wealth Insert 20B)

→ sell losers and hold winners (Wealth Insert 20C).

It is interesting that most people take the opposite approach to these three principles, both in their investments and in many other areas of their lives.

Wealth Insert 20A: Warren Buffett's 'If you were only allowed 20 investments in your lifetime'

According to Charlie Munger, most of Berkshire Hathaway's accumulated tens of billions can be accounted for by Buffett and Munger's top 10 insights. If they don't have significant insights, they don't invest.

Warren Buffett draws the analogy of a ticket with only 20 slots in it, representing the number of investments you are allowed in a lifetime. Charlie Munger quotes Buffett:

> Under those rules, you'll really think carefully about what you did and you'd be forced to load up on what you'd really thought about. So you'd do so much better.[1]

This concept, Munger says, seems perfectly obvious to him and to Buffett, but it certainly isn't conventional wisdom.

Wealth Insert 20B: up the ante when the pricing or odds are favourable

Other than index managers, whose mandate is to track an index like the Dow Jones Industrial Average, most professional investment managers aim to bet more heavily on the stocks they know well and have low pricing relative to their fundamental value.

However, the parameters for 'betting more heavily' may vary widely between managers, influenced by their investment philosophies and management style, and their representations to investors.

The more heavily they back the situations they find compelling, the greater the skill test and the more volatile their performances are likely to be — potentially resulting in underperformance or outperformance versus the market index or their peers.

In his book *More Than You Know*, investment strategist Michael J. Mauboussin reviews thinking in horserace gaming, blackjack gambling and investing — all probabilistic exercises. He notes that people with long-term success in these fields share some common approaches:

- they focus on a specific game or circle of competence and learn the ins and outs, thereby developing relative expertise
- they examine many situations
- even for the competent, favourable situations don't appear very often because the market price for bets or shares is usually pretty accurate
- hence they up the ante when the pricing is favourable.

Mauboussin observes that investing, where you need not play if the odds or expected value are unattractive, is much more favourable than casino games, in which you must bet every time in order to play.[2]

Wealth Insert 20C: loss aversion — you can go broke taking profits

Daniel Kahneman and Amos Tversky, pioneers of behavioural economics and finance, examined the human behaviours that can lead to irrational decision-making. One of these is loss-aversion. They found that, for the average person, a loss has more than twice the impact of an equal gain. Consequently, investors tend to make investments offering a higher probability of a win rather than those offering a higher expected return — the equivalent in horseracing of backing favourites more often than outsiders, even if the odds offered on the outsiders are better value than the odds on the favourites.

The related consequences of loss-aversion are the tendencies:

- to sell winners to crystallise a gain
- to hold on to losers in the hope they come good and a loss can be avoided.

These tendencies are dangerous for investors. In fact, Peter Lynch sees them as being 'about as sensible as pulling out the flowers and watering the weeds'.[3]

In 7.1 I discussed Philip Fisher's concept of investing in the life earnings of three of your classmates on graduation day. Fisher asks whether, 10 years later, you would consider selling out one of your classmates who has won promotion after promotion in a major corporation because you were offered a 600 per cent return on your original investment. Surely not!

Fisher sees the dislike of taking a loss, even a small loss, as:

> Just as illogical as it is natural. If the real object of common stock investment is the making of a gain of a great many hundreds percent over a period of years, the difference between, say, a 20 per cent loss or a 5 per cent profit becomes a comparatively insignificant matter. What matters is not whether a loss occasionally occurs. What does matter is whether worthwhile profits so often fail to materialise that the skill of the investor...must be questioned.[4]

> ### Wealth Insert 20C (cont'd): loss aversion — you can go broke taking profits
>
> In the context of opportunity loss, this could be restated as: if an investor regularly suffers significant opportunity loss because they like taking profits and dislike taking losses, then their skill must be questioned.
>
> In New Market Wizards, Jack Schwager profiled a number of great traders. Many commented on the dangers of selling winners and holding on to losers — dangers for both performance and trading psychology. Money-manager Stanley Druckenmiller commented in respect of trader George Soros:
>
> > *I've learned many things from him, but perhaps the most significant is that it's not whether you're right or wrong that is important, but how much money you make when you're right and how much you lose when you're wrong... Soros is the best loss taker I've ever seen. He doesn't care whether he wins or loses on a trade. If a trade doesn't work, he's confident enough about his ability to win on other trades that he can easily walk away from the position.[5]*

20.3 Focus on your plans

In Wealth Insert 5C I introduced the fundamental principle of the circle of competence. This is well demonstrated by the three 'investments' I made during a sporting trip to the US at the end of my first year of university: a dozen Wilson tennis racquets, 100 stainless-steel rings and a game of roulette.

I knew quite a lot about tennis racquets and made a healthy profit buying them wholesale in Miami and then selling them in both Miami and Costa Rica. On closer analysis, however, the apparent success of the first of my three 'investments' was really a failure. Unwarranted confidence from that success encouraged me to contemplate the two loss-making entrepreneurial activities that followed. So the lesson I learned here was: one profitable initiative does not make an entrepreneurial genius.

I never managed to sell the stainless-steel rings I bought in Costa Rica, as I knew nothing about jewellery and consequently bought badly; fortunately, my daughters took a liking to a few of the rings that had horseshoes on them. The cost of my failed investment was US$100. The lesson I learned here was: invest only when you understand the investment. The value of that lesson is so immeasurable that I keep the rings near my desk to this day as a reminder—and I do need regular reminding.

And the game of roulette in Freeport, Bahamas? Arguably, the theory of roulette wheels was familiar territory for me, having excelled in probability 101 at university only weeks before! Alas, my dabbling in gambling led to another failure and the loss of US$125. The first lesson I learned here was: you don't get rich at a casino. The second, and more important lesson: ignorance is when you don't know any better; stupidity is when you do know better but you don't back your knowledge. In other words, unless you're Albert Einstein, don't expect to succeed by flying in the face of fundamental scientific principles you know to be true!

Behind this little story of my early investment experiences, reinforcing the concepts of Circles of Competence, was a far more significant question: why was I wasting my time and nervous energy on racquets, rings and roulette when I was in the US representing my country playing tennis? It was something I had worked towards for almost a decade, and it warranted my undiverted focus.

The answer: I was an unchaperoned, unworldly 18 year old tasting the pleasures of overseas travel for the first time and travelling with a group of fellow sportsmen. I had all kinds of great new experiences on this trip but most of them revealed my considerable ability to have a good time and limited ability to focus on the main event.

The key lesson here is: focus on your plans! As Warren Buffett said: 'If we get on the main line, New York to Chicago, we don't get off at Altoona and take side trips'.[6]

Over to you...

Reflection

- Is one life-enriching conversation per month a realistic challenge for you?
- What events, influences or relationships have recently had a positive impact on your Life Capital? Are they still having a material positive impact? Do you believe they will continue to do so?
- Are the majority of your life-enriching conversations planned or serendipitous?
- In life, do you sell losers and hold winners? Or do you hold losers and sell winners?
- Are you good at remaining focused?

Action

- Develop and implement a strategy to increase the number of life-enriching conversations you have, and their impact.
- Identify and implement three things you can do better to improve your focus on your main game.

Principle 21
Minimise the negative impact of your failures

Achieving your goals will be easier and more likely to happen if your decisions help to minimise the impact of your failures.

Resiliency (not perfection) is the signature of greatness, be it in a person, an organisation or a nation.

— Jim Collins and Jerry Porras[1]

Your life, like mine, will inevitably include mistakes, bad luck and setbacks along the way. The challenge is to minimise their negative impacts (the focus of this principle) and, through learning, to maximise the positive benefits we take from them (the focus of 17.3).

You have many opportunities to minimise the negatives:

→ as you set yourself up before the key decision
→ as you keep an eye out for an emerging failure
→ after a failure.

21.1 Setting yourself up for good decisions

You can do a lot to set yourself up to succeed rather than fail, or at least to minimise the downside of failure, by applying two of Benjamin Graham's core principles: the 'margin of safety' (see Wealth Insert 19A) and 'thorough analysis distinguishes investment from speculation' (Wealth Insert 21A).

Wealth Insert 21A: thorough analysis distinguishes investment from speculation

Benjamin Graham considered the 'first and most basic step' in building a portfolio of securities to be to 'distinguish clearly between investment and speculation'. He defined an investment operation as one which 'upon *thorough analysis* promises safety of principal and a satisfactory return. Operations not meeting these requirements are speculative'.[2]

Your 'margin of safety' should reflect your confidence in your predictions

Consciously or unconsciously, most of the key decisions we take in life are based on assumptions or predictions about the future. How big a 'margin of safety' you might allow in a key decision would logically depend on your level of confidence in your related predictions of the future.

Predicting the future — many potential sources of failure

Imagine that you need a bigger house for your growing family, and extending your current home isn't an option. You have seen a suitable house with great development potential, so you make some predictions regarding:

→ the time delay required for the sale of your home and the expected sale price
→ your future employment and your future income

→ the costs of redeveloping the new house, the amount you will be borrowing and the interest costs.

Based on these predictions, you decide to buy the new house before selling the old one, and negotiate a six-month deferred settlement on the purchase—a margin of safety to give you some flexibility.

When you make predictions such as these, there are many potential sources of failure, incisively described in 'The scandal of prediction', chapter 10 of Nassim Nicholas Taleb's *The Black Swan: The Impact of the Highly Improbable*.

A number of Taleb's potential sources of prediction failure might be relevant to your strategy of buying a new house for redevelopment and selling your current home:[3]

→ *A major unpredictable surprise that has a big impact.* A change of government and significant interest rate increases cause property prices to fall. The only offers you receive for your existing home are well below your forecast sale price.

→ *The tendency not to reverse opinions you already have ('belief perseverance') and its sibling 'confirmation bias' (see Wealth Insert 19C).* Somewhat fixed on your original sale price estimate, you are convinced that the offers you receive seriously undervalue your old home. You've noticed a couple of sales that confirm your original expectations but have taken less notice of the many properties that haven't sold. Accordingly, after projecting the rental income on the property, you resolve to decline the offers, hold both properties and rent out the old house, with the intention of selling it when the market recovers. You end up with more debt than you would have liked, at higher interest rates than you originally forecast.

→ *Rapid forecast degradation as the projected period lengthens.* Two years later, the person renting your old home leaves and you have difficulty finding a new tenant. You resolve to sell the property and accept a price well below your original forecast. With a two-year delay on the redevelopment of your new home, your projected construction costs have now risen, as have your costs of funding because of the rises in interest rates.

→ *The one-sided effect that the unexpected has on projects*—this almost always leads to delays and higher costs. You commence the extension of your new home. Terrible weather in the early stages absorbs your one-month contingency in the project plan and puts the extension of your new home a further month behind.

→ *The neglect of sources of uncertainty outside the plan itself.* You are halfway through the redevelopment, which is now six weeks behind schedule. Your employer offers you a promotion but it depends on you moving to another city. Despite being halfway through the project, you decide that the opportunity is too good to refuse as it will give you full responsibility for a business division for the first time. You indicate that you'd like to make the move on completion of the house. You are currently six weeks behind schedule but the builder convinces you that the remaining six months of the project plan will be delivered on time.

→ *The longer the delay to date on a project, the longer the expected future delay.* Hindsight shows that your builder's estimate of six months is well short. You lose another six weeks in the closing stages because the delays have upset the scheduling and the availability of subcontractors working in the finishing trades.

→ *Viewing the world from within a model, focusing on what you know and mentally eliminating all off-model risks.* As you've almost finished the project, you learn that another factor in the poor availability of the sub-contractors was that the builder was not paying his debts. The builder is unable to complete the project and you have to bring in outside subcontractors yourself, while commuting interstate to fulfil your promise to your employer.

→ *Lack of objectivity in reviewing your performance as a predictor.* Months later, your kids are settled into their new schools interstate, you're living in a lovely rented home and you've even managed to rent out your beautiful new home. The entire sad episode is almost forgotten, except for the amount of money you owe the bank. Your boss now asks you to work on next year's budget for the business, for which you are now accountable. You take comfort in the firm's sound growth over the previous three years and in your abilities as a predictor, having put out of your mind your predictions regarding your two houses.

The big danger with predictions is your unwarranted confidence

Most dangerous in Nassim Nicholas Taleb's eyes is your unwarranted confidence in your own predictions, potentially caused by:

→ *Arrogance regarding knowledge,* with two potential effects: overestimating knowledge and underestimating uncertainty, and misunderstanding the variability of the possible outcomes (for example, experts not knowing what they don't know and underestimating the rare events).

→ *Information overload, which can be toxic in creating excessive confidence.* As an example, Taleb cites the ease with which spreadsheet cells can be created and dragged forward, creating well-presented forecasts of dubious accuracy.

And what about confidence in and reliance on others' predictions? This is potentially even more dangerous:

→ *If psychological factors bias the predictions.* A high proportion of major business acquisitions fail to create shareholder value. As Warren Buffett explains:

> *While deals often fail in practice, they never fail in projections — if the CEO is visibly panting over a prospective acquisition, subordinates and consultants will supply the requisite projections to rationalise any price.*[4]

Similar concepts potentially apply to tenders for contracts — with the winning tenderer often suffering profitless prosperity. This is particularly common with public-sector monopoly assets that are highly sought after, such as toll roads.

→ *If political factors bias the predictions.* In the case of major public projects, political factors cause nine out of 10 cost forecasts to be underestimated, according to Bent Flyvbjerg, the Danish author of *Megaprojects and Risk.*[5] A classic example was the construction of the Sydney Opera House, which took 14 years to complete and suffered a 14-fold cost overrun on the original politically motivated low-ball estimate. The same could certainly be said of the Iraq war or of reconstruction in Iraq — Donald Rumsfeld reportedly said that there wasn't much reconstruction to do![6] A good counter-example is the Empire State Building, which was

completed in a remarkable one year and 45 days during the
Great Depression, ahead of schedule and for around half the
expected cost.

→ *If the underlying assumptions are poorly communicated,* the risks in
using the predictions cannot be understood.

In *Super Crunchers,* Ian Ayres notes that people tend to make biased
predictions, be overconfident about them and slow to change them
despite new evidence. He argues that statistical projections by big
computers don't have egos or feelings like people (especially 'self-
involved experts'), they are not overconfident and, unlike traditional
experts, they tell you the quality of their predictions.

The big danger in having unwarranted confidence in your predictions,
therefore, is the risk that you leave too small a margin of safety in your
decision-making.

Accuracy/variability can matter more than the forecast itself

Nassim Nicholas Taleb would strongly counsel that the quality of
Ayres's predictive statistical procedures and the computer's assessment
of that quality totally depend on the validity of the underlying statistical
model. Taleb would, however, share Ayres's appreciation of the value of
knowing the quality of a prediction, arguing that a forecast's accuracy
and variability can matter far more than the forecast itself. He explains:

> You would take a different set of clothes on your trip to some remote
> destination if I told you that the temperature was expected to be
> seventy degrees Fahrenheit, with an expected error rate of forty
> degrees, than if I told you that my margin of error was only five
> degrees.[7]

The same issues would apply in determining your provisions for a single-
handed sail around the world, the capital needed to fund a company
until it breaks even or the amount of borrowings you can afford to take
on in a new business venture.

Unwarranted confidence in predictions leads to poor decision-making

I can vividly relate this maxim to a business experience of my own.
I was a director of a company which, in 1995, raised approximately

$200 million from the public and from banks to fund the construction of a casino in Cairns. Detailed projections were produced by experts, based on extensive data from other Australian casinos. The data was reliable because of the very tight reporting responsibilities of casinos, and the projections were thoroughly reviewed by leading accountants, bankers and casino specialists.

Note that the three sources of overconfidence previously described were present:

→ the inevitable arrogance regarding knowledge—which came from employing experts
→ the toxicity of extensive, reliable information
→ psychological factors—the collective adrenaline of those involved, especially as the licence was a monopoly issued to the highest bidder in a public tender.

Prior to opening the casino, it could very reasonably have been argued that these projections were reasonable 'best estimates' of the venture's expected revenue and profitability. They may have been well-derived estimates but they were only point estimates, based on a single scenario. Like most people, we didn't prepare several ranges of possible outcomes with estimates of the probabilities of each. Even if we had, however, we may have underestimated the possible downside due to the sources of overconfidence.

On opening, the casino's revenue levels were only 40 to 50 per cent of those projected, with major implications for the project's returns, funding and financial stability.

To this day I could not criticise the process behind our point projections, although the results in reality were different. I was among the many who reviewed them in detail at the time. However, what I am both critical and self-critical of is the fact that we allowed the availability of vast amounts of quality data on similar facilities to make us overconfident about the potential veracity of our projections. With the benefit of hindsight and subsequent years of prospectus development, we could have reflected and made the following conclusions:

→ even though we have significant potentially relevant data, this is a start-up business

→ therefore, whatever projections we make could be out by a substantial margin, not just by the roughly 10 per cent margin typically applied to well-established businesses.

Our failure to recognise the vast variability in our projections had other implications, which highlighted our failure to clearly communicate our assumptions. We believed we had communicated our underlying assumptions accurately to both our bankers and our public investors, and as point estimates, we probably did. As ranges or probability scenarios, we did not, because we did not understand the weaknesses ourselves.

In my hindsight view, the major addition our public offer document would have benefited from was due emphasis on the fact that the project was a start-up, and that therefore any investment should be considered to be speculative. You'll find this emphasis is still missing on the documentation for many other start-up infrastructure projects. Such a statement would provide an objective balance to the extensive forecasts accompanied by the names of top professional firms and institutions—and lead to more informed decision-making by investors.

Variations on these lessons apply if you're setting up a new business. On the one hand, you're courting danger if you're establishing any kind of business without a business plan that includes some financial projections and a projection of the resources it will require—including your own time commitment. On the other hand, you can only take those projections as a rough guide, with every expectation that the actual outcome will differ up or down from your projections. Accordingly:

→ Have significant spare funding capacity in case it takes longer than projected to reach a break-even cash flow, or to be ready in case there is so much growth in revenue that you have trouble funding that growth. Surprisingly, many businesses go broke at times of rapid growth.

→ Don't start the business at a time when you are distracted by other things or aspiring to have family holidays or overseas trips, because your business may demand much more of your time and energy than you project.

Other investment principles to minimise the downside of failure

---

Wealth Insert 21B: diversification to spread risk

Benjamin Graham considered adequate diversification essential if an investor is to take proper advantage of the margin-of-safety principle:

> *A margin of safety does not guarantee an investment against loss; it merely assures that the probabilities are against loss and, in the case of common stocks, that the probabilities favour an ultimate profit. The individual probabilities may be turned into a reasonable approximation of certainty by the well-known practice of 'spreading the risk'. This is the cornerstone of the insurance business, and it should be a cornerstone of sound investment.*[8]

Wealth Insert 21C: put your eggs in one basket only if you control it

Benjamin Graham and his co-authors continued:

> *There is a well-known argument against diversification based on Andrew Carnegie's maxim: 'Put all your eggs in one basket and watch the basket.'*
>
> *An investor may concentrate heavily on the shares of one corporation provided they have a personal connection with it — as an executive or as a member of a controlling group. Many large fortunes have been built up over the years by such a concentration of interest. But where the close personal connection with the company is lacking, this policy rarely succeeds.*[9]

In Wealth Insert 20A I cited Warren Buffett's concept of a ticket with only 20 slots in it — representing all the investments you are allowed to make in a lifetime. Here, Buffett departs from Benjamin Graham's view of the merits of diversification for an astute investor. While Graham promoted the benefits of diversification (see Wealth Insert 21B), he acknowledged the lesser need for diversification where the investor has significant influence or control in specific investments (Wealth Insert 21C).

The diversification of your Life Capital is a simple and practical concept if, like Charles Handy, you lead a 'portfolio' life—having a range of professional interests. It is less straightforward if you have a single employer, and in this case your diversification needs to come at other levels:

→ In respect of your human and social capital, diversification comes from the balance you maintain between job-related obligations and your other interests. As described in 8.3: don't give up your night job.

→ Be wary of putting too much of your financial capital into the company that is also the provider of your income. Many people will have realised the perils of this approach in the aftermath of the 2008 financial crisis. This is especially relevant if you do not have significant control or influence with your employer.

Managed experiments to test your assumptions

Another approach to minimising the downside of failure prior to making a key decision is to conduct experiments to test your assumptions or projections. It is vital not to skimp on your investment of money, time, attention or energy in an experiment, as the opportunity cost of running a poorly conducted test that comes up with misleading negative results can be enormous.

21.2   Keeping an eye out for an emerging failure

Even after the key decision or commitment has been made, there are all sorts of steps you can take to maximise your benefits and minimise your downside, including:

→ having in place feedback processes regarding performance; for example, up-to-date financial reports and feedback from customers of your new business

→ keeping abreast of what's happening in your core area of focus—the basket you can watch (see Wealth Insert 21C)

→ monitoring others' views or buy-in

→ avoiding confirmation bias and thereby avoiding throwing 'good money after bad' (see Wealth Insert 19C) — if, for example, the new job is a dead end rather than a bright new horizon, reassess it; if your new retail concept is not working well, don't assume anything will be solved by opening a second outlet

→ maintaining flexibility and having an open mind to react to emerging events and to deal with emerging problems

→ being ready to take decisions and actions to cut losses (see Wealth Insert 20C)

→ having objectivity — if you're an injured athlete, stop and get the right attention; if you've got the flu, don't go for a run or a gym session, and don't go in to work.

21.3   Minimising the downside of failure through resilience

That which does not kill me, makes me stronger.

—Friedrich Nietzsche

Most lives are long enough to overcome even the worst setbacks. There is one common quality in those who overcome setbacks: resilience. It's the ability to bounce back, to learn from, see past and move on from immediate problems rather than dwell on or be overwhelmed by them.

When you contemplate resilience, you might think of the following:

→ The wartime political leadership of Winston Churchill, who was famous for uttering the line: 'Never give up, never give up, never give up, never, never, never, never'.

→ The patience, dignity and forgiveness shown by Nelson Mandela during his 27 years of imprisonment — qualities that preserved his humanity and ultimately gave him his inspiration and the power to lead and inspire others.

→ The remarkable safe return of Shackleton's crew from the Antarctic in 1914, after their ill-fated but appropriately named vessel *Endurance* was trapped in pack ice and then crushed. Or the safe return of the crew of the aborted Apollo 13 lunar-landing mission in 1970.

→ Any paralympian; or quadriplegic Hilary Lister, who sailed solo across the English Channel—one of the busiest shipping lanes in the world—despite only being able to move her head, eyes and mouth.

→ Shelley Taylor-Smith who, despite severe back and walking problems, became the only woman in professional marathon swimming to hold the number one world ranking for both men and women. She won the Manhattan Island Marathon Swim five times; the last time was six months after she had been given six months to live if she continued to push herself.[10]

→ People who are carers for family members with severe disabilities.

→ The recovery from financial disaster of people like Walt Disney and Donald Trump. In some venture capital and entrepreneurial circles, financial distress at some prior point in your career is worn as a badge of honour—your CV and experience curve are almost considered incomplete if you haven't declared bankruptcy a couple of times and shown you can bounce back!

→ Authors like JK Rowling and John Grisham, who were repeatedly rejected by publishers.

So, if you are seeking inspiration by looking at the magnitude of other people's resilience to setbacks in life, you'll find it regularly occurs in most fields of endeavour. Each person's journey will be different, each one finding their strength in their own way. Understandably, there are many theories on how resilience might be learned or achieved.

Alternative approaches to building resilience

According to the American Psychological Association, the primary factor that builds resilience is 'having caring and supportive relationships within and outside the family'. The APA cites other ways you can build resilience, including:

→ avoiding seeing crises as insurmountable problems
→ accepting change as part of life
→ looking for opportunities for self-discovery
→ taking care of yourself mentally and physically.

The Mayo Clinic website <www.mayoclinic.com> offers an alternative resilience checklist, but notes that developing resilience is an individual experience.

There are many frameworks you can use for viewing resilience, including:

→ *Martin Seligman's Learned Optimism*: in his book, Seligman takes the reader on a path to acquiring optimism and thereby resilience, a key being how you typically explain to yourself negative events (see 11.3).[11]

→ *Kamal Sarma's mental resilience training based on meditation*: Sarma identifies five stages in achieving clarity of mind and thereby sound decision-making—relaxation, calm, emotional tranquillity, insight and wisdom.[12] According to Sarma, this mental resilience training will increase your skills in listening with an open and interested mind.

→ *Viktor Frankl's spiritual freedom*: Viennese psychiatrist Viktor Frankl survived the horrors of Auschwitz and immediately thereafter wrote *Man's Search for Meaning*. In Auschwitz, where both his mother and father died, Frankl learned that:

> *Everything can be taken from a man but one thing: the last of the human freedoms—to choose one's attitude in any given set of circumstances, to choose one's own way... It is this spiritual freedom—which cannot be taken away—that makes life meaningful and purposeful.*[13]

Like Mandela, Frankl found that 'in the final analysis it becomes clear that the sort of person the prisoner became was the result of an inner decision, not the result of camp influences alone'. Frankl often quoted Nietzsche: 'He who has a why to live can bear with almost any how'. As others have noted in such situations, Frankl remarked that in the Nazi concentration camps 'those who knew there was a task waiting for them to fulfil were most apt to survive'. Fundamental to Frankl's spiritual freedom and his salvation were his love for his wife, Tilly, his contemplation of her image and his vivid mental conversations with her. At the time, Frankl did not know her fate. Tilly Frankl died in Bergen-Belsen.

According to Linda Coutu, a senior editor at *Harvard Business Review* specialising in psychology and business, almost all resilience theories suggest that resilient people have three common characteristics: 'a staunch acceptance of reality; a deep belief, often buttressed by strongly held values, that life is meaningful; and an uncanny ability to improvise'. Coutu believes you can bounce back from hardship if you have one or two of these characteristics but that to be truly resilient, you need all three.[14]

The practical dimensions of resilience

Survival for Frankl in Auschwitz also had its practical dimensions. His less spiritual rules included:

→ shave daily to look younger and fit for work
→ humour can give you the ability to rise above the immediate situation
→ don't be conspicuous
→ answer questions truthfully but don't offer any unnecessary information.

In his book *Firing Back*, Jeffrey Sonnenfeld studied how a number of high-profile executives recovered from career disasters. The principal practical lessons he drew were:

→ ignore the advice of friends to lick your wounds
→ there are people who support you and are eager to help if you will let them
→ get your mission clear
→ know your story
→ comeback is not a matter of luck, it is taking a chosen path.[15]

In a sporting example, legendary Chicago Bulls coach Phil Jackson encouraged his players to meditate in order to clear their minds of distracting thoughts so they could focus exclusively on the immediate job—not thinking too deeply and instead doing things instinctively, and not being ruled by their inner critic of every move. He called this meditation 'mindfulness'—making your mind empty so it is ready for anything and open to everything.[16]

Jackson also developed a quick visualisation exercise for his players, to enable them to cool down mentally and physically during time-outs. He called it 'the safe spot'. By picturing themselves in a place they felt secure for 15 or 30 seconds, they could take a 'short mental vacation before addressing the problem at hand'.

This on-the-spot resilience is the same required of a teacher between lessons, an orchestral player between movements or an executive at a break in a meeting, in order to clear their minds of something disappointing, embarrassing or distracting that has happened. A sporting coach might engender the same attitude in players by instructing them to focus on winning the second half, regardless of whether that is enough to make up for their half-time deficit.

A single moment of transformation

Sometimes there is a single moment or step that transforms an otherwise negative spiral into a positive one. This was the case for Michael Coutts-Trotter, while in prison on a heroin-trafficking conviction.

In 2007 Michael Coutts-Trotter was appointed Director General of Education in my state of New South Wales. Two decades earlier, the 19-year-old Coutts-Trotter, a heroin user, was caught trafficking and served a three-year prison sentence. In response to extensive commentary, Coutts-Trotter told his story:

> An officer from the Salvation Army came to see me in gaol and said, 'Look, we operate a rehabilitation centre, do you think you'd like to come there?' And I would have gone anywhere and done anything to get out of gaol, so I said, 'Yes please,' and I went. And it turned my life around, it did literally save my life.[17]

Coutts-Trotter witnessed several of his fellow prisoners dealing with illiteracy while in jail, revealing to him the value of education and early intervention. 'My life shows that redemption is possible', he is reported as saying. 'That a terrible and criminal mistake, serious as it was, can be paid for and that you can move on from it.' Coutts-Trotter hoped that the publicity about his background would reassure people 'that change is possible, that there is reason to hope, that with good luck and lots of help, you can do just about anything with your life'.

Measures of resilience

There are many measures of resilience available, including the Connor-Davidson Resilience Scale (which the Mayo Clinic adapted for its resilience checklist) and Paul Stolz's Adversity Quotient (AQ), based on four factors:

→ the degree of control you perceive you have over adverse events—a gauge of your resilience and health

→ the extent to which you hold yourself accountable for improving a situation—a gauge of the likelihood of you taking action

→ your perception of how big an impact adverse events will have—a gauge of your perspective, burden and stress level
→ your perception of how long adverse events will impact—a gauge of hope or optimism.[18]

Stolz's book is titled *Adversity Quotient: Turning Obstacles into Opportunities*. Note the similarity of this title to 'turning losers into winners' (see Wealth Insert 11).

The power of resilience

In terms of the growth of your Life Capital, the most important aspect of resilience is its power—its cumulative effect over a lifetime by increasing:

→ your chances of continuing in your cause despite setbacks
→ your chances of lifting your game immediately after a disappointment
→ your chances of reversing vicious circles
→ your preparedness to take on challenges or risks.

21.4   Above all, don't dig a deeper hole

Failures of judgement or performance soon become a thing of the past if the person involved 'fesses up', acknowledges *mea culpa*, says sorry, pays the fine or whatever is necessary in the circumstances to be able to move on. In some situations, however, the initial 'failure' may be dwarfed by much more serious subsequent events, which result from the individual's reaction to that first event—especially if they are trying to defend the indefensible or cover up the trail. This principle is regularly demonstrated by somebody in the public eye; for example, Richard Nixon and Watergate.

Over to you ...

Reflection

• In your most recent significant decisions, did you commit the time and effort to thoroughly investigate and analyse the options? Were you able to consciously leave a margin for error?

- Were your most recent predictions reasonably accurate? What, if any, were the principal sources of failure or inaccuracy? Was your level of confidence in your predictions justified? Did your decision-making allow appropriately for your level of confidence?
- Have you typically shown resilience in the face of setbacks? In what circumstances have you? When and why haven't you?
- When did you last dig a deeper hole by not dealing with an issue? What recent public incidents have demonstrated others digging deeper holes? What did you learn from your or their experiences?

Action

- Next time you conduct an experiment, avoid opportunity loss by committing the money, time, attention or energy necessary to ensure a valid experiment.
- In respect of your most recent key decisions, check that you have appropriate feedback processes in place. In respect of upcoming decisions, determine the feedback and monitoring processes necessary before the decision is made.
- Analyse how building your resilience would benefit you and how significant those benefits are. (Appendix B5 may prompt further thoughts.)
- Next time you face a setback or a challenging situation, consider the significance of your resilience in that context and later assess the strength of your resilience and any learnings. Do some reading, research or thinking about how to build your resilience.

Principle 22
Making uncertainty
work better for you

**You can get better at making
decisions and thereby make both
the uncertainty and the serendipity
of the world work better for you.**

Decision-making is the art of taking risks that are worth it.

—Roger Scruton[1]

Risk and the uncertainty of outcomes are a part of everyday life. An unpleasant outcome may be a direct loss—the loss of $10 on a horserace or failure in a course at university; or it can be an opportunity loss—failure to place your intended bet on the horse that won or choosing the wrong university course.

Your first challenge when weighing up the risks involved and making a decision is to ensure that you fully understand the choice you are making—all the options and their implications, the range of potential outcomes and the follow-up decisions that may need to be taken. Your understanding can be tested and enhanced by the discipline of drawing up either a graphical representation of the decision (a decision tree) or a table showing the potential outcomes for each action under different environments (a decision table).

Decision theorists discriminate between three key types of decisions:

→ decisions where you have no idea of the probabilities of alternative outcomes (see 22.1)

→ decisions where you can assign probabilities to the alternative outcomes (see 22.2)

→ decisions where the outcomes from your decisions are affected by others' decisions (see 22.5).

22.1 Decisions where you have no idea of the probabilities of alternative outcomes

For some decisions, you may have little or no ability to estimate the probabilities of different outcomes or little confidence in any available estimates. In such circumstances, your decision rule will probably be determined by your level of optimism or pessimism.

There are decision rules to suit all types. For example, assume you have saved your first $10000 for investment and you're trying to decide whether to invest it for the next 12 months in the share market or in the bank at 4 per cent interest. Table 22.1 sets out this scenario as a decision table.

Table 22.1: one-year returns on alternative investment choices

	Share market outcome		
Investment choice	(+15%) Bull	Flat	(−15%) Bear
Invest $10000	$1500	—	−$1500
Invest $5000 and bank $5000	$750+$200= $950	$200	−$750+$200 = −$550
Bank $10000	$400	$400	$400

→ If you are an extreme optimist, you might apply a *maximax return rule*—choosing the action for which the best possible outcome is better than the best possible outcome under any other alternative. In this case you would choose to invest the entire $10 000 in the share market, as the maximum return for that choice is $1500—larger than the maximum returns under the other two choices.

→ If you are an extreme pessimist, you would be likely to apply a *maximin return rule*—choosing the action for which the worst possible outcome is better than the worst possible outcome that may arise under any other actions you could choose. In this case, you would choose not to invest your money and leave it all in the bank, as your worst possible outcome is a return of $400, whereas the two other choices have potential negative returns under one of the scenarios.

→ A pessimist with a focus on opportunity cost against alternative strategies might alternatively apply a *minimax regret rule*—choosing that action for which the maximum opportunity cost when compared with all other actions is minimised. In this case, the decision table would instead be one of opportunity costs, as shown in table 22.2.

Table 22.2: opportunity costs on alternative investment choices

| Investment choice | Share market outcomes | | |
	(+15%) Bull	Flat	(-15%) Bear
Invest $10 000	—	$400	$1900
Invest $5000 and bank $5000	$550	$200	$950
Bank $10 000	$1100	—	—

Under a *minimax regret rule* you would choose to invest $5000, as this leads to a maximum opportunity cost of $950, compared with a maximum opportunity cost of $1900 and $1100 for each of the other two choices.

In this example, the three different decision rules produce three different investment choices.

In group decision-making, the ultimate decision will often be influenced most by the person who influences which decision rule is adopted. This in turn will be influenced by their concepts or definitions of risk.

22.2　Probability-based decision-making

Decision-making is enhanced when you know not only the potential outcomes but also their respective probabilities. This is simplest when all the potential outcomes have a single measure—the most obvious measurement being dollars. In purely quantitative contexts, such as investment or gambling, probability-based decision-making uses the concept of expected value.

Wealth Insert 22A: expected value

You can hang a perfect framework of mathematics around betting on the toss of a coin, the roll of a die or most casino games. The probabilities are well defined and in most cases fairly easily and confidently calculated. Hence, to use a simple example, you know it is worthwhile betting up to $5 to participate in a game with a prize of $10 if a coin comes up heads, and zero if it comes up tails ($10 × 50% + $0 × 50% = $5). This calculation of the 'expected value' of the win (the sum of the amounts of the potential wins weighted by their probabilities) is the fundamental starting point for most probability-based decision-making. In some games, the odds of the alternative outcomes can be so accurately calculated that a rational decision is easy to arrive at.

It becomes more complicated when further uncertainties are added. In poker, this can be when you don't know the other players' cards but can read their body language; in horseracing, it can be when you can study the form or seek some inside tips. While these uncertainties bring complications, ultimately you're trying to gauge your estimate of the expected value and then buy-in for something less—giving you some margin of safety. Having found your little edge, you are therefore wanting to buy $5 of expected value for a $4.50 or $4.75 outlay, or less.

This is a core feature of financial or investment decision-making—the use of probability theory to determine the expected value of the investment or bet, so you can decide whether to place it or not. It is not surprising, therefore, that many great investors and business people attribute their success in part to earlier experience using probability theory as poker players or bookmakers' pencillers. Charlie Munger says his army poker honed his business skills—teaching him to fold early when the odds were against him, and to back heavily any big edges he had because he wouldn't have a big edge very often.[2]

It's one thing to understand probabilistic decision-making intellectually, but it's quite another step to be able to use it naturally in everyday situations—in conjunction with your instinct and experience, and a range of non-quantifiable factors that become more important the further you depart from coins and dice.

One decision-making context in which you would routinely apply probability is the impact of weather patterns on your outdoor adventuring decisions—from a hike in a national park to an ascent of Everest. You may be surprised to learn that weather forecasting is one of the most reliable areas of professional forecasting. You can apply a probabilistic approach to decide which day or month is best for your adventure—the period which, based on historical data, has the biggest chance of friendly weather and the lowest chance of foul or dangerous weather.

In determining your provisions for your adventure, you need to be aware of two potential outcomes from your decision:

→ type 1 error—that you under-provide and run out of provisions in a precarious situation

→ type 2 error—that you over-provide and take significant unnecessary weight.

The challenge for the probabilistic decision-maker is how much emphasis to place on each type of error and what margin of safety to apply.

It is also important to recognise that in many real-life situations you can take steps to increase the chances of your preferred outcome or the benefits received from that outcome. Either of these approaches can improve your expected value, as might any steps that reduce the chances or the downside of your worst outcome.

22.3 Assessments of risk

In 21.1 I showed that you confront many potential sources of failure when you try to predict the future. I also noted that a big danger with predictions, whether your own or those of others, can be your unwarranted confidence in them.

Somewhat linked to humans' poor track records in prediction is a relatively poor record in assessing risk—either the chance that something will go wrong or how bad it could be. Its manifestations range from the alarming failure rates of new businesses and a fear of change to the relative fears of death by car accident (relatively high), a falling coconut (relatively low) or a shark attack (extremely low).

Psychologically, we tend to place higher risk weighting on things that:

→ are scary (for example, shark attack)
→ we feel are out of our control or we don't understand (for example, the dumping of nuclear waste)
→ we don't expect to benefit from (for example, the use of pesticides)
→ are given a high media profile (for example, a terrorist attack or mad-cow disease)
→ are under the control of people or institutions we don't trust (for example, an economic recession if we've lost confidence in our government).

Our poor assessment of risk can lead to poor decision-making. For example, although the average person in most developed countries has a chance of around 1 in 150 of being killed in a car accident, our sense of control when driving a car makes us feel safer than when flying in a commercial aeroplane. This was especially the case in the US immediately after 9/11. However, in the three months leading up to December 2001, US road fatalities were 1000 higher than in the corresponding period in the previous year, principally as a result of people favouring road over airline travel.[3]

Anything you can do to enhance your risk-assessment skills should enhance your decision-making ability. One mode of decision-making is called 'satisficing' (a concept combining 'satisfy' and 'suffice'), where you are not trying to maximise an objective but to achieve a specific minimum level. This is a logical decision rule in circumstances where the subject of the decision is not your primary focus in life and you don't want to overcommit your scarce resources to it.

Imagine you are a university student in your final semester, and your aim is to pass all your four subjects with the minimal amount of study. In this satisficing situation, your assessment of the amount of study required for each subject to ensure a low risk of failing is an important skill. There could be no more disappointing result than to receive a distinction, two passes and a fail—probably reflecting excess but poorly allocated study and resulting in you not completing your degree on time.

22.4   Refinements in decision-making theory

In the 1730s mathematician Daniel Bernoulli recognised that the satisfaction you receive from a financial prize may not be directly proportional to the quantum of the prize. For example, you would not receive 10 times the satisfaction from winning $10 000 000 as you would from winning a million.

In order to address real-life situations where you can't measure everything in dollars, or where the dollar measures may be misleading, Bernoulli and later economists developed a theory of decision-making called 'utility theory'.

According to this theory, the utility of an outcome is a measure of its desirability or the satisfaction arising from it. Once you have measures of the utility of alternative outcomes, decision-making can then be based on a concept similar to 'expected value' but called 'expected utility', obtained by weighting the utility of each possible outcome by its probability. Under utility theory, rational decision-makers will then make the choice that maximises their expected utility.

The utility function for money is not linear. It is different for every person. For most people it would look something like figure 22.1.

Figure 22.1: the utility function for money

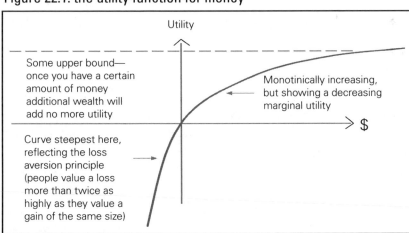

Utility theory provides a framework that can be applied to such decisions as the following:

→ whether to insure your house (despite the premium costing more than your expected claims)

→ whether to buy a lottery ticket (despite your ticket costing more than the expected value of your prize)

→ whether to go on a holiday or work the week and save money

→ whether to take the job with a big company that offers a high fixed remuneration but lower performance-based upside, or the one with a smaller company with half the fixed remuneration but a much higher upside.

That we all have different utility curves is evidenced by the fact that some people insure their assets or participate in lotteries, while others don't.

Prospect theory

In a 1979 paper, Amos Tversky and Daniel Kahneman[4] noted that utility theory provided poor explanations for humans' preferences in a variety of decision situations. For example, under utility theory and common sense, you would be ambivalent between an outcome where you receive $1000 and an alternative outcome where, on the same day, you receive $2000 and then lose $1000. While both outcomes would net you $1000 on the day, there are psychological factors at work that make you prefer the first outcome.

'Prospect theory', which Tversky and Kahneman developed to explain such situations, was one of the foundations of Behavioural Finance and Economics. Some of their conclusions are relevant both to investment decisions and to other life decisions.

Decision frames

Tversky and Kahneman used this term to refer to the decision-maker's perspective of alternative outcomes. This is controlled partly by the individual habits and characteristics of the decision-maker, and partly by the formulation of the problem. As Tversky and Kahneman pointed out, 'changes in perspective often reverse the relative apparent size of objects and the relative desirability of options'.[5] They demonstrated this through a number of decision-making problems involving money, day-to-day decisions and even human life. They defined the problem one way and then reformulated the choices in a way that did not change the underlying impact—just the framing of the impact. Many people's preferences changed with the reframing, even if any other changes were seemingly inconsequential. The simplest of their examples was as follows:

→ *Problem:* Imagine that you have decided to see a play where admission is $10 per ticket. As you enter the theatre you discover that you have lost a $10 bill. Would you still pay $10 for a ticket to the play? Of a sample of 183 people, 88 per cent said Yes, 12 per cent said No.

→ *Reframed problem*: Imagine that you have decided to see a play and have paid an admission price of $10 per ticket. As you enter the theatre you discover that you have lost the ticket. The seat was not marked and the ticket cannot be recovered. Would you pay $10 for another ticket? Of a sample of 200 people, 46 per cent said Yes, 54 per cent said No.

Tversky and Kahneman noted that when considering choices, most people see them through one frame and are normally unaware of alternative frames and the potential effects those frames might have on the relative attractiveness of different options. If they become aware of and adopt alternative frames, they might reach different conclusions.

They draw an analogy to the subject of self-control, whereby decisions taken right now can render ineffective a potential future decision. For example, the decision to choose between different levels of savings commitments or between chocolate and fruit can vary widely depending on how long before consumption the decision is made (see 4.2).

I had a somewhat related experience when I had a number of infringement points on my driver's licence and risked losing it. I deliberately reframed my driving objective as being to take as long as possible to get from A to B without holding up the traffic—amber traffic lights thus became an opportunity to stop rather than an indication to accelerate to get through before the red.

Other variations on decision frames include:

→ framing your work as experiments or as educational/learning experiences rather than as a success/fail situation (reminiscent of Edison's 'I am now well informed on 6000 ways you cannot do it')

→ before making a major decision as a company board, drafting the press release

→ asking yourself before any major decision: 'What would this look like on the front page of the newspaper?' or 'What would this look like from the other person's point of view?'

Thinking problems through both forwards and backwards

This is a variation on decision frames and one of Charlie Munger's favourite tricks. You probably do it regularly when you travel; for example, in working out the time to set your alarm at night so you can catch your early-morning flight.

The harder or more complex it is to think backwards, the more valuable it may be to do so. It's especially valuable for the big journeys in life—a four-year overseas posting, your expectation of becoming a partner in five years or the whole journey of life itself. It can help you see where things become impossible in terms of time or resources, or cause fundamental conflicts between your values and the decisions you have to take. It can also help you realise that if the people you will be depending on need to be in a particular mindset, you may have to take prior actions to get them there.

Some of the most simply defined but powerful applications of thinking backwards are:

→ in working out what you want to be, it will help to also ask the question 'What do I not want to be?'

→ in making decisions that may affect the environment, ask yourself 'What sort of world do I want my grandchildren to inherit?'

→ in deciding whether to sell something at a certain price, ask yourself 'Would I buy it at this price?' or 'At what price would I buy it?'

Charlie Munger argues that thinking things through forwards and backwards forces objectivity by making you try to disprove your initial assumptions. As I explained in Wealth Insert 19C, most people try to do the opposite—they try to confirm their initial assumptions. In psychology, this is called 'first conclusion bias' or 'confirmation bias'.

Loss-aversion

On average, across a range of experimental contexts, people appear to value avoiding a loss a little more than twice as highly as they value a gain of the same size. This 'coefficient of loss aversion' varies between people and between contexts, being higher for safety decisions than for money decisions, and higher for income than for leisure. Loss aversion in decisions reflects the asymmetry of pain and pleasure.

The more loss-averse you are, the more likely you are to:

→ sell your winning investments and retain your losers (see Wealth Insert 20C)

→ choose not to work overtime or put your money in the bank to earn interest because you don't want to pay more taxes — the benefit from the extra money may not outweigh your feeling of loss incurred by paying additional taxes

→ pay less attention to an opportunity loss than to an equal outright loss (hence the emphasis on the subject of opportunity loss in Principle 9) — this is particularly significant when reviewing and thereby learning from the outcomes of your own decisions

→ back higher probability outcomes rather than those with the higher expected utility, because you like to be right. Hence, you might contact the person you think will see you, rather than the one who you think might make the greatest difference but is less likely to say yes. Similarly, a loss-averse accountant is more likely to spend the time from 5.00 pm to 6.30 pm doing chargeable work for a client (bringing in known fees and completing a known workload), rather than going to a cocktail party where the outcome is far less certain.

Loss-aversion also impacts our negotiations: we are less likely to achieve agreement if the issues being bargained are framed as losses rather than gains.[6] We have a general tendency to avoid risk, though as Roger Scruton says:

> While the avoidance of risk may look like a rational short-term strategy, in the long run it is the riskiest strategy of all, since it leaves us unable to take the crucial decisions on which our future depends.[7]

Status quo bias

The more loss-averse you are, the more you will have an aversion to change, favouring the retention of the status quo over other alternatives.

In commerce this can result in:
- → ill-founded confidence in your strategy, even in an uncertain and changing world
- → an avoidance of the unpredictability of creative efforts.

In careers this can result in:
- → an aversion to changing habits
- → taking on similar assignments rather than those that extend your experience curve — with consequent implications for whether you end up with three years of experience or three times the same year's experience.

Sunk costs

The amount of time, effort or capital already invested in something ('sunk costs') can affect decisions in an economically irrational way — often in the same direction as status quo bias.

In economic theory, the amount you have previously paid for goods or for an investment should not influence your decision between the alternative courses of action now available. In practice, however, these sunk costs can have a significant impact on your decisions because of your loss aversion.

For example, you've bought a ticket to an uncovered stand for a football match and it's pouring with rain. Do you go to the match even though you know you're unlikely to enjoy it and you'd be much more comfortable watching the game on TV? Do you leave at half-time once you know you are definitely not enjoying it? In both decisions, you are influenced by your sunk costs. Would you have gone to the match if you had not bought the ticket in advance but could buy one at the gate?

You arrive at the same football match on a sunny day but the match is delayed for an hour and the promoters communicate very poorly with the crowd. You have the choice of ignoring the irritation of the sunk one hour and still enjoying the wonderful game or dwelling on the sunk costs and poor public relations, spoiling your enjoyment of the game.

Having the ability to ignore sunk costs is an important aspect of framing a decision. Being able to look objectively at where you are, without regard to how you got there (other than for learning purposes), is a rare and valuable gift.

Irrationality surrounding sunk costs can arise in major development projects, especially where the decision-makers wish to avoid appearing wasteful. The sunk costs effect is also known as the Concorde fallacy, after the Anglo-French supersonic aeroplane. The British and French governments continued financing the Concorde project after they knew its financial prospects were dim—largely because of the substantial amounts they had already invested.

Amazingly, there is no evidence of lower animals exhibiting the Concorde fallacy and little evidence of young children doing so.[8]

A career example of sunk costs

Career decisions are particularly difficult because most involve enormous sunk costs and potentially even greater opportunity costs.

Imagine you have completed three years of a five-year medical degree and now wish you had studied law. As described in table 22.3, you have three choices.

Table 22.3: decision choices regarding change of university course

Choice	Outcome
Leave medicine and start law	All your sunk costs studying medicine are torn up but the opportunity costs of having delayed starting law stop immediately.
Complete medicine and then start law	You incur further sunk costs studying medicine and further opportunity cost by delaying starting what you really want to do. The opportunity costs only cease once you start law.
Complete medicine and stay with it	You have no sunk costs but a lifetime of opportunity costs ahead of you.

If you were economically rational, you would ignore all sunk costs and past opportunity costs (except for learning purposes), and would weight future actual costs and opportunity costs approximately equally. In real life, however, you are more likely to give some weight to the sunk costs: three years of study. You are also likely to increase that weighting to allow for any sense of failure, bad judgement, wastefulness or public embarrassment at being seen to have changed course or 'failed'. In addition, you are likely to underestimate opportunity costs when compared with real costs, because of your loss aversion.

The term 'sunk costs' may not be perfect in the context of personal relationships. Nevertheless, envisage a couple who have been living together for eight years. She is keen to get married and have kids, while he is still unable to get his mind around either marriage or kids. At what point does the woman recognise that, in the context of her maternal ambitions, the eight years they have lived together is a sunk cost from her point of view and it's time to open herself up to other opportunities?

22.5   Game theory

Any review of decision-making would not be complete without mentioning game theory, which defines decision-making in situations where your outcomes also depend on others' decisions. For example, in a poker game the outcome from your decision to fold, match or raise is dependent on the decisions of the other players.

Game theory recognises the importance of knowing the rules of the game and the impact of other people's choices on your alterative payoffs. For example, if you are deciding whether to change employers, a decision by your boss whether to stay on or resign may have an impact on your alternative outcomes.

In the mathematics of game theory, the other players are assumed to know the rules of the game and to behave rationally by seeking to maximise their own payoffs. Neither of these two assumptions can be taken for granted in real-world situations. How often do you find that you don't know the rules of the game, or realise that you have not been acting rationally in terms of maximising your own payoff? How often do you see colleagues in that position?

Game theory has been applied to decision-making in fields ranging from economics and philosophy to politics and military strategy, from species survival to computer science. Awareness of game theory was popularised by the Oscar-winning movie *A Beautiful Mind*. Its subject, John Nash Jr, is one of eight game theorists who have been Nobel Laureates. The movie provides a wonderful example of game theory at work when Nash (played by Russell Crowe) says to his friends:

> *If we all go for the blonde and block each other, not a single one of us is going to get her. So then we go for her friends, but they will all give us the cold shoulder because no one likes to be second choice. But what if none of us goes for the blonde? We won't get in each*

other's way and we won't insult the other girls. It's the only way to win. It's the only way we all get laid.

22.6 Returns for risk

I worry less about embarrassment than about missing an opportunity.

—Nassim Nicholas Taleb[9]

Wealth Insert 22B: to achieve a high return, you need to take on some risk

Rational investors who are offered two alternative investments with the same expected return will choose the less risky one. They will choose a more risky investment only if it offers higher expected returns—sufficiently high enough to reward them for the incremental risk.

Conversely, in an informed market an investment offering a high expected return on a risk-free basis will be sufficiently sought after that its price will increase to bring the expected return closer to typical risk-free returns. Accordingly, to achieve a high return, you need to take on some risk.

The principle of return for risk is also fundamental in building your Life Capital. Some of its most basic applications would be when taking such risks as:

→ trying things you haven't tried before in order to extend your experience curve or your circle of competence

→ putting pressure on your boss in order to secure the necessary resources to do your job

→ requesting an interview with a senior person in your profession in order to get some career advice

→ making changes to your golf swing, as Tiger Woods did in order to be the best player he could be.

In 2005 an Australian golf professional accused Greg Norman of not giving enough back to the local game and failing to assist young players.

He suggested Norman was unapproachable and had snubbed young Australian golfers. The fascinating part of the story was the reaction of fellow professional Robert Allenby, who described the other golfer's claim that Norman didn't offer advice to younger golfers as 'pretty sad'. Allenby suggested that it came about because the other golfer didn't have the courage to go up and talk to Norman himself.

One of this book's core messages is that you should take the risk of asking for advice rather than standing back and not asking. The cost benefit analysis is compelling, as shown in table 22.4. For you, the cost of a knock-back is minimal but the upside from a valuable conversation is unlimited. For the other person the cost is their time (and they will tell you if you're wasting it), while the upside from a valuable conversation is unlimited. The most significant part of this upside for the other party may be the pleasure of helping you overcome a hurdle or identify the missing link in your game plan.

Table 22.4: alternative outcomes if you do/don't talk to someone

	Loss	Gain	Opportunity loss
Talk to someone	Embarrassment if they treat you with disdain	Potentially substantial; arguably unlimited	Nil
Don't talk to them	Nil	Nil	Potentially substantial; arguably unlimited

22.7   Making serendipity work for you

For thousands of years, all swans were believed to be white. With the discovery of Australia and a single sighting of a black swan, this long-held belief was disproved. Nassim Nicholas Taleb uses the term Black Swan as his metaphor for an event with three attributes:

→ it lies outside regular expectations
→ it has an extreme impact
→ despite being most unexpected, people proffer explanations for it after the event.[10]

Taleb mentions many examples of Black Swans, including:
→ major financial market collapses
→ epidemics
→ fads, fashions or ideas
→ the rise of Hitler or Islamic fundamentalism.

Taleb saw the Lebanese civil war as a Black Swan. After almost 1300 years of peaceful ethnic co-existence, the civil war transformed his birthplace from a heaven into a hell.

Wealth Insert 22C: Taleb's strategy for profiting from extreme events

Nassim Nicholas Taleb argues that academic finance theory, and its application in many financial institutions, is badly flawed in its statistical assumption that financial markets follow the normal distribution (the bell curve), when they clearly do not. That this assumption was flawed was vividly demonstrated by Black Monday, 19 October 1987. Based on bell-curve assumptions and Wall Street's historical volatility, a single-day fall that big would be statistically unlikely even if the life of the universe was repeated one billion times and the market had been open every day over that period.[11] The extreme daily volatility of world stock markets in 2008 was also totally inconsistent with the assumption that financial markets follow the bell curve.

Taleb notes that while you can't predict Black Swans, you can set yourself up to collect Black Swans of the positive kind by maximising your exposure to them. To that end, Taleb's own investment approach is:

• don't put money in medium-risk investments because no-one knows how risky they really are
• put the majority of your money in extremely safe investments and the remaining 10 to 15 per cent in a number of very speculative, leveraged situations.

Under this strategy, no major surprise can hurt you significantly, so you aren't dependent on complicated risk management and the errors that often come with it. At the same time, you're well exposed to the possibility of major positive surprises.[12]

Black Swans, Taleb says, tend to occur very often—in fact, so often that you will be unable to confidently predict events and developments in general, or Black Swans (by their definition) in particular, even in respect of your own life.

Taleb's Black Swans are relevant to our lives and careers. In today's rapidly changing world, our lives are not likely to go according to plan and we will be exposed to many Black Swans—both positive and negative.

Taleb offers some strategies:[13]

→ Distinguish between positive contingencies (where lack of predictability can be extremely beneficial) and negative contingencies (where lack of predictability can be extremely harmful).

→ Be paranoid about the possibility of negative Black Swans. Avoid them by thinking in terms of the harm certain scenarios might cause, rather than in terms of their likelihood. For example, don't put all your professional and financial eggs in one basket, regardless of how strong you think it is.

→ Don't be too narrow-minded—leave yourself open to serendipity, as you won't experience positive Black Swans unless you're exposed to the possibility of them.

→ Seize any opportunity, or anything that looks like an opportunity. You need to realise when you're getting a seriously lucky break and then be prepared to cancel everything else to capitalise on it.

Maximise serendipity by living in cities and going to parties

According to Taleb, exposure to serendipity and breakthroughs is maximised for those who live in cities rather than rural areas. He also believes that your exposure to serendipity will be maximised if you occasionally leave work behind to socialise and go to parties, opening yourself up to the opportunity of meeting people.[14]

Economics writer Tim Harford agrees with Taleb on the importance of city life, saying that cities provide an environment for people to become smarter more quickly because they are able to learn from one another. Many economists see this learning environment as a major explanation for both high city rents and the high wages paid to people who have worked in cities for long periods.[15]

While modern technology-based communications may substitute for some face-to-face contact, Harford notes that they will also make it easier for those in cities to meet new people, maintain relationships and arrange to see each other—so much so that city dwellers can scarcely avoid meeting interesting people.

Talk to people you haven't met before

Entering a room full of people, you have the choice of whether to talk to those you know best and see often, those you've never met before and those in between. Like me, you probably start with those you know best or are most comfortable with, and who probably share most of your views. Which of the range of discussions offers the greatest opportunity for serendipity?

Always carry a pen and paper

There is something simple about the advice that you should always carry a pen and paper to capture bright ideas as they occur to you, to remember things you must do or to write down the phone numbers of people you meet and want to contact. It's a simple but very powerful strategy.

Richard Branson describes a standard-sized school notebook as his most essential possession. He makes notes of all the telephone conversations and meetings he has, ensuring that he listens carefully at the time. When he gets home, he looks through his notes and follows up any good ideas.[16]

Leonardo da Vinci, perhaps the greatest genius who ever lived, was also not above using this strategy. He carried a notebook at all times so he could jot down ideas, impressions and observations as they occurred. Around 7000 pages of his notebooks still exist, and most scholars estimate that this represents only around half the total number of pages he left in his will. In 1994, Bill Gates paid $30.8 million for 18 pages of da Vinci's notebooks.

22.8 The importance of 'Yes'

A man on a London bus told British comedian Danny Wallace to 'say yes more', as 'the people without passion are the ones who always say no. But the happiest people are the ones who understand that good things occur when one allows them to'.

Wallace's autobiographical *Yes Man* describes this conversation as the epiphany of his life, turning him from a person who went out of his way to say 'no' to almost everything into someone who says 'yes' to opportunities. For one year, he decided to take up every opportunity he was offered, leading him to travel around the world several times and get married in Melbourne.

From the start, Wallace's aim was that his year of saying yes would be a learning experience—an experiment in happiness and positivity. It often took him significantly outside his comfort zone and exposed him to all manner of new experiences—from exposing internet financial scams to the world of drugs and penis enlargement.

Wallace's rule is certainly not one to emulate. Responding to every request with an indiscriminate 'yes' has its dangers for all dimensions of your Life Capital—not least for your health and safety. Nevertheless, the man on the bus had a point: good things will occur if you allow them to. So where or how do we draw the lines between 'yes' and 'no'?

Beware the compliance practitioners

In *Influence: The Psychology of Persuasion*, Robert Cialdini explains the psychology behind the reasons why people say 'yes' to requests or offers. He says that most of the thousands of tactics employed by people like salesmen, whom Cialdini calls compliance practitioners and whose main aim is to get you to say 'yes', capitalise on six basic categories of human behaviour:

→ *Consistency:* your nearly obsessive desire to appear consistent with what you have already done.

→ *Reciprocation:* your efforts to repay in kind what another person has provided you. Cialdini observes that it is actually your obligation to receive that makes your obligation to reciprocate so easy to exploit because it reduces your ability to choose whom you wish to be indebted to.

→ *Social proof:* your frequent determination of what is correct by finding out what others think is correct, especially in respect of behaviour.

→ *Authority:* your inability to say no to someone in authority.

→ *Liking:* your preference to say yes to requests from someone you like.

→ *Scarcity:* your rush to obtain something that might soon be unavailable.

Cialdini argues that our increasingly complex and rushed world forces us to simplify our decision-making through shortcuts. That is, in particular situations, rather than considering all of the dimensions, we will pay attention to just one piece of the relevant information — whatever piece of information has stood us in good stead in similar situations in the past. The compliance practitioners are well versed in these natural shortcuts and their tactics are targeted at them. Cialdini believes it is vital to understand how to protect yourself from the wiles of compliance practitioners and to fight, if necessary belligerently, to avoid any threats to the reliability of your shortcuts. He concludes:

> The blitz of modern daily life demands that we have faithful shortcuts, sound rules of thumb to handle it all. These are not luxuries any longer; they are out-and-out necessities that figure to become increasingly vital as the pulse of daily life quickens. That is why we should want to retaliate whenever we see someone betraying one of our rules of thumb for profit. We want that rule to be as effective as possible. But to the degree that its fitness for duty is regularly undercut by the tricks of a profiteer, we naturally will use it less and less and will be less able to cope efficiently with the decisional burdens of our day. We cannot allow that without a fight. The stakes have gotten too high.[17]

The need for quick decision-making that Cialdini identifies and seeks to protect will be exacerbated if you increase your flow of serendipitous opportunities by the approaches suggested in 22.7. Your quick decision-making will be most effective if:

→ you have a clear vision, strategy and decision rules against which to judge the time to say 'yes' and the time to say 'no'

→ you understand your gut strengths and know which of them you can rely on when making quick decisions

→ importantly, you have the discipline and the ability to say 'no'.

Over to you ...

Reflection

- What was the last decision in which you used probabilities or expected values? Do you use these concepts routinely in everyday life? When was the last time you could have benefited from using them and did not?
- When was the last major decision for which you made a conscious risk assessment—mental or written? What could you have done to make that risk assessment more worthwhile for your decision-making?
- Are you typically reticent to approach someone for a favour? How do you feel when someone approaches you for a favour and you are able to help them? Are your answers somewhat contradictory?
- In the past week, what things that you said 'yes' to should you have said 'no' to? And the converse? What do you learn from that about the effectiveness or weakness of any of your decision-making shortcuts?

Action

- Analyse the benefits of applying sound decision-making techniques, and thereby being a better decision-maker. What is the significance of those benefits? Appendix B12 may prompt further thoughts.
- Try to achieve some advantage or clarity by reframing a challenge or decision you are currently facing—or by thinking backwards.
- Identify a context in which loss aversion or status quo bias might regularly cause you opportunity loss.
- Identify the context in which you currently have the greatest amount of sunk costs. Identify the potential implications of those sunk costs for any forthcoming decisions.
- Identify a future important decision where your outcome will be significantly influenced by the decisions of others, and consider any allowance you should make for that in your strategy.
- Next time you are uncertain about whether to approach someone for a favour, take the risk and ensure you avoid opportunity loss.
- Next time you return from a social function, spend a couple of minutes thinking through who you socialised with, how you engaged with them and whether that approach might minimise or maximise potential serendipity.
- For one week, carry a pen and paper at all times and write down all the opportunities or significant new knowledge you encounter.

Principle 23
Conversations, information and decision-making

The more capable you are at accessing, objectively assessing and reframing relevant information, the more soundly based your decisions will be.

The goal of Herodotus's journeys? To collect new information about a country, its people, and their customs, or to test the reliability of data already gathered. Herodotus is not content with what someone else has told him—he tries to verify each thing, to compare and contrast the various versions he has heard, and then to formulate his own.

—Ryszard Kapuscinski[1]

23.1 The wisdom of crowds

In 1906 British scientist Francis Galton examined the entries in a 'guess the weight of the ox' competition. He found that the 800 entries averaged 1197 pounds—almost identical to the actual weight of 1198 pounds. This story begins James Surowiecki's *The Wisdom of Crowds*.

Surowiecki goes on to tell the story of a much more complex problem: the search for the US submarine *Scorpion*, which disappeared in 1968 returning from the North Atlantic. The search leader John Craven concocted a series of scenarios from the last known location of *Scorpion*, and then assembled a team with a wide range of knowledge—from mathematics to salvage. Then, instead of having the team work together to come up with a recommendation, he asked each individual to put together probabilities on the various scenarios. Craven then combined their guesses, using a statistical theorem, and the answer was within 220 yards of the final discovery. No single scenario was anywhere near that.[2]

The Wisdom of Crowds explains how a crowd of ordinary people can be smarter than an expert and smarter than the smartest individuals in the crowd. Surowiecki identifies four essential qualities of a smart crowd:

→ *Diversity*: different perspectives reduce the risk, especially in small groups, that a few biased or extreme individuals can exert sufficient influence to skew the group's collective decision.

→ *Independence*: when people pay most attention to their own information and views instead of worrying about what others think. Independence reduces the risk of correlated mistakes by members of the crowd. Also, independent individuals are more likely to bring new information, disagreement and contest.

→ *Decentralisation and specialisation*: enabling people to bring more local and focused sources of knowledge and opinion.

→ *Aggregation*: whereby individual opinions and judgements can be collated effectively into a collective conclusion, without losing valuable ideas.

Significantly, Surowiecki observes that you can always create the crowd to bring wisdom to the circumstances. In doing so, because you don't always know where you'll find good information, it's smarter to cast a wide net rather than wasting time figuring out exactly who should be in and who should be out. He also notes that too much discussion can make the group collectively less intelligent, because the team members end up thinking the same and making the same mistakes. This may be the outcome even though its members may individually be becoming smarter. The order in which people contribute to the discussion will also have a significant effect on its course, earlier comments being more influential.

Amazon's book recommendation engine is based on a wisdom of crowds algorithm, using ratings from purchasers of similar books. So too is Google's PageRank search program, which views every link to a web page as a 'vote' for that page—but not all links are equal, nor therefore are all votes equal. PageRank applies social network analysis (see 14.5) to determine the ranking of all the linked pages and the votes implied by those links are weighted accordingly.[3]

The use of experts

Surowiecki, like Taleb (see 21.1), considers that experts have poor track records in many fields of prediction or forecasting, and that they generally overrate the likely accuracy of their predictions. He argues that you should not have great faith in the single individual decision-maker who typically brings with them biases, blind spots and consequent mistakes, and that you should prefer collective decision-making because individuals' mistakes matter much less. He also notes that true experts are surprisingly hard to identify, and a group that's smart enough to be able to identify the expert shouldn't need the assistance of that individual.[4]

However, there are contexts in which experts are more valuable—especially in well-defined systems like the sciences or mathematics where rules-based solutions can dominate. In all contexts, the value of expert input rises when it is subject to cross-examination, yet so often decisions are taken in major commercial and political contexts without the cross-examination of those experts.

23.2   Groupthink

It seems to be easier to fool a crowd than a single person.

—Herodotus[5]

Although the term 'groupthink' was first coined in the 1950s, the phenomenon was obviously well understood by the historian Herodotus in the fifth century BC.

Psychologist Irving Janis wrote extensively on groupthink after studying its influence in a number of US foreign policy disasters (Pearl Harbor, The Bay of Pigs, the Korean War and the Vietnam War). He defined it as:

A mode of thinking that people engage in when they are deeply involved in a cohesive in-group, when the members' strivings for unanimity override their motivation to realistically appraise alternative courses of action ... Groupthink refers to a deterioration of mental efficiency, reality testing and moral judgement that results from in-group pressures.[6]

Janis identified two broad causes of groupthink: one cause is related to the group (for example, the homogeneity of membership, insulation or lack of a tradition of impartial leadership), and the other is related to a provocative situational context (for example, high stress from external threats or moral dilemmas). Janis also identified a number of symptoms of groupthink (such as illusions of invulnerability or of unanimity, direct pressure to conform or self-censorship) and a number of ways of preventing it. These included:

→ examining all effective alternatives
→ allowing each member to freely air objections and doubts or selecting one group member for the role of devil's advocate
→ setting up independent groups to work on the same problem
→ leaders not expressing opinions when assigning tasks to groups
→ members discussing the group's ideas with trusted outsiders or experts, either individually or at group meetings.

You see manifestations of groupthink in all sorts of environments:

→ in bubbles and crashes in financial markets
→ in feuding groups whose members only talk to like minds, fuelling their emotions
→ in some internet communities where most of the people are of like mind
→ in businesses where a prevalent optimistic or pessimistic mood emerges. In such circumstances, former Goldman Sachs chairman John Whitehead believes a good leader has to have a feel for the prevailing mood and be able to counterbalance it. He calls it 'leaning against the wind'.[7] This quality of leadership may be important over a sustained period, or in one-off situations where everyone's positivity or negativity is compounding to excess. The same may apply at a personal level; for example, in a period where everyone around you seems to be increasingly pessimistic, it takes personal leadership to maintain your optimism.

→ in business strategy, if groupthink favours the status quo. In *Why Smart Executives Fail*, Sydney Finkelstein highlights the strategic dangers of status quo thinking in business:

> How many times have we seen executives and organisations fully ensconced in a world of their making ... while the rest of the world goes off in another direction? ... They are true believers in trouble ... There is real danger in the status quo, and the risk is highest when true believers take over the organisation. Access to diverse sources of information is valuable to avoid becoming a company of true believers who disregard data that might tell another story.[8]

One challenge the true believers too rarely accept is to recognise that the diversity of sources of information and views is intended to strengthen the organisation and its decision-making, and not to attack it.

Finkelstein proposes that whenever a company is considering an important new course of action, groupthink will be avoided and its decision-making enhanced by seeking a minority report that makes as strong a case as possible for the seemingly second-best option. Minority reports of congressional and parliamentary committees sometimes do this. One famous example is Richard Feynman's minority report into the *Challenger* disaster. Feynman could not be convinced by his colleagues that their conclusions were consistent with the findings of their investigation. He observed that:

> It would appear that, for whatever purpose, be it for internal or external consumption, the management of NASA exaggerates the reliability of its product, to the point of fantasy ... For a successful technology, reality must take precedence over public relations, for nature cannot be fooled.[9]

Feynman argued for a suspension of shuttle launches until NASA's scientific understanding, internal communications and objectivity regarding shuttle reliability were improved.

23.3 Scuttlebutt and your big decisions

In 19.2 I focused on those big opportunities where a certain decision can preclude other alternatives. Examples include decisions about where to live, whether to change profession or change your employer, or whether to focus your time and energy on a particular project to the exclusion of other alternatives.

I noted that in such situations it is worthwhile to reflect on lessons from investors like Warren Buffett and Charlie Munger. Wealth Inserts 19A and 21A presented two of Benjamin Graham's underlying principles, which most influenced Buffett and Munger:

→ the 'margin of safety' concept.

→ thorough analysis distinguishes investment from speculation

Another major influence on the investment thinking of Buffett and Munger was Philip Fisher's focus on the identification of outstanding growth stocks. In his 1958 book *Common Stocks and Uncommon Profits*, Fisher maintained that superior returns would result from investment in exceptional companies with quality management and above average growth potential, but they could not be obtained by investing in marginal companies.

Fundamental to his search for exceptional companies was his 'scuttlebutt' method for accessing and assessing intelligence about a company's operations through the business grapevine.

Wealth Insert 23A: Philip Fisher's scuttlebutt and the business grapevine

Fisher remarks that an accurate picture of the strengths and weaknesses of each company in an industry can be obtained from a 'representative cross-section of the opinions of those who in one way or another are concerned with any particular company'. Most people, he notes, like to talk about their work and will talk rather freely about their competitors if they know they won't be quoted. So, if you ask five companies about their competitors' strengths and weaknesses, '9 times out of 10 a surprisingly detailed and accurate picture of all five will emerge'.[10]

Fisher cites other excellent sources of data and informed opinion: suppliers and customers, research scientists in universities, governments, competitors and executives of trade associations. He stresses the importance of giving people the

---

confidence that you never reveal your sources, and then abiding by this. Otherwise, you will never receive those all-important unfavourable comments.

Former employees, Fisher says, can be of immense help but they can also be harmful if you don't cross-check with others to verify the reliability of what you've been told—especially checking why the employee left the firm, so you can allow for any prejudice in their comments.

In *The Great Game of Business*, Jack Stack emphasises a similar scuttlebutt process for developing standards or benchmarks for an industrial business. He suggests talking to material suppliers, joining industry associations or studying great companies and asking them what they measure:

> *Write to that company. Call it on the phone. Ask what industry events the executives attend, and go and meet them there. If one of the executives is giving a speech, show up and stick around to ask questions afterwards. Most people are happy to tell you what you want to know unless you are a direct competitor, and even then they are often willing to swap information. Find out how many shifts they're open, what they do to make a difference. You don't need an appointment with the CEO. Talk to the guy who sweeps the floor...*[11]

Wealth Insert 23B: weight of money versus weight of competence and preparation

Philip Fisher recognised that prominent people in management receive a vast number of requests from investors for their time and they take such requests seriously because of the significance of their stock price. However, he heard from many executives that the amount of time they make available and their degree of willingness to furnish information is influenced more by the visitor's competence and preparation than the size of the financial interest the visitor represents.

Wealth Insert 23B (cont'd): *weight of money versus weight of competence and preparation*

Fisher worked and wrote in an era when the market was not as dominated by large institutional investors as it is today, the regulation of insider trading was not as severe or sophisticated, and the demands on company executives' time for market briefings were much lower. In today's environment, access to CEOs or CFOs is highly regulated and restricted. Nevertheless, Fisher's perspectives are still relevant today—although you, as a retail investor, may be talking to an investor relations executive rather than the CEO or CFO.

The scuttlebutt method is highly applicable to major decisions regarding your career, where you live, or whether to travel or continue your study. The breadth of the grapevine relevant to these situations is extensive, and insider-trading regulations do not apply. When considering most paths in your life journey, it is possible to speak to others who have been there before, whether successfully or unsuccessfully. Often there is more to learn from the unsuccessful.

When considering alternative employers, alternative businesses to buy or entry into a new industry, you can seek out the opportunity to speak to any of the following:

→ employees (current or former)
→ suppliers
→ customers
→ complainers
→ others in a similar business or using a similar business model
→ landlords
→ bankers
→ accountants
→ lawyers.

Such conversations not only assist in developing knowledge and resolving the immediate decision, they also help in making contacts or developing relationships that may be of value after the move—whether as customers, suppliers, employees, partners or mentors.

A classic example is if you are considering the purchase of a franchise from a franchisor. You have an obligation to go back to them to raise any questions you might have about their disclosure statement. Even if you don't know the right questions to ask up-front, you will be better informed about such a major decision if you discuss the opportunity with any of the following:

→ your financier's employee who deals with franchisees from this and other franchisors
→ other franchisees of the franchisor
→ competitors of the franchisor
→ customers of other franchisees of this franchisor
→ the landlord and its other tenants
→ an accountant familiar with this or similar franchises who can advise on the capital requirements and cash flow of the business model.

In the absence of such grapevine scuttlebutt, you may be setting yourself up for failure.

23.4 Accessing information and developing knowledge

When capitalising on a grapevine to access information and develop knowledge, some important principles or opportunities apply.

Independence

As I explained in 23.1, the value of your grapevine is maximised if independence of thought in your information sources is maximised. Hence, in seeking information and views from others it is preferable not to lead with: 'Fred thinks this ... I think that ...' or 'I understand from Fred that ... what do you think?'

Efficiency

You will generally receive diminishing returns from your scuttlebutt unless you are tapping into people from different disciplines, with different perspectives on the opportunity at hand.

Asking the same questions of multiple sources

This will give you valuable information, not only about the immediate issues but also about the people you've asked. It is particularly valuable if you've recently assumed a new leadership role—ask each of your direct reports the same questions about opportunities, constraints, resources and the things you should do differently, and compare the responses.

The vagaries of human memory

One argument for having multiple contacts from the same perspective or discipline is to allow for the vagaries of human memory, as Herodotus did. Around 2500 years ago, he found that people remember things differently. In effect, they remember what they want to remember: 'Everyone colours events after a fashion, brews up his own melange of reminiscences…The past does not exist. There are only infinite renderings of it'.[12] Little has changed.

No shame

Don't fall for the 'not invented here' syndrome. Never be too proud to use someone else's best practices or ideas, provided attribution is made where required or appropriate.

Design your own course

For most of life's challenges and opportunities, there is no course to teach you. The answer is to design your own—teach yourself!

When Rudi Giuliani decided to run for Mayor of New York City, he couldn't find a book about how to be a mayor, so he created his own course. He started informally with reading and then asked questions of authors, professors and elected officials. Later, he formalised his approach with seminars to explore and develop ideas for reinventing New York City. He brought in experts and asked them what they would be telling him to do if he were mayor.[13]

23.5 Objectivity, scepticism and the assessment of information

The high-adrenaline world of mergers and acquisitions highlights the importance of scuttlebutt. As Sydney Finkelstein comments in *Why Smart Executives Fail:*

> *Get information from the trenches. You have a choice. Develop your own information sources, or depend on investment bankers to identify acquisition candidates. So, you can talk to suppliers, customers, even competitors. You can rely on division managers in the competitive trenches. Ask whom they have noticed that has an interesting product or service that fits well with current offerings, that has great managerial talent and so on. Or, you can wait for the 'books' that make their rounds on Wall Street with one express purpose — to entice you to buy assets that are currently for sale at the highest price possible. It's your call.*[14]

Like Philip Fisher's reflections on the potential for prejudice in the minds of former employees (see Wealth Insert 23A), Finkelstein's comments highlight the importance of the objectivity of your sources and the advantages of healthy scepticism.

Objective cross-verification helps minimise the downside and maximises the upside. It also optimises the validity of any experiment, thereby minimising the risk of major opportunity loss.

A clear and open mind, scepticism and scuttlebutt help you pick up 'soft signals' of potential issues and opportunities. Further discussions with others, especially those you respect, and your own independent thought are the next steps in determining whether those issues or opportunities remain part of the story or are irrelevant. Your search for important soft signals can easily be hindered by the vast amount of information being generated every day, especially if you work in the overheated environment of the trading room of a major investment bank, which has every conceivable source of information feeding into its vast communication networks.

Investment is a classic example of how your judgement can be clouded with every latest and loudest bit of information. According to Michael J Mauboussin, the majority of America's high-performing investors are based not in New York and Boston, but in regional cities,[15] where they are not isolated but are one step removed from the excessive stimuli, distracting rumours and adrenaline of the financial centres. Warren Buffett said of Omaha: 'You can think here. You can think better about the market; you don't hear so many stories, and you can just sit and look at the stock on the desk in front of you. You can think about a lot of things'.[16]

This is a version of the concept of 'confusion management', devised by *Flip* author Peter Sheahan. He considers confusion management the most important asset for a leader today, who has to deal 'with ambiguity, contradiction and uncertainty while still retaining the ability to function'.[17] One of the tools Sheahan identifies for confusion management is a form of online scuttlebutt—peer-to-peer networks that 'allow users to get recommendations from people they know and trust, so they can sort through the limitless choices efficiently'.[18] Other tools include the classic technological solutions applied by Amazon in making book recommendations and the Google algorithm for identifying the most relevant sources of information.

Charlie Munger admired the value of Charles Darwin's extreme objectivity:

> He tried to disconfirm his ideas as soon as he got 'em. He quickly put down in his notebook anything that disconfirmed a much-loved idea. He especially sought out such things ... If you keep doing that over time, you get to be a perfectly marvellous thinker ...[19]

23.6 The final test: tell the story and examine it through multiple lenses

Lynch's two-minute monologue is a valuable discipline to draw upon when making most major decisions—whether personal or business.

Wealth Insert 23C: Peter Lynch's two-minute monologue

Peter Lynch has a powerful discipline for checking his thinking on potential investments. He takes the view that when you become aware of a potential investment, all you have is 'simply a lead to a story that has to be developed'. As I described in Wealth Insert 7, his first step is to put each stock into one of his six categories so he's clear what kind of story it's supposed to be. His next step is to fill in the details that help him guess how the story will develop.

The final test before making the investment is the telling of that story. Lynch likes to be able to give a two-minute monologue covering why he's interested in the stock, what's needed for the company to succeed and what stands in its way. According to Lynch:

> Once you're able to tell the story of a stock to your family, your friends or the dog... so that even a child could understand it, then you have a proper grasp of the situation.[20]

In his *Treatise on Painting*, Leonardo da Vinci suggests that when you are painting you should examine your work in a mirror so you can see it in reverse and thereby imagine that it is someone else's work, allowing you to be more objective. He also suggests leaving it for a while and relaxing so that on your return your judgement will be surer; or looking at it from a distance, so you can take in more of it at a glance and more easily identify any lack of harmony or proportion.[21]

Like Leonardo's paintings, your decisions will be more effective if you listen to your monologue from different perspectives. Charlie Munger applies a version of this approach when he thinks problems through forwards and backwards (see 22.4).

When considering a major acquisition or divestment, a CEO or company board does something analogous to Lynch's two-minute monologue by drafting a press release. They follow Leonardo's principles if they then review that draft separately from the perspectives of shareholders, staff and other stakeholders.

Over to you ...

Reflection

- When have you used scuttlebutt really effectively or seen others do so? What things impacted the effectiveness and value of your scuttlebutt?
- Are you generally an objective thinker? Are you an independent thinker? In what past contexts have you found yourself being less objective? Is your judgement often clouded by the latest and loudest piece of information?
- Where, how and why have your teams evidenced 'groupthink'? Were any of Janis's preventions tried or Finkelstein's minority report approach?

Action

- In a situation where you're missing important but obtainable information, plan an approach for obtaining it — at least in part including the use of scuttlebut.
- Try a draft press release or Lynch's two-minute monologue next time you have to make a major decision. Look at the words from many alternative perspectives — those of your mother, your partner, your boss, people in your street, members of your profession, the authorities. Also try Finkelstein's minority report approach.

Conclusion

What of it?

We are, each of us, 'decision-makers' in deciding the destiny of humankind. It is a time, then, that offers so much meaning. And yet, because of the pressures, preoccupations and priorities of life today, we don't sense this significance of the moment—or sensing it, seem unable to hold it and be inspired by it. This is one of the most profound paradoxes of our times. Recognising this can help us make the right choices—and find more meaning in our lives.

—Richard Eckersley[1]

As we have seen, your most important and most frequent investment decisions are not financial. They involve your time and energy, your mental and physical health, your relationships and learning. Together, they build your Life Capital.

By encouraging you to be aware of the size of opportunities in life, and to realise the value of engaged conversations, *Investing in Your Life* empowers you to enjoy success and satisfaction on your terms.

There is a strong analogy between how the great investors accumulate financial capital and how you can build your Life Capital. The great investors capitalise on the power of compound growth, the value of annuities, circles of competence, opportunity cost, margins of safety, diversification to spread risk, qualified deal flow, returns for risk, leverage, options, the wisdom of crowds, scuttlebutt and objectivity. All of these investment concepts have natural applications to the building of your Life Capital—a powerful and original analogy!

In summary, *Investing in Your Life* is all about recognising the following important factors:

- → Your personal development—it's an investment process, your own responsibility and your own choice.
- → You are more likely to invest your scarcest resources—your time, energy and emotional capital—in measurable aspects of life, with shorter term paybacks. You are therefore likely to underinvest in your human and social capital, both of which have longer term paybacks and limited measurability.
- → Many opportunities for building your human and social capital are far bigger than you realise. You can better identify the big opportunities in life by drawing on the concepts applied by the great investors in spotting financial investment opportunities.
- → The bigger the opportunities you see, the more likely you are to invest in them.
- → If you view conversations, relationships, opportunities, habits, learning and decision-making through the eyes of an investor in Life Capital, you may see them quite differently.
- → Leveraging off other people's Life Capital through engaged conversation is an important source of opportunity, which is more sustainable if you reciprocate. For most people, the art of conversation is an underdeveloped and underutilised skill, and a source of significant opportunity loss.
- → Your life is a marathon, not a sprint. The greatest growth in Life Capital, as in financial capital, is ultimately achieved by those with a long-term perspective who recognise the old adage 'You get out of it what you put in'.

So, 'What of it?'

… for you

You live in a world where extreme demands are placed on your time, energy and emotional capital. One of your most important skills is your ability to identify what *really* matters to you, and how the opportunities you see in life fit those concerns. *Investing in Your Life* gives you tools to help you do this better and more efficiently.

These tools will only be effective if you take time out to reflect on the significance of what lies in front of you — in the day ahead, the week ahead and any big events immediately before you. Once you recognise that you have a significant opportunity, reflect on the ways you can optimise that opportunity — taking into account its relevance to the many different components of your Life Capital. You'll be astonished by two things. Firstly, by the realisation that many factors can help you increase both your chances of success and the extent of your success (a great multiplier effect!), and consequently also your confidence. Secondly, by how much better you have become at understanding the interactions between the many components of your Life Capital. For example, seeing how your emotional capital interacts with your intellectual capital, or your financial capital with your social capital.

Investing in Your Life focuses on *why* certain opportunities are important in life. I have only touched briefly on *how* to capitalise on the opportunities themselves, because for most of your significant opportunities in life there is already a vast array of 'how to' literature available, which you can easily access on the internet or in bookshops.

For each potentially Life Capital–enriching opportunity that you identify, you have to make an important decision: to take it on or to let it pass. You need to weigh up what the opportunity will bring to your life and your chances of achieving it, given the other demands on your energy, and also the courage and emotional capital needed to capitalise on it. In doing this, don't forget to allow for the ways you can improve both your chances of success and the quantum of success by leveraging off others' Life Capital.

If you solidly embrace the principles contained in *Investing in Your Life,* you have three manageable areas of risk.

→ That you cut out opportunities for serendipity by trying to mastermind things too much. The aim of this book is to achieve exactly the opposite: you need to develop habits that are conducive to serendipity, and to avoid such habits as cutting conversations short or not having an open mind, which prevent opportunities for serendipity.

→ That you spend so much time reflecting on and talking about your opportunities that you take an eternity to make decisions or you leave little time to carry them out. While this could initially be the case, with practice you will become more like a triage nurse in the accident and emergency ward, able to quickly isolate the serious cases that warrant specialist and immediate attention. This is not a precise science so don't waste time looking for precision. If a big opportunity doesn't jump out at you, move on. To do this well, you'll need effective shortcuts to making good decisions. You'll find that you'll develop these over time through reflection on your life, what matters to you and the events around you.

→ That the development of your Life Capital lacks balance between its many components. This risk is exacerbated if you focus on building your strengths and have limited feedback mechanisms regarding your blind spots. It can also be exacerbated if you invest excessively in certain components of your Life Capital to the exclusion or dilution of others. Probably the best protection from this risk is to be aware that you are doing it, and to recognise why you are doing it.

... for you as a team leader or parent

Keep asking yourself what else you can do to encourage your team members or children to invest more in their Life Capital, and to engage more effectively with you, with each other and with outsiders.

The most significant thing you can do is to demonstrate to them through your own words and deeds your belief in the rewards from investing in your Life Capital, and in the importance of engaged conversation.

... for organisations

Investing in Your Life presents obvious opportunities and challenges for organisations:

→ how to encourage their people to invest more in their human and social capital

→ how to increase their people's awareness of the high returns available from investing in themselves

→ how to provide an environment that is conducive to such investment, and to the types of conversations that can be important catalysts to this investment.

The opportunities for an organisation are vast:

→ physical—office or plant layout, sizes of business units, communications technology

→ informational—clear objectives, discussions regarding insightful historical data and scenario planning

→ cultural—common vision, common language and stories

→ attitudinal—balanced perspectives on performance reviews, experimentation and risk taking, success and failure, diversity, internal and external collaboration

→ educational—selected courses

→ social—dinners, family picnics and celebrations of success.

The more an organisation can encourage its people to invest in themselves and to engage effectively with others, both internally and externally, the more grounded, capable and successful that organisation is likely to be.

... for researchers in human and social capital

Many subjects in human and social capital are unquantifiable. However, the analogy between the building of human and social capital and the building of financial capital may enable some researchers to analyse more effectively the growth processes that are taking place or are potentially available in their chosen field, even if they don't have sound measures of their status at particular points in time.

For example, a full analysis of the impact of successful microfinance programs for women in third world countries should go well beyond an analysis of the impact on financial or economic capital. It should also cover its significant potential impact on the following:

Human capital

→ Women learning to be entrepreneurs.

→ Women's self-worth, self-reliance and independence, and consequently their ability to take more control of their lives and make decisions about matters that are important to them and their families, including their health and their education.

→ Women's self-discovery, greater creativity and licence to push their boundaries.

→ Women's increased ability to be mentors or role models for others in their communities.

Social capital

→ The impact on the status of women in their communities.

→ The building of peer support and peer pressure—with its impact on areas well beyond financial concerns.

→ The building of institutions in a community—potentially extending beyond the initial lending activities to include much-needed savings, insurance and money transfer services

→ The impact on working conditions.

→ access to mentors and the emergence of role models

→ The building of the credit-worthiness of poor women individually and collectively.

→ The greater mobility of women as their networks widen—offering options not previously available.

Almost all the above non-financial benefits are recurring, rather than being one-offs; hence most of these benefits should be valued like an annuity. Also, the interaction of these many forms of increased human and social capital with the women's increased financial capital has the potential to create a virtuous circle—compounding benefits that go well beyond any impact based purely on economic analysis.

The benefits might not be able to be measured precisely but, as in the analogy with financial capital, if they are positive, recurring and compounding, over the long term their impact will definitely be substantial.

... for teaching

As engaged conversation is a major catalyst in building human, social and financial capital, the opportunity cost of underdeveloped conversation skills is vast. It is also a major contributor in many societies to the persistence of inequality from generation to generation.

This situation is exacerbated by underinvestment in education, especially public education, and by the absence from virtually all school, university or professional courses of teaching on engaged conversation or social literacy; for example, perceptions of trust, participating in and reading social situations, and building relationships and networks.

John Field's *Social Capital*, which provides an excellent review of contemporary research and thinking about social capital, concludes with the suggestion (in respect of the UK):

> ... *perhaps there should be a national programme for social literacy, not only for schoolchildren but also—and perhaps primarily —for adults.*[2]

I am convinced that Field's suggestion is very valuable. It is also challenging, as it would require significant experimentation, and therefore risk some 'failures', before the most effective and most acceptable programs are developed. One of the biggest challenges is to gain the buy-in of those who are intended to benefit from such programs, as people with low social literacy can be somewhat distrustful of external agencies. It is also challenging for policymakers, because the benefits will be difficult to isolate and measure, and will principally accrue in future rather than current electoral cycles.

... for policymakers and proponents of policies

Any public investments in social capital have difficult hurdles to jump, including concerns that their impacts may be negative rather than positive. It is therefore important that policymakers or proponents of public policies analyse the full dimensions of the impact of such investments—recognising, as per the microfinance example above, the recurring and compounding benefits that can emerge.

This mode of thinking is important when deciding which investments to make. It is also important in structuring the public investments to achieve the utmost they can in multiple and mutually supportive areas—to increase the chances of recurring benefits (annuities) and virtuous circles (compounding).

Applying this logic to Field's concept of a 'national programme for social literacy', the return on investment would come through the direct and compounded effects of the following:

- → the program helping people build their social literacy and introducing them to new networks
- → people's wider networks and stronger networking skills enhancing their access to resources and opportunities in many forms—with potential benefits for their economic and financial performance, their educational performance, their health and their contribution to society
- → people's greater access to resources and their enhanced performance collectively helping to build their confidence and self-esteem, and thereby helping to build their capacity to take on new challenges
- → adults whose social literacy is enhanced being better able to influence the social literacy of their children, and being more likely to communicate to their children the importance of social literacy and the value of any social literacy program available to them.

These benefits cannot be quantified, but once again we can note that they are positive, recurring and potentially permanent, and have the characteristics of a virtuous circle. Hence, by making the analogy with the growth of financial capital from annuities and compounding, the benefits will ultimately be very substantial—even if the majority of them emerge well beyond the next election.

To conclude, I believe that the analogy I have drawn between the long-term accumulation of human and social capital and the long-term accumulation of financial capital can be of value in many areas of public and private life. The value of employees' human and social capital is being increasingly recognised by good businesses, despite its intangible nature. I particularly challenge governments and international agencies to recognise the value of human and social capital, and the returns from investing in them. My hope is that they will accelerate such investments accordingly, despite the challenges of the current economic downturn.

I wrote *Investing in Your Life* principally for individuals like you. You have one major advantage over both governments and public companies: you are not accountable to the electorate or to shareholders in short-term cycles. Hence, you can choose to place serious weight on the longer term benefits that accrue from investment in your Life Capital—greater opportunities, income, contribution, companionship, satisfaction or pleasure. You can do so on your own terms, in your own good time, in the context of your passions and plans, and by leveraging off the Life Capital of others through engaged conversation.

Appendix A
Some life assets

The following life assets potentially apply to everyone:

Social assets
→ the family and community into which you were born
→ the community and the environment in which you live
→ having an enriching family and social life.

Human assets
→ *Spiritual assets*
  • understanding what makes your life meaningful at the deepest level—in other words, your personal mission
  • your experiences and learning as you search for and think through the ultimate meaning and motivation in your life.
→ *Physical assets*
  • your health (physical and mental) and fitness
  • your work–life balance and feeling good
  • your energy levels, including the ability to have a restful night's sleep, to handle stress, to relax and to concentrate.

→ *Intellectual assets*
  - being observant or inquisitive
  - having a good memory (including for names).
→ *Intellectual and emotional assets*
  - having a sense of humour
  - having experience, self-knowledge and self-awareness
  - clarity of direction and focus
  - the ability to recognise opportunity and to make decisions
  - good communication — having the ability to listen and to talk
  - the independence of judgement needed to say 'no' — even to those in authority
  - the ability to ask for feedback effectively.
→ *Emotional assets*
  - self-awareness and empathy
  - self-belief and self-reliance
  - the ability to absorb, even to welcome or seek, constructive criticism
  - the ability to move on and not overemphasise bad events
  - the ability to bounce back from adversity — resilience

The following life assets might be more selectively relevant to individuals or specific careers:

Social assets

→ your personal contacts/networks/relationships/colleagues/partners/ champions — the people you choose to surround yourself with
→ your human information channels
→ your reputation and brand
→ your Circle of Influence
→ your deal or opportunity flow and client introductions
→ having a coach or mentor you can work with
→ having a good tax adviser.

Financial assets

Human assets

→ *Intellectual assets*
  - your technical and professional qualifications
  - your ideas-generation capacity and intellectual property
  - your ability to talk or work across multiple disciplines
  - your ability to manage a large amount of assets or businesses.
→ *Intellectual and emotional assets*
  - your current job and previous experience

- your knowledge and competence in your immediate work environment
- your objectivity and judgement
- your ability to identify good people
- your ability to lead and manage large numbers of people
- your ability to deal with ambiguity, uncertainty and contradiction.

→ *Emotional assets*
- having a worldly mind-set and the ability to adapt

→ *Physical assets*
- the ability to move around freely and internationally to follow opportunity
- the ability to handle an arduous travel schedule or to handle stress, without becoming ineffective
- if you're really lucky, good looks! According to Robert Cialdini:

> *Research has shown that we automatically assign to good-looking people such favourable traits as talent, kindness, honesty, and intelligence. Furthermore, we make these judgements without being aware that physical attractiveness plays a role in the process ... attractive people are more likely to obtain help when in need and are more persuasive in changing the opinions of an audience.*[1]

→ *Cultural assets*
- your artistic preferences
- your mastery and use of your language
- your grasp of grammar, spelling and self-expression
- your manners
- your qualifications.

→ *Symbolic assets*
- your reputation, prestige and honour
- your right to be listened to.

Appendix B

Sizings of benefits from selected opportunities to invest in your Life Capital

B1: Constructive feedback and reporting relationships

1   Benefits from receiving constructive feedback positively
- → Some one-off performance benefits in the immediate future
- → Some recurring performance benefits (annuity)
- → You get better at receiving and dealing with feedback, and consequently you are given more feedback (virtuous circle — compounding)
- → Your constructive response is reciprocated by the other person and the relationship grows (virtuous circle — compounding)
- → With the stronger relationship, numerous other aspects of your life become easier or more effective; for example, reporting, access to information, access to resources (virtuous circle — compounding)
- → The other person ultimately becomes one of your champions and introduces opportunities to you (free options)
- → As you get better at receiving feedback, and give more thought to how feedback is given, you are likely to get better at providing it (virtuous circle — compounding); see 2
- → Each of the above performance and relationship benefits is potentially applicable to feedback in all of your domains — home, work and leisure — and in all of your major relationships (multiplicity).

2 Benefits from giving feedback constructively
- → You pass on the potential of receiving the many virtuous outcomes identified in 1. (*options*); if, however, you provide feedback lazily or destructively, you destroy that potential (*opportunity cost*)
- → If you are providing feedback to a number of people, the above impacts are in total proportionally bigger (*multiplicity*).

3 Benefits from more effective upwards reporting: An *annuity* for the term of the reporting relationship of the following benefits:
- → Better information flow for you and your team
- → Better knowledge of and input to strategic issues
- → Better access to proper resourcing
- → Better capacity to influence outcomes because of better knowledge base
- → Greater resilience because of your better understanding of tough decisions
- → More effective problem-solving
- → More constructive feedback (see 1)
- → Less wasted time and energy, less micromanagement, greater effectiveness, better performance and more satisfaction
- → More opportunities for networking and learning (*options*).

If you master how to report upwards effectively, these benefits may extend to other future reporting relationships.

B2:   Work–life balance — time — energy

1 Benefits from more effective negotiation with others
- → The impact on your total workload from negotiating better with clients regarding the basis of assignments; with colleagues regarding their contributions and your access to resources; with support staff regarding delegation; and with your life partner or family regarding the sharing of the load at home, bringing in outside help or regarding their expectations (*multiple* reductions of the number of hours worked per week)
- → Having much greater time for your personal and family life and your outside interests (*leverage*, implicit in the A = B – C formula) leaves you refreshed and more effective, and able to complete your work in fewer hours (virtuous circle — *compounding*)
- → Avoids the negative impacts of an absolutely full diary

2 Negative impacts of an absolutely full diary
- → Your use of your time and energy is poor, and you become drained and less effective (vicious circle — *negative compounding*)
- → Poor preparation means meetings are less effective than they should be (*opportunity loss* and wasted time *compounding* your diary problems)

→ Poor preparation means you learn less at meetings—both in terms of content and also in terms of learning about others attending the meetings (*opportunity loss*)

→ No time for reflection immediately after conversations or meetings means some of the potential benefits are lost; for example, good opportunities are overlooked, soft signals are missed, follow-up commitments are forgotten (*opportunity loss*)

→ Others are not as impressed with your contribution and may be less keen to work with you in future (*multiple opportunity loss* because of the number of meetings you attend and the number of people at each meeting)

→ You're always in a rush between meetings so you are often unengaged in conversations and miss opportunities to help others (*opportunity loss*)

→ In the event of something negative occurring (which is more likely if you're rushed), you don't have any time to process what's happened and to clear your head before the next event (*potential negative compounding*)

→ People think you're too busy and unavailable so they don't offer you opportunities (*opportunity loss*).

Given the 80/20 rule, it is madness to have an absolutely full diary on a regular basis and suffer the consequent level of opportunity loss. The situation is made even worse if you are left with no time for thinking and preparing for the week ahead, with consequent loss of both opportunities and effectiveness (a *negative compounding impact* on many other issues).

B3: Successful behavioural change

1 Benefits from increasing the probability of successful behavioural change include an increased probability of gaining each of the following:

→ Ongoing direct benefits from the behavioural change (*annuity*)

→ Learnings from the successful change process (*annuity*)

→ Impact on your confidence generally and on your confidence to undertake other behavioural change (*annuity of options*)

→ Impact on others' perception of you (*potentially compounding* with other factors).

As a consequence of the increased probability, you have a higher expected value and hence are more likely to make and persist with the necessary investment.

2 Benefits from being able to identify the low-hanging juicy fruit may include the following:

→ The higher probability that you'll invest (increasing the *expected value*)

→ The higher probability of your investment being successful (increasing the *expected value*)

→ Success increases your confidence to tackle other behavioural change (*potential annuity of options*)

3 Blind spots can include not listening, not having an open mind, not giving others the opportunity to tell their stories, not noting down opportunities and forgetting many of them as a result, sticking to comfort zones and risk aversion. Identifying and dealing with a blind spot that is causing serial opportunity cost can transform an *annuity of opportunity cost* into an *annuity of opportunities*.

B4:   Pessimism and flexible optimism

Pessimism can have the following negative effects:

→ You are less likely to see opportunities or to take on and persist with them—including many opportunities identified under other headings in this appendix (*annuity of opportunity loss*)

→ Your pessimism will impact on the optimism of others who engage with you and on their desire to team with you (*vicious circle—negative compounding*).

Achieving a change from pessimism to flexible optimism may help you overcome these negative impacts.

B5:   Resilience

Some benefits from building resilience include the following:

→ The downside from events that go against you will be reduced (you avoid an *annuity of vicious circles—an annuity of negative compounding*)

→ You are more likely to be prepared to take on risks or experiment because the downside for you from failure has been reduced (you avoid an *annuity of opportunity loss*)

→ People are more likely to want you on their team if you are more resilient and are more open to pursuing opportunities (*annuity of options*)

→ You are less likely to be pessimistic (see B4).

B6:   Your circle of competence

There are many benefits to be gained by widening your circle of competence. These include the following:

→ More opportunities are potentially available (*annuity of options*)

→ The range of people with whom you can engage with confidence widens (*annuity of options* over relationships)

→ There is potential cross-fertilisation with concepts from your existing areas of expertise (*virtuous circles — compounding*)

→ You are less likely to overuse your existing assets (and hence it is less likely they become liabilities).

B7: Your life assets and liabilities

Understanding your life assets and liabilities can have the following benefits:

→ Understanding when you can best use your assets increases your opportunity set (*annuity of options*) and reduces the risk that you use your strengths inappropriately and they become liabilities (*avoids loss*)

→ Knowing your liabilities enhances your ability to work around them (*annuity of avoidance of loss*)

→ Knowing where you can improve or where you can learn from others gives you opportunities to enhance your Life Capital (*annuity of options*), as well as offering a greater chance of converting liabilities into assets

→ Realising how you need to invest in your assets to preserve and build them

B8: Learning methods

Using your optimum learning methods can have the following benefits:

→ Your human capital will grow faster

→ Your engagement gap will be shorter, making you more effective quicker (*leverage*)

→ You will know the things you really need to know sooner, and not feel that you have to be seen to know everything (see B9)

→ You will derive more pleasure and be more likely to persist, succeed and gain more confidence (*virtuous circle — compounding*)

→ Others will be more impressed with you and your progress, so your relationships will benefit (see also B1)

→ You are likely to be a better teacher

B9: Thinking you have to be seen to know everything

Negative impacts may result from thinking you have to be seen to know everything; they may include the following:

→ Less enjoyment because of being on guard (*annuity*)

→ Slower learning (which probably *compounds* the underlying problem)

→ Covering up problems and less likely to engage with others to solve issues (*vicious circle — negative compounding*)

→ Less awareness of opportunities and less take-up of opportunities (*annuity*)

→ Your defensiveness leads to less open and ultimately poorer relationships (*vicious circle — negative compounding*)

B10: Conversation

There are numerous benefits of more engaged and leveraged conversation, including the following:

→ You will identify more opportunities (*annuity of free options*)

→ You will have more qualified deals at decision time (*leverage*)

→ You will make better decisions because of better information (*higher expected value*)

→ Your relationship building will be enhanced (*virtuous circles — compounding*)

→ You will learn more (annuity).

B11: Collaboration

Being an effective collaborator can have many benefits, including the following:

→ More opportunities come your way (*options*)

→ These opportunities are in wider and wider fields and with better and better collaborators (*virtuous circle — compounding*)

→ Collaboration is easier and more enjoyable (the investment is less onerous)

→ More success and wider learning from the collaboration

→ The leveraged impact on your relationships of under-promising and over-delivering — leading to more potential relationships and more champions (further *options*).

B12: Decision-making

You will enjoy an annuity of the following benefits by applying good decision-making techniques.

→ You are more likely to take measured risks so you will capitalise on more opportunities, and your probability of success is higher (these

compound to produce a significantly higher *expected value* of the outcome)
→ Your decision-making will be respected by others and this may help build relationships (*options*).

B13: Benchmarking

The following are potential benefits each time you apply sound benchmarking:
→ You have a measure of the size of change that is possible
→ You see more objectively what is possible and what may not be possible, helping you to set your goals more realistically
→ Seeing the size of the potential change gives you energy for improvement
→ You will have a better understanding of where and why you fell short this time (performance attribution) so your learning will be accelerated.

B14: Not dealing with issues

There are many potentially negative impacts of failure to deal with a significant medical discomfort (for example, persistent neck problems or headaches):
→ ongoing discomfort
→ other potential medical problems as a consequence
→ poorer concentration and reduced effectiveness
→ less engagement and less positive engagement with others and hence deteriorating relationships.

All the above are annuities of impact—the term of the annuities is until you have resolved the medical issue.

Notes

Preface

1   L Babcock and S Laschever, *Women Don't Ask: Negotiation and the Gender Divide*, 2003.

Introduction

1   Other than where specifically identified, the quotes from and information about Bono are taken from *Bono on Bono: Conversations with Michka Assayas*, 2005.

2   J Tyrangiel, 'The Constant Charmer', in 'Time Magazine Persons of the Year', *Time*, 26 December 2005, p. 36.

3   N Gibbs, 'Time Magazine Persons of the Year', *Time*, 26 December 2005, p. 25, and interview with Bono on ABC TV's *Enough Rope* with Andrew Denton, March 2006.

4   Gibbs, p. 24.

5   R Tomlinson& F O'Brien, 'Bono Inc', in *Bloomberg Markets*, March 2007, p. 74.

6   Tomlinson & O'Brien, p. 73.
7   Tomlinson & O'Brien, p. 80.

Part 1

1   S Scott, *Fierce Conversations: Achieving Success at Work and in Life, One Conversation at a Time*, 2002, p. ix.

Principle 1

1   P Monk, 'The Retreat from Pythagoras', in *Australian Financial Review*, 30 June 2006.
2   H Mackay, *Advance Australia—Where?*, 2007, p. 100
3.   J Harley & D Batson, 'From Jerusalem to Jericho: A study of situational and dispositional variables in helping behaviour', in *Journal of Personality and Social Psychology*, 1973, vol. 27, no. 1, pp. 100–08.
4.   R Mellick, 'Neurology of Laughter', in *Australian Financial Review*, 22 February 2008.
5.   R Putnam, *Bowling Alone: The Collapse and Revival of American Community*, 2000, p. 19.
6.   R Putnam, lecture at Lend Lease Corporation, 19 August 2005.
7.   JS House, University of Michigan, Salt and Light weblog.
8.   Putnam, p. 327.
9.   M Kundera, *The Book of Laughter and Forgetting*, 1979, afterword.

Principle 2

1   S Singh, *Fermat's Last Theorem*, 1997, p. 43.
2   Singh, p. 4.
3   M Seligman, *Authentic Happiness: Using the New Positive Psychology to Realise Your Potential for Lasting Fulfiment*, 2002, p. 37.

Principle 3

1   M Gladwell, *The Tipping Point: How Little Things Can Make a Big Difference*, 2000, p. 27.

2   The 'Rule of 70' is most accurate for interest rates less than 5 per cent per annum. For higher rates up to about 10 per cent, the similar 'Rule of 72' is more accurate.

3   Berkshire Hathaway Annual Report, 2007.

4   City of New York Finance Department, 2008 Land Tax assessment.

5   US\$253 billion = US\$24 $\times$ $(1.0623)^{382}$.

6   D Goleman, *Working with Emotional Intelligence*, 1998, p. 35.

7   J Livingston, 'Pygmalion in Management', in *Harvard Business Review*, 1969 (reprinted in *Best of HBR: Motivating People*, January 2003, p. 103).

Principle 4

1   WG Bennis & RJ Thomas, *Geeks and Geezers*, 2002, p. 17.

2   A Deutschman, 'Change or Die', in *Fast Company*, Issue 94, May 2005, p. 53ff.

3   T Schelling, 'The intimate contest for self-command', in *The Public Interest*, Summer 1980, pp. 95–96.

4   Tim Harford, *The Logic of Life*, 2008, p. 60.

5   Harford, p. 64.

6   D Goodgame, 'The game of risk: How the best golfer in the world got even better', in *Time*, 14 August 2000.

Principle 5

1   C Ellis, *Winning the Loser's Game: Timeless Strategies for Successful Investing*, 2002, p. 8.

2   R Eckersley, 'What's it all about', in *The Sydney Morning Herald*, 25 March 2000.

3   R Eckersley, 'The politics of happiness', in *Living Now*, March 2007, pp. 6–7; R Eckersley, 'A Headlong rush to riches and unhappiness', in *Canberra Times*, 25 October 2005.

4   R Eckersley, 'Old ways of finding happiness still work', in *Canberra Times*, 6 March 2003.

5   C Munger, 'A lesson on elementary, worldly wisdom as it relates to investment management and business', lecture to USC Business School, 1994.

6   C Munger.

7   M J Mauboussin *More than You Know* 2006 pp. 7–13.

8   R Yallop, 'Slams baby', in *The Australian*, 15 January 2002

9   B Jhoty, 'Oarsome Competitor', in *Australian Men's Health*, February 2008, p. 70.

10. Garry Kasparov, *How Life Imitates Chess*, 2007, p. 68.

11. P Senge, *The Fifth Discipline: The Art and Practice of the Learning Organisation*, 1990, p. 14.

12. G Kasparov, *How Life Imitates Chess*, 2007, p. 75.

13. W G. Bennis & R J Thomas, *Geeks and Geezers*, 2002, p. 176.

Principle 6

1   S Finkelstein, *Why Smart Executives Fail: And What You Can Learn from Their Mistakes*, 2003, p. 148.

2   P Hughes, *Spiritual Capital — An Important Asset of Workplace and Community*, 2008, pp. 14–15.

3   J Newcombe, *Newk: Life On and Off the Court*, 2002, pp. 13, 14.

4   Newcombe, p. 89.

5   Interview with Ian Thorpe on ABC Radio's PM, 21 November 2006, and Janet Hawley, 'Thorpe's lethal stroke we'll never see', in the *Sydney Morning Herald*, 24 March 2007.

6   Interview with Shane Gould on ABC Radio's Conversation Hour with Richard Fidler, 9 March 2006.

7   A Damasio, *Descartes' Error: Emotion, Reason and the Human Brain*, 1994, pp. xxi, xxiii.

8   M Gladwell, *Blink: The Power of Thinking Without Thinking*, 2005, pp. 63, 252.

9   F Molloy, 'Training the Teens', in *Fast Thinking*, Autumn, 2007, p. 95.

10. S Covey, *The Seven Habits of Highly Effective People*, 2003, p. 54.

Principle 7

1   C Ellis, *Investors' Anthology*, 1988, p. 267, quoting from *The Life of P. T. Barnum*.

2   P Lynch, *One Up On Wall Street*, 1989, p. 156.

3   P Lynch, *One Up On Wall Street*, 1989, chapter 7.

4   C Handy, *The Elephant and the Flea*, 2001, p. 132.
5   $(1.2)^{10} = 6.2$, $(1.2)^{20} = 38.3$, $(1.2)^{30} = 237.4$

Principle 8

1   From Emerson's 1841 essay, 'Compensation'.
2   A Snyder, *What Makes a Champion! Fifty Extraordinary Individuals Share Their Insights*, 2002, p. 26.
3   S Finkelstein, *Why Smart Executives Fail: And What You Can Learn from Their Mistakes*, 2003, p. 2.
4   Finkelstein, p. 42.
5   G Shearing, *Lullaby of Broadway*, 2004.
6   V Frankl, *Man's Search for Meaning*, 1946, p. 129.
7   I Cockerill, *Solutions in Sports Psychology*, 2002, p. 186.
8   J Kimberley, *Antarctica: A Different Adventure*, 2007, pp. 2–3.
9   G Gordon & N Nicholson, *Family Wars: Classic Conflicts in Family Business and How to Deal with Them*, 2008, pp. 101–4.
10 Ibid. pp. 85–9.
11 Ibid. pp. 125–31.
12 Tiziana Casciaro and Miguel Sousa Lobo, 'Competent Jerks, Lovable Fools and the Formation of Social Networks', in *Harvard Business Review*, June 2005, p. 95.
13 Eugene O'Kelly, *Chasing Daylight*, 2005, pp. 114– 15.

Principle 9

1   D Gilbert, *Stumbling on Happiness*, 2006.
2   F Schwed Jr, *Where are the Customers' Yachts*, 1940, p. 54.
3   This fact and the diversity of such inventions was only discovered by the extensive work of Englishman Joseph Needham, commencing in the 1940s and ultimately documented in 18 volumes. Needham's remarkable story is now well told in Simon Winchester's *Bomb, Book and Compass*. Winchester notes: 'The three inventions that Francis Bacon once famously said had most profoundly changed the world—gunpowder, printing and the compass—Needham found all had been invented and first employed by the Chinese'.

4 C Munger, 'How do you get worldly wisdom? Just take the best models from all disciplines', lecture to Stanford Law School Course, 1996 (reproduced in *Outstanding Investor Digest*, 29 December 1997).

5 'Knowledge summary series: 360-degree assessment', www. entrepreneur.com; F Shipper and J Dillard Jr, 'A study of impending derailment and recovery of middle managers across career stages', in *Human Resource Management Journal*, Winter 2000.

Principle 10

1 T Schwartz, 'Manage your energy, not your time', in *Harvard Business Review*, October 2007, pp. 63 ff.

2 E O'Kelly, *Chasing Daylight*, 2007, pp. 14, 73.

3 O'Kelly, p. 78.

4 C D Ellis (ed.), 'The loser's game', in *The Investor's Anthology*, 1988, p. 176.

5 GB Shaw, *Maxims for Revolutionists*, 1903.

6 JC Whitehead, *A Life in Leadership: From D-Day to Ground Zero*, 2005, p. 106.

7 T Harford, *The Logic of Life: The Rational Economics of an Irrational World*, 2008, pp. 145–157.

8 MJ Mauboussin, *More Than You Know: Finding Financial Wisdom in Unconventional Places*, 2006, p. 117.

Principle 11

1 M Seligman, *Authentic Happiness: Using the New Positive Psychology to Realise Your Potential for Lasting Fulfilment*, 2002, pp. 8–9, 49, 116, 134 ff, 175–176, 249.

2 J Stack, *The Great Game of Business*, 1994, p. 115.

3 M Newman, *Emotional Capitalists: The New Leaders*, 2008, pp. 73–74, 83.

4 M Seligman, *Learned Optimism: How to Change Your Mind and Your Life*, 1990, pp. 207–9, 292.

5   M Seligman, *Authentic Happiness: Using the New Positive Psychology to Realise Your Potential for Lasting Fulfilment*, 2002, p. 178.

6   M Buckingham, *Go Put Your Strengths to Work*, 2007, pp. 5–6, 55, 85.

Principle 12

1   P Senge, *The Fifth Discipline: The Art and Practice of the Learning Organisation*, 1990, p. 113.

2   P Lynch, *One Up on Wall Street*, 1989, pp. 182–184.

Principle 13

1   R Branson, *Losing My Virginity*, 2002, p. 142.

2   R Flesch, *The Art of Clear Thinking*, 1951, p. 144.

3   MJ Adler and C van Doren, *How to Read a Book*, 1972, p. 270.

4   J Newcombe, *Newk: Life On and Off the Court*, 2002, p. 55–56.

5   D Lynch, 'Ask Why not, instead of why', in *Australian Financial Review*, 25 October 2005.

6   S Douglas, interview with Brother Colm O'Connell, <www.mensracing.com>, January 2005.

7   A Snyder, *What Makes a Champion! Fifty Extraordinary Individuals Share Their Insights*, 2002, p. 217.

8   F Smith, *Australian Financial Review*, 17 October 2006.

9   N McMahon, *Sydney Magazine*, 1 July 2008, p. 29.

10 P Senge, *The Fifth Discipline: The Art and Practice of the Learning Organisation*, 1990, p. 142.

11 A Snyder, *What Makes a Champion! Fifty Extraordinary Individuals Share Their Insights*, 2002, p. 199.

12 R Kapuscinski, *Travels with Herodotus*, 2007, p. 264.

13 This was the experience of former Goldman Sachs chairman John Whitehead, author of *A Life in Leadership: From D-Day to Ground Zero*, 2005, p. 240.

14 S Levitt & Stephen Dubner, *Freakonomics*, 2005, pp. 118–119.

15 E Spragins, *What I Know Now: Letters to My Younger Self*, 2006, p. xvi.

Principle 14

1   R Putnam and K Goss, *Democracies in Flux: The Evolution of Social Capital in Contemporary Society*, 2002, p. 8.
2   J Coleman, 'Social Capital in the Creation of Human Capital', in *American Journal of Sociology*, Volume 94, Supplement, p. S109.
3   Rudolf F , *The Art of Clear Thinking*, 1951, p. 160.
4   C Fischer, 'Network analysis and urban studies', in *Networks and Places: Social Relations in the Urban Setting*, 1977.
5   T Harford, *The Logic of Life: The Rational Economics of an Irrational World*, 2008, chapter 5.
6   Harford, p. 164, referencing the work of economists Ed Glaeser, David Cutler and Jake Vigdor.
7   R G Fryer, 'Acting White: The social price paid by the best and brightest minority students', in *Education Next*, Winter 2006, pp. 53–59.
8   D Goleman, *Working with Emotional Intelligence*, 1998, p. 203.
9   T DeLong, J Gabarro & R Lees, 'Why Mentoring Matters in a Hypercompetitive World', in *Harvard Business Review*, January 2008, p. 121.
10 R Lowenstein, *Buffett: The Making of an American Capitalist*, 1995, pp. 107–9, 398.
11 B Groysberg, 'How female stars succeed in new jobs', in *Harvard Business Review,* February 2008.
12 B Gates, speech given at Harvard University, 8 June 2007.
13 Figures sourced from www.hitwise.com.
14 *Time*, 13 December 2006.
15 D Tapscott & A Williams, *Wikinomics: How Mass Collaboration Changes Everything*, 2006, p. 43.
16 'Joined-up thinking', in *The Economist*, 7 April 2007, p. 61.
17 A biomarker is a measure of the disease that can be used for detection and assessing response to therapy.
18 'It's getting crowded in here', in *Newsweek*, 13 September 2008.
19 Tapscott & Williams, pp. 264–265.
20 M Granovetter, 'The strength of weak ties', in *American Journal of Psychology*, May 1973, and *Getting a Job: A Study of Contacts and Careers*, 1995.

21 See <www.commonsenseadvice.com/human_cortex_dunbar. html.>
22 R Putnam and Kristin Goss, *Democracies in Flux: The Evolution of Social Capital in Contemporary Society*, 2002, p. 7
23 D Goleman, *Working with Emotional Intelligence*, 1998, p. 207.
24 D Goleman, *Working with Emotional Intelligence*, 1998, p. 158.

Principle 15

1 *Vanity Fair*, July 2007, p. 74.
2 S Covey, *The Seven Habits of Highly Effective People*, 2003, pp. 186–187.
3 P Sheahan, *Flip: How Counter-intuitive Thinking is Changing Everything — From Branding and Strategy to Technology and Talent*, 2008, pp. 65, 118.
4 C Handy, *The Elephant and the Flea*, 2001, p. 140.
5 J Whitehead, *A Life in Leadership: From D-Day to Ground Zero*, 2005, p. 106
6 P Lynch, *One Up on Wall Street*, 1989, p. 256.
7 C D. Ellis (ed.), *The Investor's Anthology*, 1988, p. 81.
8 Ellis, p. 84.
9 Putnam and Goss, p. 7.
10 S Covey, *The Seven Habits of Highly Successful People*, 2003, pp. 188–199.
11 Covey, pp. 206–214.
12 W Bennis & P Biederman, *Organising Genius*, 1997, p. 205.
13 *Vanity Fair*, July 2007, p. 34.
14 F Reichheld, *The Ultimate Question*, 2006, pp. 19–20
15 Reichheld, p. 28.
16 Reichheld — in order — pp120, 4 and 9, 44, 117, 173, 14
17 E Spragins, *What I Know Now: Letters to My Younger Self*, 2006, p. 27.
18 J Lowe, *Damn Right! Behind the Scenes with Berkshire Hathaway Billionaire Charlie Munger*, 2003, p. 59.

Part VI

1   C Handy, *The Elephant and the Flea*, 2001, pp. 14, 215.

Principle 16

1   TH White, *The Once and Future King*, 1958.
2   P Senge, *The Fifth Discipline: The Art and Practice of the Learning Organisation*, 1990, pp. 131–132, 136–139, 152–156.
3   G Colvin, 'What It Takes to be Great', in *Fortune*, 19 October 2006.
4   C Handy, *The Elephant and the Flea*, 2001, p. 120
5   C Margerison, *Action Learning for Managers*, International Management Centre
6   M Newman, *Emotional Capitalists: The New Leaders*, 2008, pp. 17–18.
7   I Ayres, *Super Crunchers: Why Thinking-by-Numbers is the New Way to be Smart*, 2007, p. 98
8   Senge, p. 18ff.

Principle 17

1   P Senge, p. 143.
2   P Arden, *It's Not How Good You Are, It's How Good You Want to Be*, 2003, p. 122.
3   G Kasparov, *How Life Imitates Chess*, 2007, pp. 34–35.
4   M J. Mauboussin, *More Than You Know: Finding Financial Wisdom in Unconventional Places*, 2006, pp. 90–1.
5   W Bennis & PW Biederman, *Organising Genius*, 1997, p. 21.
6   R Rubin, *In an Uncertain World: Tough Choices from Wall Street to Washington*, 2003, p. 37, 54.
7   C D. Ellis, *Winning the Loser's Game: Timeless Strategies for Successful Investing*, 2003, pp. 102, 110.
8   C Bellis, J Shepherd and R Lyon (eds), *Understanding Actuarial Management: The Actuarial Control Cycle*, 2003, p. 2.
9   Senge, p. 289.

Principle 18

1   D Goleman, *Working with Emotional Intelligence*, 1998, p. 205.
2   F Cavarretta, 'Impact of intrateam diversity on team performance variance: Two ways to take chances', Proceedings of the 66th Annual Meeting of the Academy of Management, 2007.
3   Senge, p. 220–31.
4   Senge, p. 234.
5   C Argyris, 'Good communication that blocks learning', in *Harvard Business Review*, July–August 1994, p. 81.
6   Chris Argyris, 'Teaching smart people how to learn', in *Harvard Business Review*, May–June 1991, p. 100.
7   Senge, pp. 249–251.
8   P Evans & B Wolf, 'Collaboration rules', in *Harvard Business Review*, July–August 2005, p. 103.
9   A Roddick, *Business as Unusual: My Entrepreneurial Journey*, 2000, p. 6.

Part VII

1   K Sarma, *Mental Resilience: The Power of Clarity: How to Develop the Focus of a Warrior and the Peace of a Monk*, 2008, p. 18

Principle 19

1   L Iacocca, *Iacocca: An Autobiography*, 1984, p. xv.
2   *The Economist*, 25 March 2006, p. 67.
3   B McLean & P Elkind, *The Smartest Guys in the Room: The Amazing Rise and Scandalous Fall of Enron*, 2004, p. 15.
4   M Yunus, *Banker to the Poor: Microlending and the Battle Against World Poverty*, 1998, p. 98.
5   B Graham & D L. Dodd, *Security Analysis*, 3rd edition, 1951, pp 45, 76.
6   M Buckingham, *Go Put Your Strengths to Work*, 2007, p. 173.
7   R Cialdini, *Influence: The Psychology of Persuasion*, 1984, p. 37.
8   Mauboussin, p. 69.
9   P Singer, 'What should a billionaire give and what should you?', in the *New York Times Magazine*, 17 December 2006.

10 R Bailey, 'National wealth is more cultural than economic', in *Weekend Australian Financial Review*, 20 October 2007.

Principle 20

1   C Munger, 'A lesson on elementary, worldly wisdom as it relates to investment management and business', lecture to USC Business School, 1994.
2   Mauboussin, pp. 27–8.
3   Lynch, p. 245.
4   P Fisher, *Common Stocks and Uncommon Profits*, 1958, p. 16.
5   JD. Schwager, *The New Market Wizards: Conversations with America's Top Traders*, 1994, pp. 207-208.
6   C Loomis, 'The Inside Story of Warren Buffett', in *Fortune*, 11 April 1988.

Principle 21

1   J Collins & JPorras, *Built to Last: Successful Habits of Visionary Companies*, 1994, p. xii.
2   B Graham, DL Dodd, S Cottle and C Tatham, *Security Analysis: Principles and Techniques*, 4th edition, 1962, pp. 47–49.
3   NN Taleb, *The Black Swan: The Impact of the Highly Improbable*, 2007, p. 149.
4   Annual letter to shareholders of Berkshire Hathaway, 1982.
5   B Flyvbjerg, 'Design by deception: The politics of megaproject approval', in *Harvard Design Magazine*, Spring–Summer 2005, p. 56.
6   I Ayres, *Super Crunchers: Why Thinking-by-Numbers is the New Way to be Smart*, 2007, pp. 114–15.
7   Taleb, pp. 160–163.
8   Graham, Dodd, Cottle & Tatham, p. 55.
9   Graham, Dodd, Cottle & Tatham, p. 55.
10 Snyder, pp. 157–160.
11 M Seligman, *Learned Optimism: How to Change Your Mind and Your Life*, 1990, p. 30.

12 Sarma, pp. 23, 30, 74, 96, 149.
13 V Frankl, *Man's Search for Meaning*, 1946, pp. 86–87, 201.
14 D Coutu, 'How resilience works', in *Harvard Business Review*, May 2002.
15 J Sonnenfeld, *Firing Back: How Great Leaders Rebound after Career Disasters*, 2007, pp. 259–274.
16 P Jackson, *Sacred Hoops: Spiritual Lessons of a Hardwood Warrior*, 1995, pp. 115–120.
17 *Sydney Morning Herald*, 12 April 2007, and *The World Today*, 11 April 2007.
18 See <www.peaklearning.com>.

Principle 22

1   R Scruton, *The Focus*, Vol. X/1, p. 36.
2   J Lowe, *Damn Right! Behind the Scenes with Berkshire Hathaway Billionaire Charlie Munger*, 2000, p. 36.
3   J Kluger, *Why we worry about the things we shouldn't... and ignore the things we should* published in *Time*, December 4 2006.
4   Kahneman was awarded the 2002 Nobel Prize for Economics for his work with Tversky, who died in 1996.
5   A Tversky & D Kahneman, 'The Framing of Decisions and the Psychology of Choice', in *Science*, Vol. 211, Jan 1981, p. 453.
6   A Tversky & D Kahneman, 'Loss Aversion in Riskless Choice', in *Quarterly Journal of Economics*, November 1991, p. 1056
7   R Scruton, 'Courage and doubt: decision-making is the art of taking risks that are worth it', in *The Focus*, Vol. X/1, p. 36.
8   H Arkes & P Ayton, 'The Sunk Cost and Concorde Effects: Are humans less rational than lower animals?', in *Psychological Bulletin*, Vol. 125, No. 5, 1999, pp. 591–600.
9   Taleb,, p. 296.
10 Taleb, p. xvii.
11 R Lowenstein, *When genius failed: the rise and fall of long-term capital management*, 2000, p. 72.
12 Taleb, p. 205.
13 Taleb, pp. 203, 206–10.

14 Taleb, pp. 208–9.
15 T Harford, *The logic of life: the rational economics of an irrational world*, 2008, p. 176.
16 Branson, p. 502.
17 R Cialdini, *Influence: The Psychology of Persuasion*, 1984, p. 280.

Principle 23

1   R Kapuscinski, *Travels with Herodotus*, 2007, p. 103.
2   J Surowiecki, *The Wisdom of Crowds*, 2004, pp. xx–xxi.
3   I Ayres, *Super Crunchers: Why Thinking-by-Numbers is the New Way to be Smart*, 2007, pp. 40–2.
4   J Surowiecki, *The Wisdom of Crowds*, 2004, pp. 276–278.
5   Herodotus, *The Histories*, circa 450 BC.
6   I Janis, *Victims of Groupthink*, 1972, p. 9.
7   J Whitehead, *A Life in Leadership: From D-Day to Ground Zero*, 2005, p. 277.
8   S Finkelstein, *Why Smart Executives Fail: And What You Can Learn from Their Mistakes*, 2003, pp. 129, 134.
9   R Feynman, *Personal Observations on the Reliability of the Shuttle*, Appendix F, Rogers Commission report into the Space Shuttle Challenger disaster, June 1986.
10 P Fisher, *Common Stocks and Uncommon Profits*, 1958, p. 17.
11 J Stack, *The Great Game of Business*, 1994, p. 108.
12 Kapuscinski, p. 262.
13 R Giuliani, *Leadership*, 2002, p. 56.
14 S Finkelstein, *Why Smart Executives Fail: And What You Can Learn from Their Mistakes*, 2003, p. 100.
15 Mauboussin, p. 17.
16 A Smith, *Supermoney*, 1972, p. 182.
17 P Sheahan, *Flip: how counter-intuitive thinking is changing everything — from branding and strategy to technology and talent*, 2008, p. 22.
18 Sheahan, p. 40.
19 C Munger, 'Worldly Wisdom Revisited', address to Stanford Law School, 1996.
20 P Lynch, *One Up on Wall Street*, 1989, p. 172.
21 M J Gelb, *How to Think Like Leonardo da Vinci: Seven Steps to Genius Every Day*, 1998, p. 54.

Conclusion

1   R Eckersley, 'What's it all about?', in the *Sydney Morning Herald*, 25 March 2000.
2   J Field, *Social Capital*, 2003, p. 90.

Appendix A

3   Cialdini, p. 171

Index

If you found this book useful...

...then you might like to know about similar books published by John Wiley & Sons. For more information visit out website <www.johnwiley.com.au/trade>, or if you would like to be sent more details about other books in related areas please photocopy and return the completed coupon below to:

P/T Info
John Wiley & Sons, Australia, Ltd
155 Cremorne Street
Richmond Vic 3121

If you prefer you can reply via email to: <aus_pt_info@wiley.com.au>.

Please send me information about books on the following areas of interest:

☐ sharemarket (Australian)

☐ sharemarket (global)

☐ property/real estate

☐ taxation and superannuation

☐ general business.

Name:

Address:

Email:

Please note that your details will not be added to any mailing list without your consent.

Printed in Australia
03 Oct 2019
718825

9 781742 169316